# Symptoms of Fascism

# Symptoms of Fascism

ARUN SHOURIE

VIKAS PUBLISHING HOUSE PVT LTD
New Delhi Bombay Bangalore Calcutta Kanpur

**VIKAS PUBLISHING HOUSE PVT LTD**
5 Ansari Road, New Delhi 110002
Savoy Chambers, 5 Wallace Street, Bombay 400001
10 First Main Road, Gandhi Nagar, Bangalore 560009
8/1-B Chowringhee Lane, Calcutta 700016
80 Canning Road, Kanpur 208004

COPYRIGHT © ARUN SHOURIE, 1978

ISBN 0 7069 0696 9

1V02S8401

Printed at Dhawan Printing Works, 26-A Mayapuri, New Delhi 110064

*For*
*my mother and father*

# Preface

This book is a collection of essays round and about a traumatic experience in the political life of our country.

The essays were written and published when the events were unfolding themselves. They use these events to focus on issues that transcend the events, on issues that have significance for the system as a whole.

Like so many authors, I have often felt like a paralytic watching a rising flood. The portents are clear and you keep trying to alert everyone you can reach to the coming danger. Few listen. And no one acts in time.

Successive experiences of this kind lead one to look beyond the events of the moment, to reflect on the system as a whole, to reflect most of all on one's practice: is there anything worth saving in the system? is there anything in it that will save whatever it is in it that is worthwhile? are we addressing issues that concern the people? are we addressing the right audience?

Like many others I am filled with foreboding today. For I feel that our polity lost quite sometime ago the will to solve its problems within a liberal framework. Now it seems to be losing the ability to even contain them within such a framework.

Today, the owners of industry and agriculture are strong, well organized and impatient; a powerful, unthinking, mercenary state apparatus is in place; the middle class is exhausted; the poor are unorganized and lost in fumes of false-consciousness.

Freedom, such as it has been during the last thirty years, has been an upper and middle class affair in our country. Large sections of these classes are now a constituency for fascism. Others among them do not have the maturity to act with restraint—they press their sectional demands in ways and to the point where these break down the very system which at least allows them to press their demands, and they—so vociferous and militant when the going is easy—do not have the courage to stand up to an assault on the very system that allows them their relative freedom.

The poor would fight if they perceived that the liberal system works for them. But they know by their daily experience that it does not work for them, that, in fact, it work *against* them. They know from their daily experience that the policeman, the administrator, the politician is not a referee, that he is an agent of the propertied. They know from their living experience that "law" is but the convenience of the powerful. They have seen again and again that even though they throw out one bunch of politicians and parties after another, the new ones turn out to be no different from the old.

Is it any wonder then that they do not fight for preserving the present arrangements? "But did they not throw out the Emergency dictatorship?" They did indeed. But if things have to go *that* far before the interest of the masses can be aroused then the present arrangements cannot last. For the steady day to day erosion—which is proceeding at full pace and to stem which the poor are neither alert nor organized and equipped—that erosion will ensure that the system will be defenceless by the time the final blow comes. And the blow, when it comes, will hurt the poor most: for then, as we saw during the brief Emergency, there will be no restraints on the well-to-do at all. It will also reopen basic questions—right from the unity of the country on down—that we have thus far taken as settled.

This is the perspective that those who feel with and for the people of our country, those who feel for our country itself, have to bear in mind. Each of us has to comprehend the nature of the current drift. And each of us has to examine his own practice, each has to ask himself what it is that he will be doing when the next avalanche comes. For come it will.

> *Shauk ka imtihan jo hua,* as Faiz would remind us,
>   *so hua*
> *Jism-o-jan ka zian jo hua so hua*
> *Sood se peshtar hai zian aur bhi*
> *Dosto, matame-jism-o-jan aur bhi*
> *Aur bhi talkhtar imtihan aur bhi.*

ARUN SHOURIE

# Acknowledgements

The essays included in this volume have appeared in *Seminar*, *Mainstream*, *India Today*, *Economic & Political Weekly*, *Samagrata*, *Deccan Herald* and *Indian Express*. I am grateful to the editors of these journals and newspapers for publishing them and for allowing me to include them in this volume.

Contents

PRELUDE

1 On Keeping Silent  3

THE EMERGENCY

2 The Coup as a Portent  13
3 Symptoms  43
4 The Role of Popular Movements—A Gandhian Perspective  144

MRS GANDHI

5 Creeping Paranoia  177
6 Liar: An Appropriate, if Unparliamentary Word  187
7 On Dealing with a Politician  201

THE SEQUEL

8 Yesterday's Bullies  209
9 Kidnapped, Not Arrested  225
10 The Shah Commission and Our Future  239

## NEW BEGINNINGS

11 Intellectuals and the Interregnum 247
12 Proposals for Bihar Students 272
13 The Janata Year 279
14 Lessons of an Inquiry 318
   *Index* 323

# Prelude

Prelude

# 1  On Keeping Silent*

Each day brings news of a novel way in which our leaders have violated the law. Each day we hear of yet another norm that has been struck down. Each day brings news of a fresh scandal.

As the situation has worsened our leaders have become more audacious in violating laws, in flouting norms. Consider just a few events of the past months. Our leaders foist a fraudulent plan on the people and then, with unabashed cynicism, bury it amidst hysterical shouts of world-wide inflation, of forces beyond our control. They discuss the resignation of an economist with cynical chants about how talk of realism is defeatist, of how "every dream shall become a reality and every reality a dream." They manipulate the appointment of the Chief Justice—confident that the episode will soon be forgotten. With a complete disregard for norms they pump scarce commodities into a state, sanction dubious projects for it, make reckless promises to every interest group within it (promises and outlays that ultimately leave the state bankrupt)—all to keep themselves in office. A state government manipulates restrictions on the movement of rice for a few days to enable its friends to make a killing. Another decrees a farcical ceiling on the price of wheat in Bombay and,

*October 1974.

three weeks later, lifts it—pushing *jowar* prices to astronomical heights and thus helping its friends, the large *jowar* farmers in the state. The same government abets wholesale adulteration of high quality seed. A newspaper press is burnt in one State. Instead of investigating the matter the State Government heaps fresh financial difficulties on the paper. In another State another government shuts off power to a newspaper. And the Centre—instead of restraining these acts—conspires to have an editor dismissed. While all this is being done, of course, the PM assures a professor in distant Trivandrum that she is "against censorship, even in its mildest forms." Thousands upon thousands of young men and women are kept without trial in prisons while government spokesmen engage in a cynical game about "the correct number of those under detention." Corpses are found lying around in cities; horrible accounts pour in of men selling their wives and children, of mothers abandoning their children, of women collapsing within sight of ration shops and gruel kitchens. And government spokesmen play literary games—about the semantic difference between starvation ("on the one hand") and sundry maladies ("on the other"). One could go on and on.

As the situation has worsened, the perspectives of our leaders have changed in two ways. One, they no longer think of the distant future; they are just concerned about the next turn of events. Second, they think less and less about the country, about ultimate objectives, about institutions; their only thought is about staying in office. They rationalize this preoccupation with the argument that if they lose their offices, they lose all; that then they will have no way of ensuring that the country marches towards those luminous goals. Each of them—in the states even more visibly than at the Centre—is grabbing now: as if all are convinced that the game will be up soon and that, therefore, the only sensible thing to do is to grab whatever one can lay one's hands on. As our leaders are in this frame of mind, we can be certain that they will act without restraint, that cynical and authoritarian acts will soon be the order of the day.

Times of crises such as the present one impose a great responsibility on each of us. For the real tragedy of such times—and the real cause of the drift into an authoritarian nightmare—is not that a few leaders become rapacious, that they start breaking laws, disregarding norms or destroying institutions. Rather

## On Keeping Silent

it is that common men remain silent, that we acquiesce.

Each of us rationalizes his silence in many ways. We should bare these arguments so that they are seen to be what they are—specious alibis.

The first of these is a plea of helplessness: "what is the use of my speaking out, of my not going along; what can protest by one individual accomplish?" Each of us must realize that our leaders—whether they be in politics or administration or business—work with your hands and mine: their evil is wrought with our hands. We—as officials—collect money for them. We—as industrialists—contribute to their coffers. We—as workers—adulterate goods for our employers. We—as economists—work assiduously to make the politicians' lies seem plausible. If a colleague is dismissed, we—as professionals—manoeuvre to get his place.

In a very real sense, therefore, the country is not being undermined by a handful of leaders or business tycoons. The higher a person is in the hierarchy the cleaner he keeps his hands, the better sterilized his chambers. The minions—you and me—are the ones who do the dirty work. And this is precisely the reason why we are not as helpless as the first alibi would have us believe and why our protest and non-cooperation will not be inconsequential.

The second alibi is somewhat more assertive: "but how can I be sure that the things you say are true? How do I really know who is behind the ouster of that editor? Where is the evidence?" By a curious irony, the leaders use this alibi for not moving against their corrupt colleagues—they allege that they too lack specific evidence of wrong-doing. How hollow their words sound when they plead their helplessness thus. And yet so many of us employ the same alibi to justify our silence, to go on as if nothing were happening around us. We can assess the true worth of the alibi by recalling how it was used by millions in Japan to shut their eyes to the rise of militarists in the 1920s and in Germany to ignore the things that the Nazis were doing.

"But surely the government must have its reasons; it must know things that it cannot reveal, that you and I do not know." This too has been a highly serviceable alibi. It is one of the favourite devices of government propagandists when they are eager—as they almost always are—to snatch the benefit of doubt for themselves. A vague hint about the victim being a "foreign agent," some whispers about the conspiracies of foreign powers who do not approve of "our socialism" (our socialism? my foot—it is the laughing stock of the world), a hint or two about his "communal leanings." Yet citizens the world over have learned again and again that governments never know more than they reveal. They know much less. The Americans are the latest to have been taught this lesson again: their presidents and governments kept assuring them that there was more to the Vietnam War than they could reveal. Hardly a day passed when "national security" was not invoked as a reason for demanding the trust of the people. In retrospect we can see what a massive hoax it all was. We can see how wrong were the people who kept quiet on the plea that "the government must know things that you and I don't." And we can now see the terrible cost of their silence.

"But, listen, why are you getting so worked up about this latest step? All this has been going on for a long while. I mean, why are you so excited about the fact that an editor has been fired? After all—let's face it—we have never really had a free press. Nothing new has happened. It is just that you are learning the facts of life for the first time." This is a much more sinister alibi—for at each moment it seems quite plausible. Each new violation builds upon others that have preceded it and thus seems to be just a minor extension of things to which all are already accustomed. Yet it is no more defensible for that reason: even as we reassure ourselves that the latest pebble rolling down the hillside does not really mark a qualitative change, that pebbles ("and much larger ones than that") have been rolling down for quite a while, suddenly one gives away and the avalanche starts, suddenly it is too late to run for cover.

To realize the full significance of an authoritarian act—one that violates norms and laws—one has to look ahead and speculate the end of the journey. In all probability the act itself involves only a handful of people and it is usually centred around a very special constellation of circumstances. The ouster of one editor, after all, involves only a few individuals. Yet its true significance transcends these individuals. In this particular instance it informs every two-penny politician in the country that he can do what he will for muzzling the press. It warns every editor that the government shall use means that are as devious as it thinks are necessary to win the forthcoming elections and, by God, if he prints anything about these he will go the way of the dismissed editor. Even more important than the inconvenience an authoritarian act causes its immediate victims and even more important than the signals it sends out to the others, each of these acts corrodes our conscience; it dulls our vigilance, it accustoms us to more tarnished norms, to lower standards. And in this way it prepares the way for the next—and more audacious—authoritarian act.

We are often lulled by the calm that follows each act. Soon the act fades in memory and in retrospect it always appears to have been inconsequential: "all that noise and fuss you made for just one editor; you see, don't you, how comfortably off he soon will be in his new job and even you must have noticed that the heavens have not fallen since he was fired." Yet the onlooker must realize that each act seems inconsequential in retrospect largely because it has since been buried amidst the clamour of even more audacious acts; that it has helped pave the way for these subsequent acts and that, therefore, in fact, it has been far from inconsequential.

"But surely you exaggerate; you are just extrapolating; how do you know things will go that far; we must retain a sense of proportion in these matters; a single step in one direction does not mean that we will persist to the end on that course." Yet we have learned again and again that once the authorities break a norm they use the new-found licence as much as they feel they need to for attaining their ends; and, as we noted earlier, as the situation worsens these ends become more and more parochial and the time-horizons become shorter and shorter. When leaders start violating norms the citizenry can be certain that such evils as are possible will indeed be foisted upon it by the leaders and that these will come to prevail in a shorter time than most reasonable men would think possible.

"But we must be patient. I agree that the act you mention is not quite in accordance with the spirit of the law. In fact, I will go along with you and say that it is unpardonable. But there is no reason to get excited about the whole thing. It is just a passing phase. I know them—I have known them for years. They are as dedicated to these ideals as you and I are. But, after all, you will agree that they have to stay in office. If they lose the elections how will they work towards the ideals that you and I and they, ideals that all of us, hold so dear? Listen, we have to be practical; we have to look the other way now and then. You just wait and see. Once they are assured a new five-year term, things will be entirely different." We should not fall for this low-means-but-high-ends deception; nor for the dedicated-but-helpless-leader bit. We do not need this bunch of ministers and "leaders" for attaining our goals, for ensuring well-being and freedom to our people. What we need for achieving these goals are the institutions, the norms and the values that the authoritarian acts of these "leaders" are destroying.

"But I am just an engineer. You are talking of things that are far wider than my job. You see, I am a specialist. I do the job I have been assigned. That's the limit of my duty. Our country isn't going to be saved by shouting about vague principles but by each one of us doing the job that has been assigned to him." The "specialist" who mouths this alibi is after the leaders' hearts: they love no one more than the quiet cog. Yet it is surely obvious by now that the labours of each of us will be set to naught by the erosion of our polity. For each of us to "busy himself with the task at hand" is quite the most certain way of committing collective suicide. Thus, even as each of us does his job he must concern himself with, and devote time to, the larger issues—he must assess the large consequences of his acts and the larger consequences of the acts of others.

This brings us to the final alibi: "but I have to keep my job; I have a family to support." There are many responses to this. For one thing, it just does not wash for many of us: many of us who aid and abet wrong-doing are well off, we can get other jobs than the ones we hold at present. For another, it is almost always possible to retain one's job and yet refuse to be an accomplice. The only cost may be a transfer or that one loses one's chance of a "promotion." Surely, in times such as these, the lures of a large city or of a larger name-plate are not worthy pursuits. How can we put them in a scale against the interests of our country, the survival of norms and institutions in our polity? But in a vital sense all these partial responses skirt the issue.

The basic point is the following one: even if the consequence of standing up today is that we may lose our jobs we should not think of this as a cost. A flood threatens us. If each of us busies himself with grabbing what he can, with gathering together and stuffing his possessions into his little sackcloth so that he may make a run for his life when the time comes, if each of us busies himself in this rather than in helping to strengthen the embankments, all of us shall surely be swept away —we, our families and all those stuffed sackcloths. We must think of our polity and of our country now. It is already very late and entities much larger than ourselves or our families are at stake. We must heed Iqbal:

*Vatan ka fikr kar nadan, musibut ane wali hai,*
*Teri barbadiyon ke mashwaren hain asmanon men.*

# The Emergency

## 2  The Coup as a Portent*

Indira Gandhi's recent machinations to hang on to office have attracted a great deal of attention. But her coup is just a symptom, the "concentrated expression of long tendencies," the flash that in a moment enables one to see the landscape that surrounds one. We should look beyond these machinations, beyond the twists and turns of daily pronouncements, and seek answers to basic questions. What forces have made the democratic paraphernalia inconvenient for the ruling classes in India? What does the coup tell us about the future evolution of India's polity? Which classes benefit from the new arrangements and which classes are liable to be harmed? How must the Indian people prepare themselves during the coming decade?

The fundamental questions can be answered only in the perspective of decades, not in that of months or even of a year or two. Moreover, to understand the significance of a particular event we must analyze the potential inherent in it. If the analysis is confined solely to specific steps that have already been taken—as we would confine it if, for instance, we were arguing a criminal case in a court—it could never be the basis for preventive action. By the time all the evidence was in, the

*October 1975.

new set-up would have congealed, the new power relationships would have been consolidated, and it would be too late to do anything except write histories of the events. Rather, in assessing political developments we should keep in mind the twin lessons that the progress of technology during the past hundred years holds out for us: that things which seem barely possible at one stage do come to pass at the next and that they come to pass sooner than anyone expected they would.

The decades, then, and not the coming months or a year or two.

# I

India's post-independence polity was characterized by one of its leading intellectuals as an "intermediate regime"—in the sense that the class that lay between the owners of the means of production and the workers held formal political power.[1] Even as its members manned the state apparatus, this class—henceforth, the intermediate class—relied on industrial capitalists and large commercial interests for finance and on the rich peasantry for mobilizing rural support.

[1] K.N. Raj, "The Politics and Economics of 'Intermediate Regimes'," *Economic and Political Weekly*, July 1973. In this paper Raj elaborated categories that were set out by the Polish economist, Michael Kalecki. While there are many nuances to the demarcation of groups in the Indian polity, the following discussion employs these three broad categories. First, the owners of the means of production—the capitalists and the rich peasantry. Second, the industrial and agricultural proletariat; members of this class own only their own labour power; most of them (in particular the millions in agriculture, small industrial units and service establishments) are unorganized. Third, the intermediate class that lies between the preceding two classes. Some members of this class own tangible means of production (e.g., the self-employed trader or artisan); some, such as the bureaucrat, own intangible means of production (Raj refers to "certain kinds of knowledge and skills—administrative, managerial, scientific, technical, etc."); others do not own any means of production. In all cases, however, income from property is not very large compared to the income from their own labour. Some sections of this class are very well organized (e.g., the senior bureaucracy in India); others are fairly well organized (e.g., the lower level clerical and administrative personnel of the government and its enterprises); others have yet to be organized.

The indecisiveness and contradictory character of Indian policies during the past 25 years arose from the inherent heterogeneity of the intermediate class as well as from the fact that throughout this period it was pursuing two contradictory objectives. On the one hand, it took measures to improve its power and economic status vis-a-vis the owners of the means of production. On the other hand, because of its economic dependence on the owners, it sought to ensure that the interests of its patrons were not harmed in practice. For this reason it advocated many contradictory policies and failed to implement any one of them whole-heartedly. Each of its policies was a blunt double-edged weapon: "double-edged" because while one edge aggrandized the interests of the intermediate class, the other safeguarded those of its patrons. And "blunt" because the heterogeneity of the class itself as well as the conflict between its objectives meant that in practice no measure could be implemented forcefully.

This characteristic is best seen in the socialist legislation and rhetoric of Indian governments during the past 25 years.

The intermediate class opted for "socialism" and state capitalism so as to increase its power vis-a-vis that of the owners of the means of production.[2] Each nationalization directly transferred assets and—as in the case of bank nationalization—economic power from the owners to members of the intermediate class who manned the state apparatus. Expansion of the government's role in the economy as well as vastly expanded public sector outlays created new opportunities for these members. The license and quota superstructure erected in the name of "socialism" centralized patronage in their hands. Owners—including the great captains of industry and commerce —had to come to them as applicants. Moreover, the socialist *ambience* put the owners of capital, land and financial assets on

---

[2] And not, as Daniel P. Moynihan would have us believe, because it could not, for reasons of sentiment or intellectual inertia, free itself from the notions of Britain's Fabian socialists. Cf., Daniel P. Moynihan, "The United States in Opposition," *Commentary*, March 1975. Obviously, individuals like Jawaharlal Nehru had been influenced by Britain's Fabians. But the peculiar character of socialist rhetoric and legislation and its actual fate in practice owed itself to the class interests and composition of the intermediate class.

the defensive. Indeed, at times they were pushed into being apologetic.

This, however, was only one edge of the socialist weapon. For instance, industrial controls ended up creating a completely protected market for the owners of industry—a market from which both foreign and domestic competition were excluded, one in which both entry and production were restricted. And the vast legislation on land reforms led nowhere. It was indeed symptomatic that in spite of all the sloganeering and legislation about land reforms during the past 25 years, the rulers successfully thwarted all proposals to conduct even a census of holdings that would identify owners and tenants—to say nothing of proposals to tax agricultural incomes or of proposals to make owners pay for the higher land values that resulted from public investments. Similarly, while the laws decreed rates of taxation that were among the highest in the world, little effort was made to enforce them.

Other features of the polity displayed the same ambivalence. Thus, while the intermediate class centralized patronage so as to increase its relative power vis-a-vis the owners, it ended up deploying much of it on behalf of the same owners—using jobs to buy off the leaders of blocs (like trade unions, castes and the like) so that they in turn would keep the blocs in line and keep them from revolting against the system. The attitude of the intermediate class to universal suffrage and parliamentary institutions was no different. On the one hand, it used them as instruments to put the owners on the defensive—each electoral bout became an occasion for proclaiming radical goals, for drawing the people's attention to the alleged perfidy of the owners. On the other, it cooperated with the owners in using these institutions, first, as instruments for displacing feudal interests and, later, as instruments for fooling the masses into putting their faith in an illusion—the illusion that they could reform the system from within, that they could affect the outcome by pledging their votes to one party or one leader rather than another.

This whole arrangement was necessarily an unstable one. It separated economic and political power and vested the latter in a class that—because of its inherent heterogeneity as well as its economic dependence on the economically powerful class—was incapable of acting swiftly to wrest economic power to itself. The results made it an untenable one.

First, it greatly inconvenienced the owners of the means of production. The socialist rhetoric pictured them as culprits. Progressive laws—even when experience showed that ultimately ways would be found to get around them—compounded their uncertainties and dampened their enthusiasm. They clearly saw that socialist legislation and the expansion of the government's role in the economy was concentrating enormous patronage in the hands of sections of the intermediate class—the bureaucracy and the political elite—and that, just as agents will often embezzle their employers, these sections were using it to set themselves up on their own. They had begun to demand attention, deference, favours, tribute. Moreover, workers and the poorer sections of the intermediate class began to use the new freedoms to organize themselves. This inconvenienced the owners in many ways. In particular, the unionized sections now interposed themselves as a fulcrum between the two senior patrons of the regime—big industry and big peasantry—and thus threatened their alliance. For instance, whenever the regime tried to placate large peasantry by guaranteeing higher floor prices for the grain it purchased, its efforts to do so would automatically lead to demands for higher wages by the organized sections and thus inconvenience the owners of industry.

Second, the indecisive policies of such a regime, buffeted as they were from one verbal pole to another, were unable to deal with the economic problems facing the country. Private capital was not allowed to run forward on its own, yet the regime was unable to mobilize resources for expanding the public sector at a rapid enough rate. Utilization of existing capacity as well as the creation of new capacity declined. From the late 1960s, the growth rate fell to a level where the per capita income of the country grew by no more than 0.5 per cent a year. The per capita availability of basic commodities such as food-grains, pulses, edible oils, and coarse cloth began to decline or remained constant at miserably low levels. The proportion of the population that could not afford even the level of consumption which was required for maintaining body weight, grew to almost one-half of the total. Unemployment almost certainly increased.³ As one would expect, the vulnerable sections were the ones that were hurt the most. While the owners and the better off members of the intermediates class—the senior bureaucrats, for instance—had little difficulty in finding jobs for their friends and relatives, the average industrial worker had to support a larger and larger number of unemployed relatives.

Increased privation naturally had various consequences. Organized workers, sections of the lower middle class and even some groups of professionals became more militant and on occasion began actually to disrupt production. The educational system—always an excellent barometer—literally broke down in large parts of the country. Students threatened and often beat up teachers and proctors, question papers were "leaked," "mass copying" became the order of the day, teaching standards plummeted.

Governments were pushed into taking countermeasures. The Bihar and Bengal governments resorted to terror. Others tried to contain the pressures by various devices. For instance, in giving jobs, approving contracts, and the like, most states began discriminating heavily in favour of their residents, in favour of the dominant castes and—as in the Punjab—in favour of the dominant religious group. Some state governments formally announced what was euphemistically termed a "sons of the soil policy" under which employers were officially asked to discriminate in favour of natives or long-term residents of the state.

Moreover, the gap between promises and performance became so large that rulers found it more and more difficult to

---

³The Indian government has stopped collecting data about unemployment. Indirect evidence, however, is still available to indicate what is going on. Thus, for instance, the 1971 Census indicated that while the labour force grew by 42 million in 1961-71, only 15 million found employment in the organized and agricultural sectors. Using the definitions of the 1971 Census consistently for both 1961 and 1971 the figure showed that the participation rate for women was almost halved—from 23 per cent in 1961 to 12 per cent in 1971. Once again using the 1971 definitions consistently, the number of "cultivators"—i.e., those who had some rights to the land—actually fell by 15 million and the proportion of agricultural labourers—i.e., of those who till the land without having any rights to it—even the rights of one holding an oral lease—to all rural workers rose from about 17 per cent to about 31 per cent.

win votes just by radical slogans. Larger and larger amounts of money had to be deployed to win and fix electoral contests. Big business was, of course, very willing to help its agents out. The stench of corruption, however, was a necessary consequence and this further discredited the regime. The money the politicians obtained from their patrons—though large—was never enough to do the job. The state exchequer had to be brought into play. These outlays and the distortion of priorities that inevitably followed began to affect the financial stability of the regime.

As the situation worsened, intellectuals of all hues used the freedoms of speech and writing to reveal the lies of the rulers, the discrepancies between their promises and their performance, the widespread corruption and abuse of office. In the end, the objective situation and the incessant clamour actually began to affect the people's perception of their rulers—they began to undermine the legitimacy of the regime.

The situation thus came about in which, on the one side, large sections of the population were becoming restive, the basic problems of poverty and unemployment were becoming worse, agents (i.e., those who held nominal political power) were setting themselves up as masters, the legitimacy of the agents was being undermined by the licence of free speech; and, on the other, the patrons of the regime (i.e., the owners of the means of production) had to shell out more and more to prop up their agents, they had to put up with increasing militancy of their employees and, in spite of all this, they were not free even to enjoy to the full the protected market that had been created for them; in fact, they were having to continually justify their existence, to do things apologetically and surreptitiously.

As the situation deteriorated during the last decade, those who held formal political power began, on their own behalf and on behalf of the owners, to prepare the polity for the inevitable *denouement*.

During this period the formal powers of the State were expanded step by step and the rights of the citizen were dismantled. The stratagem was always the same. In the name of the State the regime would assume a specific power to combat an evil—inequitable land tenures today, smuggling, black money, the evasion of foreign exchange regulations or anti-adulteration laws tomorrow. The new powers would not be used—as they were never meant to be used—against the principal culprits; these, after all, were the patrons of the nominal rulers. The evil would persist, grow, become more and more odious. The regime would plead that it was helpless against the resourceful culprits, that it needed additional formal powers. As it commanded overwhelming majorities in the legislatures, it would soon obtain these powers. This cynical game was played year in and year out.

Just as the formal powers of the regime were being enlarged, the state apparatus was greatly strengthened. New, highly mobile and well equipped para-military forces were created: the Border Security Force, the Central Reserve Police, the Industrial Security Force. Internal political intelligence activities were expanded manifold. By 1974 the Central government alone was spending on the police apparatus 52 *times* what it had spent in 1950. In addition, during 1974 the state governments spent on the police apparatus twice the amount spent by the Central government. (These figures exclude the vastly increased expenditures on the army, navy and air force of the country—forces that, so long as they are not politically educated, are a reserve force available to the rulers, a force that can be deployed against the people whenever it suits the rulers' interests that this be done.) Over the years, in one engagement after another, against Naxalites in Bihar, Bengal, Andhra today, against unionized workers in the railway colonies tomorrow, this expanded police apparatus was brutalized. Gradually it was accustomed to intervening on behalf of, and to working hand in hand with, the local strong men, the local landlords, the employers.

Finally, idealism and respect for norms was ground out of all who manned the state apparatus. Liberals like Nehru had themselves foresworn all efforts to educate these functionaries in political terms. The general atmosphere of corruption, irresponsibility, cynicism, in which everyone around each functionary seemed to be working solely to his personal advantage, completed the job. Within the political arena advancement came to depend on outdoing others in palace intrigue, on hauling in illicit money, on one's facility in mouthing fraudulent slogans, on one's readiness to use audacious and strong-arm methods—

on precisely the norms that would filter only political rogues to the top.

## II

Small wonder then that in mid-1975 a dozen functionaries acting in the name of "the Prime Minister" were able to herd thousands and thousands of citizens into prisons in a perfectly "legal" manner. As often happens at turning points in history, the anxieties of the ruling class were ultimately embodied in one individual, Mrs Gandhi. Just as the owners had begun to feel that they could no longer maintain their assets and hegemony without winding up the democratic show, Mrs Gandhi too was cornered in such a way that she became convinced that she could not maintain her personal position without resorting to police methods. The popular movements of 1974 and 1975 which drew attention to corruption, mal-administration and other basic ills—and which ultimately came to focus on Mrs Gandhi as the fountainhead of much that was wrong—performed the historic task of jolting the polity out of its slumber, of forcing the regime to bare its true face.[4]

Events in mid-1975 showed how well the polity had been prepared for the changeover. The cumulative effect of sifting leaders by crooked norms was made dramatically obvious. Nobody within Mrs Gandhi's party could raise a finger at her as all of its members were culpable. In May-June 1975 she was plagued by judicial and other difficulties and many within her party felt that she should be replaced. Yet none of them dared to speak out against her in public. Each had indulged himself in many ways and all knew that she had the books on them. In private discussions her supporters invariably used one last argument on her behalf: even if she had done much wrong, her contenders were no better; if, given her entanglements with the courts, she could not be trusted to push electoral reforms with any vigour, could her leading contender be trusted to pursue tax

---

[4]Indian intellectuals have been asking each other to read two of Karl Marx's classics, *The Class Struggles in France* and *The Eighteenth Brumaire of Louis Bonaparte*, and to infer the many, almost literal, parallels.

reforms? Apart from many other things that were rumoured about him, had he not "forgotten" to pay income taxes for nine years in a row? The fact is that the entire political elite—in this sense, the members of legislatures were indeed representative—had advanced by the same norms and, as far as their social practice was concerned, there truly wasn't any reason to choose one of them rather than another.

And the consequence of having made sure that personnel who manned the state apparatus remained beyond the pale of political education was also made obvious. During the critical weeks the police and the administrators reacted to orders like a mere machine. Functionaries just stopped thinking for themselves and carried out orders they received from persons they had not even heard of before.

In all this, Mrs Gandhi's significance lies only in that by her own conduct she has exemplified the instincts, objectives and stratagems of the ruling class and its determination to safeguard its interests.

She set herself up as the champion of the poor, of the toiling masses. She courted radicals. She sponsored progressive laws. But when it suited her purpose, without a moment's hesitation she replaced all her previous oratory about freedom, democracy, and socialism by new slogans—slogans that the world had heard so often from usurpers: productivity, discipline, faith in the Leader. While she had talked a great deal about the rights of the workers, she now proclaimed that in a poor society such as India, where millions are unemployed, the workers—by virtue of just having jobs—form a privileged group. While she had often proclaimed her life-long dedication to democratic ideals, to human rights, to the inalienable rights of each individual, she now declared that the arrest of thousands of her opponents was not a serious matter as the numbers arrested were but a small proportion of India's vast population. To avoid embarrassing contrasts with her previous proclamations her functionaries simply prohibited editors from reprinting her earlier slogans and speeches—just as they banned the reproduction of the writings of Mahatma Gandhi, Jawaharlal Nehru and Rabindranath Tagore.

By her recent actions in herding her opponents into prison, mutilating the Constitution, snuffing out democratic rights, Mrs

Gandhi has demonstrated how rulers, how ruling classes, will tolerate, even sponsor, "reforms" and the like but—whenever they feel that their vital interests are about to be hurt, whenever they feel cornered—they will strike back, as a snake that has been stepped upon. And she has shown that, when threatened, the ruler, as the class he exemplifies, will use *all* the weapons he can command. Neither he nor the class will let constitutional provisions, norms, precedents block the way.

Moreover, by the ease with which she has pulled off her coup, Mrs Gandhi has shown that unless those who oppose the ruler or the ruling class are able and willing to use *all* means to combat the ruler or the class—in particular, the audacious and authoritarian means that the ruler will surely deploy—they will be helpless. Petitions, letters, appeals, articles, symbolic gestures —means that have some relevance as long as everyone abides by the rules of parliamentary democracy—will get them nowhere.

Finally, recent events in India have demonstrated that halfbaked "socialism" only paves the way for a fascist takeover. The liberals, the Fabians, the intermediate class as a whole, expand the role of the state in the affairs of a society and they strengthen the state apparatus ostensibly to fulfil this role. But the apparatus they set up is a mere machine. Neither the personnel who man it, nor the masses—nor, indeed, the intermediate class as a whole—are willing to fight to keep it from usurpers.

The personnel who man it turn out to be equally willing to serve masters other than enlightened liberals. After all, the liberals have made sure that the personnel are kept "politically innocent." They have just been taught to obey the powerful. They have not been taught the significance that institutions and norms have for the country and the people at large. Quite the contrary. Their experience has accustomed them to the fact (and they have themselves participated in ensuring) that institutions are just entities to be molded to suit the rulers' convenience.

The masses do not rise to defend parliamentary institutions and the like for a simple reason. The intermediate class— because of its internal heterogeneity, its own class interests and its dependence on the owners—is not able to use the institutions decisively on behalf of the masses. Nothing in the experience of the masses, therefore, tells them that abstractions such as democratic rights or constitutions have any significance for their struggle to subsist. As for the apparatus itself, they have seen it being deployed more often in favour of their masters rather than on their behalf. Hence they are apt to dismiss the all-important struggle for this apparatus as just another contest among the well-to-do.

Finally, the intermediate class itself is too heterogeneous to rise swiftly. Members of each section have been weaned on values that place their personal interests as individuals above all else. Thus they busy themselves in protecting these interests by swiftly switching their loyalty to the new rulers, by rationalizing the new order, by becoming its reliable and anxious agents. To the extent that members of the class think as a class, they dread the proletariat and identify with the owners. They do not aspire to transform society. They just want to set themselves up in business, to become little owners themselves. That they have few possessions only increases their attachment to them. Hence they want "security above all," "order at all costs." They reason that while a regime of the owners—at whose expense they were trying to increase their status and assets—may diminish their relative influence, a regime of the proletariat will do away with them altogether. Thus, when the crisis comes, they cast their lot with those very usurpers whose historical function it is to wrest power from them.

### III

Mrs Gandhi's coup marks a transition. From now on power will not be exercised by representatives of the intermediate class. Power will be exercised by the representatives of the means of production, owners who are now fully alert to their interests as a class. Whereas the intermediate class failed in its attempt to unify the loci of political and economic power by aggrandizing its economic power at the expense of the owners of the means of production, the latter will now unify economic and political power by adding the latter to their quiver. Once the regime settles down—with those who seized power in June-July 1975 or with another bunch in command—its principal characteristics will be as follows.

Big business and big peasantry will be the dominant classes.

Their alliance will be much more open than in the past. And they will use the state apparatus much more overtly than in the past to serve their purposes. In particular, they will use it to crush organizations of the poor (such as trade unions) and of the lower rungs of the intermediate class (symbolized in the current crisis by the Hindu nationalist party, the Jan Sangh). Furthermore, they will use the apparatus to scotch all new attempts to organize the poor. The brutal manner in which the railway strike was crushed in 1974 will be the model for operations in urban areas, and the brutal manner in which the state apparatus has been used to cut down all who were attempting to organize and awaken the poor in Bihar and Bengal will be the model for operations in the rural areas. The regime will move to herd labour and the poor into organizations of its own so as to manage them better. Acts against employers will be viewed as acts against the State and will be dealt with accordingly.[5]

The country will be parcelled out into fiefdoms, each fief in the charge of a strong man. He will be free to do as he pleases in his fief so long as he maintains "order" and so long as he is loyal to the group that holds power in Delhi. This is the way in which Bengal has been "pacified" since 1971: the state, in particular Calcutta, which contains one-sixth of its population, has been parcelled out among local toughs; they have been free to do as they please within their jurisdictions—to help their friends along, to dispose of their enemies, to collect money from the citizenry—so long as they have restored "order" and shown allegiance to the provincial satrap in Calcutta.

Once the regime has consolidated itself its class backers will demand and obtain a free hand for themselves. The role of the public sector in industry will be greatly reduced because it comes in the way of the ambitions of private big business by preempting important industries and because its expansion

---

[5]One of the first acts of the new regime—a signal that it gave immediately to owners of industry—was to ban strikes. It tried to make out that workers had been going on strikes not because of the objective factors we have sketched in Section I but because of the permissive license of democracy, because they had been misled by professional agitators. Employers immediately started taking advantage of the ban and of the new climate of fear to retrench employees, in particular to retrench those who were leaders of their fellow-workers.

entails drafts on the resources available to the private sector for its expansion. Monopoly capital—the section that has been most inconvenienced by the socialist atmospherics of the past 15 years—will be the chief beneficiary. With its resources and links with the regime, it will expand most rapidly. And as the most expeditious way for it to grow is to adopt wholesale the products, processes and equipment that have already been developed abroad, it will persuade the regime to relax restrictions on foreign capital.[6]

Policies have never been very "socialist" as far as Indian agriculture is concerned: hence, fewer changes will be needed. The only difference will be that the policies will now much more overtly favour the big peasantry. Outlays will be concentrated more openly in the more prosperous areas. When funds are channeled to rural areas ostensibly to help artisans, landless labourers, and small farmers they will be more audaciously

---

[6] In the first six months the regime has already announced various steps in this direction. Restrictions on expanding output of what were hitherto dubbed as low priority items are being dismantled. Indeed, the vocabulary itself is being altered. Until a few months ago ministers used to rail against the production of luxuries. Now they refer to television sets as necessities for communication; now they tell us that goods like refrigerators are not luxuries *per se*; it just so happened, they say, that in the past the government imposed such heavy taxes on them that none but the very rich could buy them; hence, the impression got around that they were luxuries. They now say that as factories have in any case been set up to produce goods that only the rich can afford, it is only logical that they should be given raw materials etc., to manufacture the goods. (Until yesterday all the talk was of retooling these factories for the masses.) Regulations for paying bonus to workers have been amended to accord with the demands of industrialists. Functionaries of the regime have announced that foreign capital will be welcome in the "core" industries. (Until recently the argument used to be that, as the state must occupy the commanding heights of the economy, industries in the "core" sector were precisely the ones which should be kept out of the reach of foreign capital.) The government has announced an extremely generous scheme to enable tax evaders to declare their past incomes. Far from being penalized for concealing their incomes over the decades, they have been assured that they will be asked no questions. It has also been decreed that these people will have to pay taxes on their hitherto undeclared income on rates that they are substantially *lower* than the rates that are applicable to citizens who declare their income honestly.

diverted by the strong man who controls the countryside. The regime will desist from procuring even the five-odd million tons of foodgrain it has tried to procure at less than market prices in the past to keep the public distribution system going. It is entirely probable, then, that efforts to supply a minimum of foodstuffs to the potentially volatile sections through the ration shops will be curtailed or they will become even more dependent on imports than has been the case thus far.

Democratic rights—especially those of speech and association—will be sequestered. Indians are already being told that they have abused these rights. Mrs Gandhi has said that the press had taken to printing "all sorts of things" about her, her family and her colleagues, that it has been advocating "defiance of authority," that the agitations against her were not among the people but only in the newspapers, that the press and the intellectuals had seriously undermined the self-confidence of the country. The regime already controls radio and television. It will soon "restructure" the press. The ostensible purpose will be to dilute the hold of the large business houses over the newspapers. The real purpose will be to make journalists and editors responsible to nominees of the regime. Big business will not mind this change. It is more concerned with the reality of power and it knows that even as it loses a few newspapers it is ceding them to its own regime.

The principal mode for curbing the rights of speech and association, however, will not be one of introducing formal changes in the ownership of newspapers or the composition of their boards but of altering the atmosphere in which debate and discussion take place. Distinctions between the party, the government, the State, the Leader will be blurred so that criticism of the party, the government, the Leader or his coterie will become an act against the State itself.[7]

[7]Mrs Gandhi's apotheosis has already begun. Just as the National Socialist Youth used to proclaim in the 1930s that "Adolf Hitler is Germany, Germany is Adolf Hitler" the President of the Congress Party has proclaimed that "Indira is India, India is Indira." Every few days bring forth an assertion like the following: "There are few instances when an individual becomes identified with the life of a nation. Mrs. Gandhi has provided one such instance." An artist has portrayed her as the Hindu goddess, Durga. Mrs Gandhi is said to have approved the

## IV

*But will India not grow more rapidly under such a regime? Would such growth not automatically help everyone—especially the poor?* From the point of view of the owners of the means of production, the object of the changeover is not to remove obstacles to production but to remove obstacles to profit. The quickest way for the owners of industry, for instance, to maximize profits will be to use imported capital-intensive technology to produce goods that the rich want. The formal indices of growth may well be higher. But growth of this kind will not alleviate unemployment nor will it furnish goods that the poor need, but do not have the wherewithal to obtain.[8] We noted above that a licensing system had been set up in India ostensibly to direct investments to priority industries. Indian industrialists used every stratagem to convert it into an instrument for ensuring easy profits for themselves and their agents in precisely the manner that a monopolist employs to maximize his profits and to ensure a quiet life for himself: they used it to restrict entry, eleminate competition and restrict production.

It would be naive to expect that when at last the regime is

---

representation, and the paintings are being exhibited around the country by the Ministry of Information and Broadcasting. Editors have been told to give prominence to her speeches and her photographs. And so on.

A similar apotheosis is afoot for the party. The Speaker of the Lok Sabha, India's equivalent of the House of Commons, has already said that India should be transformed into a one-party State. Some time ago, another member of Mrs Gandhi's party had put forth an elaborate thesis arguing that the country needed a "limited dictatorship." The point is not that these functionaries have read some stock phrases. If they were just incompetent plagiarists it would not be a very serious matter. But the statements represent much more: they truly reflect the instincts of the new rulers and on this account they should not be dismissed lightly.

[8]Industrial production (excluding that in the lost provinces of Manchuria) grew by six per cent a year during the Nanking decade in China—the precise decade during which the fate of the Kuomintang regime was decisively sealed. This rate was no different from the rate of growth for the 1912-36 period as a whole. To the great satisfaction of its officials and Western observers, Pakistan's industry grew by 12 per cent a year during the Ayub regime—the years during which seeds were sown for the breakup of that country.

openly their own, India's capitalists will now suddenly turn altruistic and start producing goods that the poor need—even though there is little profit in them—or that they will suddenly start using labour-intensive techniques—when the quickest way for them to maximize their earnings is to adopt wholesale the capital-intensive techniques that have already been developed abroad. The new regime will not solve problems of poverty and unemployment. It will merely suppress them. For it has not assumed powers to help the poor. Rather, it has assumed them to protect big business and the big peasantry from what it sees as one vast and multiplying horde: the proletariat, the lower middle class, the landless and the small tenantry.

We have already noted that one of the immediate objectives of the regime is to wrest away from the poor the right to organize or, at best, to render it totally ineffective by herding the poor into organizations of its own. Even a little reflection and one simple fact will show that the right to organize themselves is vital for the poor: only one section of the Indian poor was able to maintain—just maintain, not raise—its real wages until a few years ago and this was organized industrial labour. The real wages of others declined. (And even organized labour was not able to maintain its real wages in the face of massive inflation during the past few years.)

Similarly, it is an error to think that other democratic rights, such as those of free speech and movement, are important only for the country's voluble intellectuals. Indeed, the intellectuals and other sections of the upper strata do not need these rights. With their resourcefulness, they will have little difficulty in making deals with regimes of the Right. In any case, a number of them have the option of migrating to other parts of the world. It is the poor man who suffers yet another irreparable loss.

In the past, one of the principal reasons why the poor in a famine or drought area ultimately received some relief was just that their privations were reported and commented on, and thus became an obvious embarrassment for the regime. Similarly, when during a drought, thousands of them flocked to metropolitan areas in search of scraps of food, of jobs—any jobs—free speech and publicity alone dampened the zeal of the regime to get them out of sight, to push them out of the cities. Under the new set-up it is entirely possible that some future usurper will use censorship laws not very different from the ones that have been employed this time, to forbid coverage of their privation and destitution. After all, under the new laws journalists are not, among other things, to report anything that "discourages" the people or causes "disaffection" toward the regime. Could it not be claimed at some stage that realistic accounts of famine and drought are liable to "discourage" the populace and cause "disaffection" toward the regime? What alternative would the poor have then except to suffer and die quietly?

*But has the regime not announced a 20-point economic programme already? Does it not contemplate many progressive steps to help the poor?* Indeed, much is being made of the 20-point programme. It is the most amateurish and cynical one among the scores and scores of programmes that have been touted before Indians during the past 30 years. The 20 points are just a patchwork list put together hastily to deflect resentment against the June 25 crackdown by promising something to everyone. The measures bear little relation to each other. All of them are tired old slogans, each having been listed on numerous previous occasions. The true fate of progressive measures is revealed by the complete abandonment of the brave targets and meticulous calculations of the Draft Fifth Five Year Plan, presented to the country with much fanfare in December 1973. It was to revamp Indian society by transferring precisely calculated amounts of consumption from the top 10 per cent of the country's population to the bottom 30 per cent. Little is heard of the Draft now, and the finalization of the Plan has been postponed indefinitely.

*But is there not a difference now? Surely the government knows that this time it just has to deliver on its promises.* The poor people of India have been waiting for a decade hoping that somehow this eventuality would come to pass. When Nehru died in 1964—and especially because he died after his halo had been diminished by the Sino-Indian conflict—commentators were quick to reassure the people that hence-forth Indian governments would have to stand solely on their performance, that the days when they could coast along on the residual glory of the independence struggle, when they could rely on the charisma of men like Nehru, were gone. The same refrain was repeated in 1969 when Mrs Gandhi split the Congress Party:

"Now that she has evicted the old guard, she'll really have to fulfil the people's hopes. She can't blame the party bosses for holding her back any longer." And yet again, after Mrs Gandhi won the 1971 elections on the promise of banishing poverty: "She has gone so far out to raise the people's expectations; surely, she'll sink if she does not live up to her promises now." And yet again after the 1971 victory in Bangladesh: "The people have put up with a lot on account of Bangladesh; they have followed her to the man; she has all the power she needs and more; she just can't fall back on any alibi now."

Just as today there is much ado about abolishing rural indebtedness, three years ago there was just as much fanfare about imposing ceilings on landownership. Seminars, conferences, rallies were held. Reports were prepared, resolutions were proclaimed, laws were passed. We now learn that the old familiar story has been repeated again: the regime proclaims a ceiling of X acres; the landowners quickly subdivide their holdings among relatives and alter the land records. Thus far, less than one-tenth of the area that was expected has been sequestered.[9]

V

Once the regime has consolidated itself it will go in for corruption on a South-east Asian scale. For Indians the epithet "Maruti" describes the coming set-up.[10] In the past the risk of

[9] To get an idea of what ultimately happens in rural India to land that is taken over for distribution among the poor the reader should examine the report of the Harchand Singh Committee. This committee was appointed by the Punjab legislature to determine the manner in which land meant for the landless and for untouchables was actually distributed. Reporting in 1973, it uncovered a scandalous state of affairs and reported how the land was actually appropriated by prominent politicians, administrators, police officers and other well-connected personages and that this was done in each case at a fraction of the prevailing market price.

[10] A number of scandals have been aired over the past few years in connection with the facilities that Mrs Gandhi's son has been given to produce an automobile, the Maruti. The facilities have been used intensively and, it seems, very lucratively. No automobile has yet come on the market. Now that the possibility has arisen that Mrs Gandhi can bequeath to her son the biggest corporation in India—i.e., the country

exposure, of people getting to know, alone restrained the rapacity of India's rulers. Once freedom of speech is taken away and the press is "restructured" nothing will restrain them. And many factors will goad them on. Domestic and foreign businessmen will be eager, even impatient, to make quick deals and only too ready to lubricate the wheels for this purpose. Moreover, the new regime itself must move rapidly to give its functionaries a stake in the system.

*But has the government not already announced a drive to weed out corrupt officials?* Every dictator launches these drives from time to time both to put up a show and to get rid of uncooperative officials. Thus, for instance, Chiang Kai-shek often berated Kuomintang officials saying that their sole objective seemed to be to "become official and get rich." He warned them repeatedly that "if we do not weed the present body of corruption, bribery, perfunctoriness, and ignorance, and establish in its stead a clean and efficient administration, the day will soon come when a revolution will be started against us as we did against the Manchus." And the record shows that he often ordered the suspension, punishment and even execution of officials on the grounds of corruption. Here, however, is a retrospective evaluation of his anti-corruption drives:

> Chiang's efforts to eliminate corruption were both spasmodic and selective. Indeed, he tolerated corruption among his most intimate advisers and even within his personal family. There is, therefore, cause to suspect that Chiang used his periodic crackdowns on corruption less as a means to eliminate it than as a device to control his subordinates. For the subordinates, most of whom were in some degree corrupt, had reason to fear that if for any reason they lost the Generalissimo's goodwill, they were vulnerable to punishment for malfeasance in office. Even if Chiang's intentions were not so Machiavellian

---

itself—steps will be taken to rid the family of the Maruti embarrassment. For instance, the regime could nationalize the automobile industry as a whole. Such a move would have the twin advantages of removing an embarrassment for the family and at the same time appearing to be another blow for socialism.

and if he was sincerely committed to wiping out corruption, he was backing a huge and entrenched system. Broadscale corruption therefore persisted throughout the Nanking period.[11]

Instead, the regime's need to placate loyalists will come to affect economic policy and economic administration more and more. For there is only one way of assuring them a regular as well as a substantial income and this is to give them access to the State's coffers, to formally associate them with the government machinery so that they may obtain their tribute automatically. Apart from enlarging corruption this association will almost certainly lead to financial profligacy: crash programmes of various kinds will become the order of the day—for alleviating drought, for helping the landless and the artisans—for raising agricultural output, for helping unemployed engineers start businesses; undertaken in the name of the poor, these programmes will invariably end up helping the well-to-do, the well connected, and in the meantime they will impose a heavy burden on the exchequer.

Unable to mobilize resources at home, unable to do even as much as it has done in the past (in terms of procuring domestically produced foodgrains, for instance,) the regime will be dependent on foreign aid. As the West is the principal dispenser of aid, the regime will be much better disposed toward the West than has been the case thus far. With its talk of "productivity" and "discipline" instead of "socialism," with its new and permissive attitude to private capital and foreign capital, the regime will be much more palatable to the West also. (The timing is indeed propitious for the new regime in India. The United States in particular will be keen to hedge its bets in Asia in view of uncertainties that now surround its Chinese connection.)

Aid will be rationalized in many ways. A higher score on growth indices will be taken as evidence of better performance. "In any case," we will be told, "it is all very well for you to go on talking about the character of the regime, but there are starving people out there and we must send in the aid if only to feed

---

[11]Lloyd Eastman, *The Abortive Revolution*, Harvard University Press, Cambridge, 1974, p. 20.

them." The point, of course, is that even as aid temporarily keeps a few from starvation, it will be shoring up a regime that is preventing precisely those fundamental transformations that are prerequisites for forging an economy that functions for the people.

The rationalizations will just provide a veneer. Essentially, foreign aid will be a political operation—a device for sustaining a regime that is pro-West in its inclinations, a device for weaning India out of the orbit of, say, the Soviet Union, a device for adding a fourth focus, in addition to Japan, China, and Iran, in the Asian theatre. Even as the "practical men" busy themselves with the great game of Realpolitik, the West will once again emerge as the prop of an anti-people regime in the Third World.

## VI

Within India, growing poverty and unemployment—even as the economy is being bent to benefit the well-to-do—and growing corruption, will erode the regime's legitimacy. This, quite apart from the compulsions that have been listed earlier, will lead the rulers to repress people more and more. The increasing resort to repression, in turn, will make the regime more and more dependent on the police and armed forces of the country.

Over the past few years as it was compelled to call upon the police and the armed forces more and more often to keep the people in line, the regime went out of its way to placate policemen and personnel of the armed forces. Their salaries were raised, their dependents were given many benefits, their service conditions were greatly improved. From now on the rulers will both need and fear the armed apparatus. Quite literally, their lives will depend on its good humour. The rulers will know that should some generals, say, decide to seize power, the rulers will have no way to stop them on their own.

Thus, efforts to placate the police and the armed forces will be redoubled. They will soon be given a stake in the system; they too will be incorporated directly into the governmental machinery with administrative appointments, senior posts in public and private enterprises, ambassadorships and the like. The general atmosphere of malfeasance as well as the anxiety of the rulers to humour them will provide many opportunities for corruption. And as the class background and values of officers in the police and the armed forces are not very different from those of the elite in general, we can be certain that they will go in for it on a large scale. Simultaneously, the rulers and their allies in the armed forces will have to manipulate promotions and appointments at all levels. For, experience the world over has shown that just a handful of officers can topple a regime.

Of course, none of this may ultimately succeed in keeping the armed forces from seizing power themselves. For a while the forces will be content with the new attention, secure in the knowledge that the regime is now overtly dependent on them, happy at learning that the civilians, the bureaucrats are being put in their place, that the country is being "disciplined." Soon enough, however, some officers will begin to reason that the attention and favours of the rulers are not from any special affection for the armed forces, but rather are symptoms of the regime's nervousness and vulnerability, an acknowledgement that real power lies with the armed forces. Why not grab it openly then? Why be back-room boys forever? After all, if discipline is what the country needs, who can instil it better than the armed forces?

Were a formal takeover by the armed forces to come about in the near future—i.e., before the ideological and political level of the forces has been raised—it would not change the character of the regime. At present the ideological predispositions of the bulk of the officers in the armed forces are not different from those of the new rulers. The only difference would be that, even in a formal sense, India would then have entered a period of coups and countercoups.

In an atmosphere of increasing factionalism, assuming coups and countercoups—and of corruption and manipulated promotions and appointments that are in the cards in any case—the fighting capabilities of India's armed forces will erode. For a while this deterioration will be masked by a greatly enlarged weapons programme—a programme that the regime will almost certainly go in for. Not only will big business benefit from it but the rulers know that there is scarcely a better way of keeping the armed forces happy than by giving them better and bigger arms.

It is only necessary to add a word about India's relations with its neighbours to complete the scenario.

A regime of the kind we have described will certainly be a supernationalist regime, with visions of regional hegemony, with memories of Greater India. Such an ideology, autonomous developments in neighbouring countries (we must remember, after all, that all of South Asia has passed into the hands of mountebank dictators) and internal compulsions will all lead the regime to take an active interest in the affairs of its neighbours. India will be the status quo power in the region. A regime of the kind we have described cannot, after all, support, welcome or even tolerate progressive movements in neighbouring countries. The alacrity with which the Indian government helped the Ceylonese government to put down the insurrection of 1971 will be the pattern of the future.

As a status quo power dominated at home by an anti-people regime, India will be in the business of propping up the local counterparts of Big Minhs, strongmen Kanhs, the Thieus and the Kys—anyone, in fact, who shows the slightest promise of keeping the place quarantined, who collaborates with India in stamping out progressive movements in his country, who collaborates by hunting down Indian progressives should they take sanctuary in these countries. It is entirely possible that in the near future Bangladesh will become ungovernable for reasons of its own, that the insurrection in North Burma will continue to elude the regime in Rangoon, that within India repression will be severest where it has been practised longest—i.e., in Bihar, Bengal and the North Eastern states—that this will incite counter-violence by the people and, thus, that the eastern one-third of the subcontinent will be the theatre in which the above scenario will be acted out first.

Should the regime in Delhi get caught in quagmires of this kind, secessionist groups will see an opportunity for striking out on their own. And they will not lack patrons abroad. In this sophisticated age it would be entirely in character for some super power to start building bridges to these groups even as it shores up the regime in Delhi. Its sole objective would be to ensure that, should one of these groups become a serious proposition, the group must be favourably disposed toward that particular super power.

## VII

The forecasts sketched above point out the direction in which the Indian polity is liable to evolve. A polity does not advance along a straight line. We should not allow twists and turns along the way to obscure the main direction of advance.

It is entirely possible, for instance, that in the coming months Mrs Gandhi will relax the new restrictions, that she will make conciliatory gestures, that she will allow the status quo ante to be restored in many respects. But these moves will not be significant. The relaxations will just be tactical moves on the part of one individual and her coterie—moves prompted by a fortuitous event (like the recent assassination of a neighbouring autocrat, Sheikh Mujib in Dacca), or by the calculation that they will benefit the rulers. At best they would just be the gift of one individual, a gift that can be sequestered at will. In each case the concession will be in form, not in essence.

It is entirely possible that a full-fledged authoritarian regime will not come into being under Mrs Gandhi, but under the new bunch that is now acquiring its education in capturing and using power. But the important deed has already been done. On behalf of the ruling class, Mrs Gandhi has signalled that whenever things become inconvenient for them, the rulers will use dictatorial methods without hesitation. And she has demonstrated (and the lesson will not be lost on any subsequent usurper) that rulers who move audaciously can indeed pull it off. Indeed, the principal consequence of an audacious act is that it facilitates over time as well as over space the next, more audacious one. It erodes standards, it accustoms people to high-handedness. The next time around the usurper will not even bother to go through the charade of constitutional amendments and arguments in courts. He will just grab power and hold it aloft as his sole testimonial.

Moreover, it is well to remember that pressures which have brought the Indian polity to its present pass are going to be even more intense in the coming decades. If the addition of 42 million to the labour force during 1961-71 seemed an awful lot, the reader should recall that during 1971-81 not 42 million, but 65 million will be entering the labour market. If the current urban population of 120 million seems very large, the reader should recall that Calcutta and Bombay alone are expected to have populations of 20 million each by 2000.

The main thrust of the preceding forecasts is that, as the Marxists would say, the situation in India will be ripening for big changes. Basic problems such as poverty and unemployment will be getting worse. The regime will be beholden to, and more and more visibly allied with, foreign, private and public, capital. It will have become an apparatus that derives its power from arms rather than from ideals or from its proximity to the people. This will lead it to rely on the armed apparatus more and more and to involve the latter more directly in governing the country. The armed apparatus will lose some of its professionalism as appointments are manipulated, as corruption and factionalism grow within it. At the same time the regime will be tempted into ill-advised foreign adventures in its neighbourhood.

In all these ways the situation will be acquiring a focus: the struggles for democratic rights, for economic emancipation of the masses and against economic imperialism will all become aspects of a single struggle.

The outcome, however, is not certain. Revolutions do not follow ripeness automatically. Suffering and repression do not awaken people by themselves. After all, in spite of decades, indeed centuries, of exploitation and privation, the Indian people are somnolent. Privation has not inflamed their anger. It has just ground down expectations and left them feeling helpless. They do not know the nature of the regime. They do not know how their own sufferings are related to the nature of the regime. The bulk of them are completely unorganized. The few who are organized are lost in narrow economism—in agitating for a slightly higher wage here, a slightly better cost-of-living allowance there.

Thus, a heavy and serious responsibility devolves on those who have the interests of the country and the people at heart. In the face of determined efforts of the entire state apparatus to suppress progressive movements they must now prepare the people for a protracted struggle—a struggle to emancipate the people and at the same time to safeguard the integrity of the country.

This is not the occasion or place to set out in detail the form such a movement must take. But it would be appropriate to mention four general lessons for the movement that follow from the preceding analysis.

First, the movement must be one that thinks for itself. Instead of wasting time in exegetical polemics about scriptures written abroad, progressive sections in India should analyze the concrete reality that surrounds them. In particular, the movement must analyze the implications that a well-developed, professional, unified, highly mobile and extremely well-equipped state apparatus has for the strategy and prospects of progressive movements. In a sense, thus, the situation is much more difficult than the one that confronted Mao in the 1920s and 1930s. "Formula Maoists" will contribute as little to the emancipation of the Indian people as "formula Marxists" (whom Mao chastized so severely and so often) contributed to the Chinese Revolution. The movement must analyze the dismal record of progressive movements in India thus far.

For instance, it must assess the consequence of the assumption that has governed the actions of many progressives in India—that the Congress was not a party of one class but a coalition of all classes and that, thus, the task of progressive sections was to strengthen the supposedly progressive factions within the Congress. It must analyze the consequences for the orthodox Communist parties in India of looking to outside powers—be they the Soviet Union or China—for inspiration, guidance and, as in the case of the Moscow-oriented Communist Party of India, for help: how this reliance led them to adopt erroneous paradigms, how it alienated nationalist sentiment within India, how the powers on which these sections were relying made deals with the rulers in India in pursuit of their own interests and how they then forced their followers in India to toe the rulers' line. It must analyze the consequences of the romantic assessment about the people's readiness to take up the fight that misled groups like the Naxalites.

Second, it must focus primarily on the dispossessed masses. For it is clear that in the ultimate showdown no one else will fight on their behalf. Even as it does so, however, it must educate those who man the state apparatus. It must seek at least to neutralize large sections of them so that they do not train their guns on the people.

Third, for awakening, educating and organizing the dispossessed masses it must engage them in political and revolutionary activity and not try to tempt them into its fold by narrow economism. The Indian trade union movement, for instance, has been rendered almost entirely ineffective by economism. The so-called progressive leaders of the trade unions have been busy winning workers over to their particular union on the promise that by joining their unions rather than that of their rivals the workers would maximize their chances of obtaining higher emoluments. As a result the workers' political awareness has remained abysmal and ultimately the initiative even in trade union matters has gravitated to the regime. For in the end it has been up to the regime to concede the demands of one union rather than another and thus to signal the workers that it pays them to join unions of its choice.

Finally, the movement must foreswear all forums that the regime itself prescribes—courts, legislatures, elections. For the regime has demonstrated times without number—and Mrs Gandhi's coup is just the latest demonstration—that these forums are meant to serve the regime and not the people, that it will not allow others to outmanoeuvre it in these forums, that whenever things become inconvenient it will just change the rules of the game. Instead of wasting time in elections, legislatures, courts and the like, it must pit the masses against the regime so that the masses see the true face of the regime, so that they experience its determination to protect the privileges of its patrons, so that they get acquainted with the means it will employ to do so.

The task is an arduous and protracted one. Not only are the Indian people politically innocent but from now on the regime will use every means to destroy every effort to organize and educate the masses. Even though the outcome will not be settled for decades, the beginning should not be deferred. There is little time to lose. It is already very late. Three decades have gone by and today the position is that the ruling classes have a fully fashioned state apparatus at their command and the people have nothing.

## POSTSCRIPT*

The essay has been reprinted without any changes. Even a footnote in which I might have used some figures a bit uncritically has been retained.

Much of what it forecast has already come to pass. Our polity has turned out to be thinner than even the most sceptical among us suspected. The suddenness with which the enthusiasm of the first half of 1975 disappeared, the suddenness with which nobodies were built up and received acclaim, the suddenness with which others who many thought were "powerful" were cut down, the total absence of an organized force that could resist the state apparatus and the readiness of the functionaries to "carry out orders," even as they apologized for doing so...all these indicate how thin a polity our's is.

Events of the past two years have also shown how far we have already gone in creating a dual society. When Pitambar Pant was asked in the early sixties to ascertain the amount of foodgrains that would be required in 1975/76 to maintain "the minimum standards of living in India," he and his colleagues in the Planning Commission had come to an estimate of 148 million tons. Later analysts commenting on the norms that had been used to arrive at this estimate pointed out that the figure was an under-estimate by 10 per cent to 30 per cent. An exceptionally good monsoon in 1975/76 gave us, on the government's claims, 118 million—a full thirty million tons less than the minimum that was required for those spartan "minimum standards of living." And yet food prices fell—millions hovering near starvation and food prices falling?

The new slogans of export-led-growth indicate the garb in which our policy-makers want to formalize a dual society in India: the national rich will ally themselves with the international rich; the national poor will be kept down and put out of sight with the force of arms.

Is this the society Gandhiji fought for?

Does the announcement of elections not change all this? How I wish that were the case. Like so many others I will do what little I can to ensure that democratic forces triumph.

*February 1977.

I fear, however, that the announcement, the timing, the manner, serve on the contrary to confirm the analysis. The people have not wrested the elections from the rulers. In fact, most thinking people cannot even figure out what it is that made Mrs Gandhi schedule the elections. Apprehensions about a worsening economic situation? The taunting example of Zulfi? The calculation that the opposition would not be able to get together and will, as has been its custom in the past, defeat itself? An astrologer? Thus, far from wresting the elections from Mrs Gandhi, many cannot even figure out how this gift has suddenly landed in their laps.

Like everyone else, I, of course, hope that all of us will use the gift to good purpose. If the elections are held and if by some chance the opposition wins, we will have a brief respite. But I fear that the longer term pressures will reassert themselves soon enough. Therefore, the long term task remains unchanged.

# 3 Symptoms*

A number of leaders—Pandit Nehru more than most—have warned us to be on the guard against fascism. This essay describes some symptoms by which the reader may recognize the phenomenon when he chances upon it. From time to time I will also draw from the description some inferences about the proper ways of dealing with the phenomenon.

The essay will deal largely with symptoms alone. Lively controversies surround attempts to determine the "true" nature of fascism—of whether it is best viewed as "the characteristic of an era," as "the last, most acutely monopolistic and imperialist phase of capitalism" or as something else. Academicians are still debating the matter and, we can be certain, they will continue to do so for quite a while. I will side-step these controversies and address myself to the practical problem of helping the reader recognize the beast when it suddenly appears. I should state that upon reviewing the record I find much merit in one particular view of the nature of fascist rule and that this view underlies much of what I will be saying in this essay. This is the view that Rauschning put forward in the late 1930s.

Rauschning was a high Nazi official, once the President of

*May 1976.

the Danzig senate, and one of the very few high ranking Nazis who resigned their position when they discerned the character of the rulers and the regime. In a famous book—*The Revolution of Nihilism*—he characterized the fascist rulers as "nihilists," as ones whose sole objective was domination and who would ultimately perform only one function—the clearance function. I do not agree with much of what Rauschning said and, in a basic sense, I have little sympathy for his point of view—his point of view is conservative, even aristocratic. But I think that in his basic characterization of the rulers and the regime he put his finger on a central characteristic—a characteristic that all of us, the supporters and opponents of such regimes as well as mere onlookers, will do well to keep in mind.

An initial problem is the problem of riches. There is so much material that one must summarize—for academicians and others have been at the game for long. And there are so many symptoms that need to be listed—for one of the features of such regimes is that ultimately they come to affect all aspects of the society, economy and polity so that their consequences are visible in many spheres.

Moreover, I would want not just to list the symptoms that would be apparent after the regime has been installed for many years but also to give a hint or two about the initial stages of such a regime—the *coup*, the consolidation and so on. There are two reasons for doing so: first, many of the characteristics that will later mark the regime make their initial, and in many cases their most dramatic, appearance in the first months; second, if one is to deal with the beast one must be able to spot it early enough; there is little use in being certain about its identity after it is firmly in place on our chests. Hence, as a description of the initial stages is of some practical import, we have the problem of integrating it with an account of the characteristics that will mark the regime.

Some of the features—the slogans, the rhetoric, the laws, the reactions of the *dramatis personae* etc.—have such a familiar ring to them that one has to keep reminding oneself that all this is not just being manufactured for the occasion but was actually written by authors who were observing or recounting other, distant episodes. So as to convey some of this flavour to the reader I will cite lengthy passages from accounts of Hitler and

## Symptoms

Mussolini. These passages will sometimes interrupt the text. But, as they are too pertinent to be shunted off to footnotes, the reader will have to bear with me and read at two levels—he will have to read what I have to say and at the same time go on absorbing the long citations at a sort of subliminal level.

Most of the material I will cite is about Hitler and Mussolini. Of course, these are extreme cases and one can discern a number of the same features in the regime of many a small pretender—Franco, Peron and so on. But I'll stick with Hitler and Mussolini: the characteristics are most visible in their regimes and both of them—as well as many of their henchmen—were by far the more intelligent, articulate and candid. Moreover, spotting a series of similarities with the regimes of Mussolini and Hitler is much greater cause for alarm than with those of a Peron or a Franco.

Finally, when the regimes of Mussolini and Hitler were in full bloom they received a louder and more unequivocal chorus of applause the world over than the Francos or Perons ever did. If they—with all the promise they seemed to have held for the eyes of even critical observers like Bernard Shaw, H.G. Wells *et al*—if even they brought their people to such a sorry state in the end, then those who argue that regimes which bear these characteristics may do some good have a much harder case to prove.

I realize, of course, that there are several differences between different fascist regimes and many an academician has made his reputation differentiating one from the other. As my objectives are heuristic ones this essay deals with characteristics that are common to them all. I will ignore the internal differences between the regimes and rulers.

### I. The Takeover

A fascist takeover is preceded by a worsening objective situation and a stalemate of different classes. Parts of the working class are organized—usually along narrow economism. They are increasingly hard-pressed but they are unable to get their way; neither rhetorical militance nor occasional harassment of the owners, as in a few strikes etc., secures their objectives for them. They are unable to use legal means to change the balance and are equally unprepared to mount an insurrection. But their rhetorical militance as well as their occasional strikes etc., are enough to alarm the owners, to make them lose self-confidence, to convince them that they can no longer handle the situation by ordinary means. They are enough also to spread fear and insecurity among the middle classes.

The would-be usurper fans these anxieties—if he is out of power (a Hitler in the 1920s or a Mussolini before the March on Rome) he helps paralyze the system, if he is in office he lets things get worse. Thus, he does what he can to help create a "planned defeatism," till confusion, lassitude and disgust, and exasperation overtake the populace, till citizens begin to feel that "perhaps democratic institutions are not suited to our national character," till they start feeling that perhaps "a strong hand" alone can deliver them from their troubles.

The usurper—who has done as much as anyone to paralyze the institutions, who has done as much to fan anxieties and sow despair—then steps forth as the strong man who will save the state. In reality his *coup* is just a grab for personal power but the preceding manipulated disorder enables him to present his grab as a bold and necessary move to save the country from chaos. The events in Germany up to the Reichstag fire and those in Italy leading up to the fascist March on Rome provide perfect examples of this sequence.

## The Legality Strategy

The usurper is careful at this stage to keep up the appearance of "legality."

Democratic constitutions are framed on the premise that citizens and politicians will abide by their spirit. The determined usurper thus has no difficulty in finding articles, clauses—the letter—to stab the spirit. He is careful to invoke an article or a clause at each step; among other things this methodical and step-by-step assault sets him (a Hitler) apart from his impatient plebian colleagues (the Rohms and others). At his trial in October 1930 Hitler had taken his famous "legality oath" in which he swore that he would refrain from any but constitutional methods in pursuing power.[1] He stuck to this oath.

[1]Karl Dietrich Bracher, *The German Dictatorship*, Praeger, 1970, p. 186.

## Symptoms

Similarly, even as his gangs were beating up workers, even as he and his colleagues were planning assaults of various kinds, Mussolini stuck it out till the King formally invited him to form a cabinet. Quite obviously, if the usurper is already in office—as Hitler was at the time of the Reichstag fire—it is that much easier for him to stage his *coup* "legally."

The morning after the Reichstag fire Hitler goes to the aging Hindenberg and gives him a highly coloured account and persuades him to issue an Emergency Decree. The Emergency Decree is issued under Article 48 of the Wiemar Constitution.

'The Presidential dictatorial powers—that is, the emergency powers granted by Article 48 of the Weimar Constitution—furnished the desired leverage. In drafting the far-reaching emergency powers of the President, the fathers of the Constitution had had in mind the protection of the Republic in times of crisis and had invoked them only in this sense. But the restrictions and controls set on these powers proved to be fatally inadequate.... A double defect of the Weimar Constitution made this possible. First, in the overwhelming opinion of scholars, the Constitution did not preclude the erosion and abrogation of its substance by constitutional means. This basically is what had been happening since 1930, and particularly after 1932; the process was completed in 1933 with the Reichstag fire decree and the Enabling Act.... But here a second weakness of the Weimar constitutional and governmental system offered a way out of the seemingly insurmountable dilemma created by the legality strategy, namely the possibility of a Presidential government without and even against the will of parliament and of democratic public opinion. The gist of the growing body of literature on this theme is that the Presidential dictatorial powers under the famous-infamous Article 48 of the Weimar Constitution, intended specifically to protect the democratic order against radical efforts to overthrow it in the early postwar years, now, under a President with a different orientation, served diametrically opposite purposes. In the days of the Bruning Government (1930), and certainly during the authoritarian Papen and Schleicher Cabinets (1932), it became apparent that the possibility of an extra—let alone anti—parliamentary government would inevitably paralyze parliament and parties. The ever-present possibility of invoking emergency powers offered a convenient escape-hatch from political responsibility, and at the same time prepared the population for the type of authoritarian ideas of government which were being bandied about with growing force by propagandists and in the universities. The catastrophic repercussions of the world-wide economic crisis, together with the public esteem enjoyed by a President receptive to such authoritarian concepts, turned the possibility of throttling democracy by authoritarianism into reality.'[2]

This simple device—of proceeding step-by-step, of, as Hitler would say, "using the weapons of democracy to destroy democracy"—pays handsome dividends.

'...now the willing collaborators in the civil service and the courts, on which National Socialism, lacking its own specialists, was so dependent, were able to find reassuring legal provisions; after all, given such apparently unexceptional legal foundations, there was no basis for any real objections to a government, however turbulent and violent, and however regrettable some of its "excesses" (which were, however, "exceptions"). Wasn't it a good thing—so state the files of many a high official of that time—that the irresistible revolution was carried out in so legal a fashion? It was, therefore, only logical to do everything in one's power to assure this legal revolution every technical and administrative success....'[3]

'The effects of the pseudo-legal one-party decree of July 14, which Papen and his conservative colleagues also voted for without demur, were inestimable. The law violated the Enabling Act, in itself pseudo-legal, on which Hitler's legislative dictatorship based itself. For this reason, Hitler's twelve-year

---

[2] Bracher, *op. cit.*, pp. 192-194.
[3] *Ibid.*, p. 197.

reign must also in a formal juridical sense be considered unlawful. Regardless of the Enabling Act, Hitler now was able to command a two-thirds majority in his one-party parliament any time he wished to legalize the violation of restrictions still found in the Constitution and Enabling Act. Open legal opposition against the rule of National Socialism had become impossible. And the possibilities of legalizing arbitrary acts insofar as this was considered necessary for the mollification and deception of the civil service and judiciary, the population and Army, the business community and the outside world, were unlimited. This perfected legalization machinery also made superfluous the drafting of a new constitution, which Hitler had mentioned in the past. It was far easier to operate with one's own law, decrees, and regulations, in the course of which the Weimar Constitution was repeatedly violated and broken but never formally repealed. Even though this was nothing more than the "formal-juridical garb of legality" (Arnold Brecht) of an already accomplished act of government, it was highly effective in deceiving and mollifying a legalistically oriented civil service and judiciary. Even today, apologetic analyses and trials of National Socialists are surrounded by the fiction of legality with which the Third Reich was able to bind "loyal" jurists and specialists, civil servants and soldiers, to its despotic rule, beginning with the introduction of the mandatory Hitler salute to the legalization of the terror and murder decrees which were carried out, or at least respected, by those servants of state....'[4]

'But leverage against both the Left and Right was not all of the profit Hitler derived from the Enabling Act. By virtue of the act, the entire apparatus of the government bureaucracy was at Hitler's disposal. This included the judiciary, which was indispensable to his far-reaching plans. The act offered a basis that satisfied both the consciences and the craving for security of the bureaucrats. Most government officials were pleased to note the legal nature of this revolution, which in spite of the many isolated outrages contrasted so favorably

[4]*Ibid.,* p. 226.

with the chaos of 1918. This legality, even more than the antidemocratic traditions of the civil service made them ready to cooperate. Moreover, a special decree had been issued, which made non-acquiescent civil servants liable to punishment. What is more, resistance would have equalled illegal action. There are those who to this day maintain that there was no definite break, that the parliamentary republic glided by degrees into totalitarian dictatorship. But examination of all the facts reveals that within the process of the legal revolution the revolutionary elements far outweighed the legal ones. The public was duped by the brilliant trick of having the change of scene take place on the uncurtained stage, so to speak. But the real drama consisted in a revolutionary seizure of power confirmed by the Enabling Act. . . .'[5]

'Not the least of (the advantages) was that few people realised the comprehensive scope of their (i.e., the usurper's and his clique's) activities. Here again, the crucial steps were hidden from view. When the revolution was officially staged, on January 30, 1933, it had in reality scarcely begun; when its successes were celebrated any sort of remonstrance had become useless: the seizure of impregnable power had become an accomplished and unalterable fact.'[6]

The usurper knows the value of conditioning the populace and he knows that nothing conditions it as well for the next dictatorial act as the dictatorial step he takes now. This—and not the formal powers it contributes to his quiver—is the principal contribution of each assumptive act. Thus, apart from the formal powers it gave Hitler, the most consequential aspect of the Emergency Decree was that it was a *fait accompli*: among the many excuses on which the parliamentaries persuaded themselves to later vote for the Enabling Act was the excuse that its enactment was, after all, just a formality, that the real seizure of power had aleady taken place by the Emergency Decree.[7]

[5] Joachim C. Fest, *Hitler*, Harcourt Brace Jovanovich, New York, 1973, p. 142.
[6] H. Rauschning, *The Revolution of Nihilism*, Longmans, Green, New York, 1939, p. 15.
[7] Fest, *op.cit.*, p. 410.

At every step the usurper is full of the most solemn promises, of his most personal assurances.

Thus, Hitler assures everyone that the Emergency powers will be used only in exceptional circumstances: 'Before the house was the so-called Enabling Act—the "Law for Removing the Distress of People and Reich (Gesetz zur Behebung der Not von Volk und Reich)," as it was officially called. Its five brief paragraphs took the power of legislation, including control of the Reich budget, approval of treaties with foreign states and the initiating of constitutional amendments, away from Parliament and handed it over to the Reich cabinet for a period of four years. Moreover, the act stipulated that the laws enacted by the cabinet were to be drafted by the Chancellor and "might deviate from the constitution." No laws were to "affect the position of the Reichstag"—surely the cruelest joke of all—and the powers of the President remained "undisturbed." Hitler reiterated these last two points in a speech of unexpected restraint to the deputies assembled in the ornate opera house.... "The government (Hitler promised) will make use of these powers only insofar as they are essential for carrying out vitally necessary measures. Neither the existence of the Reichstag nor that of the Reichsrat is menaced. The position and rights of the President remain unaltered.... The separate existence of the federal states will not be done away with. The rights of the churches will not be diminished and their relationship to the State will not be modified. The number of cases in which an internal necessity exists for having recourse to such a law is in itself a limited one." The fiery Nazi leader sounded quite moderate and almost modest.'[8]

But, as events are quick to show, the facts of the matter are going to be very different. The Emergency powers—and more— are to be used in everything but exceptional circumstances, against everyone but "social and economic criminals." The Reichstag is truly abolished in deed; its sole function henceforth

---

[8] W. Shirer, *The Rise and Fall of the Third Reich*, Simon and Schuster, New York, 1960 p. 198.

is to be to extend the Enabling Act from time to time (i.e., on those occasions when Hitler had not already extended it by fiat) and to rubber stamp decisions that have already been made. The candid and far seeing Goebbels had accurately forecast this state of affairs when, once the Emergency was declared and when someone was citing the figures about electoral returns, about their position in the legislature and suggesting that they would still need the collaboration of other parties, he had exclaimed: "What do figures matter now? We're the masters in the Reich and in Prussia." In an editorial he, therefore, openly advised the Reichstag "to make... no difficulties for the administration and let things take their course."[9]

As for Hitler's assurances that Emergency powers were just being acquired temporarily to counter an urgent danger to the country, well, the Emergency powers were never relinquished. The Enabling Act—which originally had a term of only one year—was extended on one pretext or another till the regime itself collapsed in 1945.

*Taking Stock*

I could continue to cite many passages and to draw attention to many aspects of the "legally" staged *coup*, but we should pause and take stock of what has gone thus far.

The first point to note is that the immediate, proximate event that apparently triggers off the crisis has little or nothing to do with it.

'In Nuremburg, Goring admitted that the wave of arrests and persecutions would have been carried out in any case, that the Reichstag fire only acclerated those processes.'[10]

Far from the immediate event causing the crisis, the efficiency and thoroughness with which the takeover is accomplished shows that the would-be usurper was lying in wait for just such an event. Indeed, in the ensuing confusion it is never entirely clear whether the alleged event or provocation actually occurred, or if

---

[9]Fest, *op.cit.*, p. 399.
[10]*Ibid.*, p. 396.

it occurred, who was responsible for it. (We shall return to this point later.) In any case, whatever the facts be regarding the particular incident (the Reichstag fire or the alleged conspiracies of Rohm) we know that the usurper has had as much to do with creating the general atmosphere, the overall stalemate, as anyone else. We have only to recall the role of Mussolini creating the parliamentary and extra-parliamentary crises leading up to the March on Rome to see that this is so.

The second point is to realize that the act of usurpation is a power play; it is a political act. It is futile to take a narrowly legalistic view of the *coup* and to go around rushing to the courts thinking that somehow they will keep the country from the usurper. The usurper's view of the courts is a very simple one: he will listen to them if they go along with him; he will tell them to go to hell, if they don't. Incidentally, his view of the legislature is no different. Thus, while he is pushing the Enabling Act through the Reichstag, we find Hitler telling it "to grant us what in any case we could have taken."[11]

To return to the courts, the judges—as much out of a desire to save their own skins as out of illusions ("we must grant him this bit so that he is satiated and grabs no more," that "we must put our faith in his professions so that he gets over his paranoia, this obsession of his that everyone is out to get him"), as out of the narrow legalisms on which they have been weaned—the judges make things easier for the usurper. When the record is reviewed it is at once obvious that many of the acts of the usurper were illegal even in a narrow, technical sense.[12] Even so the facade of legality stayed in tact because those who—like the judges—were meant to uphold "Law" never asked what "legality" means, they never took a stand on principle. Even when they thought that they were "standing up to" the usurper, they were only acting out the role of editorial assistants to him. He and his clique would take some action. When this was brought to the attention of the judges they would pronounce that the measure was not permissible under Act Y, article X, clause Z as these stood then.

---

[11]*Ibid.*, p. 409.
[12]For examples in Hitler's case, see Bracher, *op. cit.*, pp. 195-196, 211.

All the usurper had to do was to issue a decree amending the offending clause or have the Reichstag rubber stamp an alteration. Satisfied that their protest had been taken note of, the judges would henceforth acquiesce in the same steps which they had so recently pronounced impermissible. In functioning thus, they functioned merely as editorial assistants to the usurper and his clique—advising him and his cohorts about ways of perfecting the text, dotting their i's and crossing their t's. At a time when they could have played their role in the defence of liberty only by the widest possible view of "Law," they buried their heads in the sand and took shelter behind narrower and narrower legalisms.

Even these little shows of independence—these moments of hesitation before falling in line—did not last long. For, as we shall see, a new concept of "Law," a demand for "committed" civil servants (and by that time judges were officially dubbed to be just another category of civil servants) soon overwhelmed them. To expect that rushing to these judges will safeguard liberty or that these narrow legalisms will save the citizenry from a determined assault is to act the fool. Indeed, as we already noted, Hitler soon discovered that it was so easy to distort the Wiemar Constitution, to pulverise courts, the legislature, to bully judges, legislators, civil servants, etc., that he never formally repudiated the Wiemar Constitution—even though he had spoken of giving the country a new constitution.

It is futile to take a legalistic view of the usurper's assault not only because the courts cannot or will not defend a people but also because the usurper is not acquiring real political power by formal legislation, amendments and so on. He is acquiring it because of the willing (or unwilling) collaboration of the State apparatus in enabling him to overcome his opponents—through street violence, arrests, kidnappings and so on.[13] Such formal laws etc., as are passed from time to time are not the causes of his power but the manifestations of it.

The third lesson that stands out is that the usurper must be resisted at the first step. The longer resistance is delayed, the

---

[13]In the case of Hitler see *ibid.*, p. 187; for Mussolini see Nathanael Greene, *Fascism, An Anthology*, Thomas Crowell, New York, 1968, pp. 167-168.

## Symptoms

greater will the price be that the polity will have to pay for ridding itself of the burden. In the first anxious months the usurper works ceaselessly to create the impression of being an avalanche, of being "an irresistible tide."[14] He knows that he can survive only if he overwhelms, only if he is quickly able to convince everyone that "it is futile," as Hitler would say, "to rebel against the firmament."[15] The facts, of course, are very different. Resistance is easiest in the first few months.

> Thus, we have Goebells telling us later on: 'If the enemy had known how weak we were, it would probably have reduced us to jelly.... It would have crushed in blood the very beginning of our work...'[16]

The situation in Italy was no different. When the March on Rome manoevuers began, the Quadrumvirate decided to direct the campaign from Perugia and installed themselves openly at a local hotel: 'A platoon of soldiers could have seized the "High Command" of the fascist revolution if some NCO had taken the initiative. Actually the opposite happened for three fascist delegates called on the prefect at about midnight on the 27th and summoned him to give up his powers to the fascist command....'[17]

Hence, resistance must be mounted at the first step. If people sit back in the belief that "resistance should have been mounted yesterday, today is too late," events will surely teach them that tomorrow will be later still. Acts that have some significance in the first weeks, have no meaning a few months later.

> '...What is needed is a definite decision, not a mere tactical deal or bargain. It is precisely by their attitude of putting up with things as they are in the hope of affecting "appeasement" and a slowing down of the general course that all the leading personalities on whom the thinking people had rested their hope that something of value might, after all, come out of the

---

[14] Greene, *op.cit.*, p. 116.
[15] Fest, *op.cit.*, p. 210.
[16] Rauschning, *op.cit.*, p. 112.
[17] A. Rossi, *The Rise of Italian Fascism, 1918-22*, Howard Fertig, New York, 1922, p. 300.

deal of 1933, have thrown away the opportunities they once had of exerting influence. . . . The logic of the process takes charge, upsetting all plans and calculations. "All that is left to do is to submit to force and it will be wise to submit with good grace". . . . I was anxious to resign but was advised by influential personages not to do so, as the course of events could only be preserved from taking a dangerous turn if the leadership was not left to fall into the hands of the desperate elements of the Party. Subsequent events have shown the error of this "wait and see" policy. If such men as von Neurath and Schacht, who shared responsibility under the new regime, had put up opposition in good time, in 1934-35, if they had brought to bear the whole weight of their personal influence, they might still have been able to do a good deal. When they fell from power recently, their disappearance made no difference. . . .'[18]

The fourth lesson is implicit in the remark of Hitler that "only one thing could have broken our movement—if the adversary had understood its principle and from the first day had smashed, with the utmost brutality, the nucleus of our new movement. . ."[19] i.e., if the opponents had used the only means that could have stopped us, namely our means. It is the misfortune of democracies that they cannot be defended against fascist assault by democratic means.

The helplessness of democratic parties in such a situation illustrates the general point. At best, they are just electoral machines. Even when they are equipped for petty rascalities (gathering funds for elections, obtaining jobs and contracts for their supporters etc.) they are ill-prepared to withstand the sudden swoop of the usurper. They have no secret arm; they have no underground channels of communication that can be suddenly activated. Habituated to the ways of an open, easy-going polity they are neither ready nor quick enough to change their *modus operandi*. In fact, even as they wail against the intentions of the would-be usurper (as the social democrats and communists were

[18] Rauschning, *op.cit.*, pp. *xiv-xv*.
[19] Daniel Guerin, *Fascism and Big Business*, Pathfinder Books, New York, 1973, pp. 111-112.

*Symptoms* 57

doing in Germany and Italy) they are so habituated to the old ways that they don't quite believe their own propaganda.

Thus, even as they scream that a fascist take-over is imminent they do not prepare themselves for it. Indeed, even on the eve of the takeover we find themi mmersed in their old, theological disputes about drafting manifestos, about drawing up common economic programmes.

When in Italy coalition governments were floundering because of internal weaknesses and were unable to deal firmly with the fascist gangs, the socialists stood by—debating the true nature of the crisis. In February, 1922, Tasca reports, their support would have enabled the democratic forces to deal with the fascists; by mid-1922, not just their support but their collaboration was needed. Instead they continued with their debates. And the hour for even their collaboration being of any use passed. Mussolini saw all this and correctly commented: 'In the meantime plenty of water is flowing under the bridges of the Tiber and it is probable that the collaboration offered by the collaborationists will soon have so diminished in value that they will not be able to find a dog to collaborate with them.' And this is exactly how things turned out.[20]

In those crucial and vital months we find them still relying on the old instruments—petitions to Presidents, speeches in legislatures and, as we have seen, appeals to courts. But these are pathetic gestures. All these instruments are suddenly out-of-date: bayonets made of water, as Mussolini's scribes would say. I have already listed y the fate of appeals to courts. We can gauge how futile petitions and "protests for the record" are by anticipating our narrative a bit.

When Hitler began taking over provincial governments one after another one did not fall readily. This was the government in Bavaria. The liberals had hoped that resistance to Hitler could be mounted from Bavaria: the state had a strong sense of regional identity and was keen to emphasise its independence of Prussia, it had held out for conservative and

[20]Rossi, *op. cit.*, p. 201.

monarchical restoration and so on. Little came of all these hopes. For, instead of using the time to prepare for resistance, the provincial politicians just kept petitioning the aging—and, by now, almost senile—Hindenberg. Each time Hitler's men would make some disruptive moves, the provincial politicians would shoot off yet another cable to Hindenberg, they would go and seek assurances in person, they would confine themselves to legal depositions and hope that the State Court would issue a constitutional verdict in their favour. Hindenberg—powerless, lost in a mental haze—would readily offer his personal guarantee that the Constitution would be upheld at all costs, that there was no question of toppling provincial regimes illegally, that Nazi commissars would not be sent. . . .

'In this situation, the decree of February 28 was passed. Its second paragraph contained this handy provision, long before the adoption of the Enabling Act: "If a state fails to take the necessary steps for the restoration of public safety and order, then the Central Government is empowered to take over the relevant powers of the highest state authority." This, together with the rigorous stipulations about the suspension of basic rights, made possible the arbitrary interference in local government and consequently in the federal structure of Germany. Although the decree dealt only with temporary interventions, they were in fact of a permanent nature, as was the decree itself, which was never rescinded. The subjugation of the states was completed in short order; events followed one another in swift succession. The interpretation of the decree was left solely to the judgment of Minister of the Interior, Frick. If he thought that a state he disapproved of because it had not yet been brought in line was not dealing harshly enough with opponents of the current course, he could order and justify executive action against that state even without Hindenburg's approval. When the Minister President of Bavaria on that same February 28 once more told Hindenberg of his misgivings he again received the by then incredible assurance that the President had no intention of sending Reich Commissars. . . .

. . . 'But protests based on legality and rule of law had become futile. Clinging to the fiction of the inviolability of the state showed a fatal misunderstanding of the power situation. Such legal resistance by tested methods was hopelessly unequal to the technique of the pseudo-legal seizure of power....On March 1, Held was summoned to Berlin and, in an official meeting with Hitler, given strong warning; the Chancellor even invoked the threat of calling out the Reichswehr against Bavaria's plans. Held retreated, so as to deprive Hitler of a pretext for intervention. Once again, the dilemma of the policy of legal opposition became evident. It could not prevent the final blow, which was not long in coming....

'On March 8, with the forcible subjugation of the other states in full swing, Hindenburg reassured the Bavarian delegate once again, and stated almost indignantly that he would finally like to have his promise believed that no Reich Commissar would enter Bavaria. Even Hitler gave similar assurances; however, he added that even in Bavaria the pressure from below might become so great that the Reich would have to intervene.... While Hindenburg was still making reassuring promises and Hitler pretended ignorance, the Munich SA stood poised to force the resignation of the Bavarian Government. On the morning of March 9, in response to renewed Bavarian protests, Berlin still pretended ignorance, though the Nazi coups were being carried out in all other states. While Held was still feverishly consulting with his Police Minister and the Police President of Munich, the SA was readying itself for the first blow.... Held tried to postpone a decision....

'Once again Rohm, Epp, Wagner, and Himmler had to leave with empty hands. But now Berlin intervened. The document appointing Epp had been in readiness at the Reich Ministry of the Interior all along, and the decree of February 28 was invoked. The Bavarian envoy learned of Epp's appointment at 7:00 P.M. through the press department of the Central Government although the Bavarian Government had not yet been officially informed. Held immediately wired his protests to the President, stating that Frick had exceeded his jurisdiction, for conditions in Bavaria by no means justified intervention, and that Hindenburg's guarantees had thereby been violated. The only answer was a telegram from Frick to Held containing the official notification and making Bavaria the last German state to be politically coordinated. A similar telegram with the appropriate instructions was sent to Epp. When Held sent a telegram to Hindenburg expressing his bitter disappointment, he received a reply via Meissner the next day (March 10) making obvious the utter impotence of the President: Epp's intervention was "made by the Reich Government on its own competence," and Hindenburg would ask Held to refrain from calling on him and to address his complaints to Hitler directly . . . . The resignation of Held became a mere formality. On March 16, Epp vested all powers of government in the National Socialist "Ministerial Commissioners"; fantastic accusations—treason, separatism were levelled against the former government . . . .'[21]

Nor were events in other states any different: '. . . .And on the evening of March 8, Frick, contrary to all promises, appointed the National Socialist Lieutenant. . .as Reich Police Commissioner, on the stereotype grounds that the "maintenance of public safety and order in Wurtemberg was no longer assured under the existing police administration." This simply meant that "public safety and order" were identical with a National Socialist seizure of power. . . .'[22]

The lessons thus are that democratic parties must, if they are to stand up to the usurper, realize that at moments such as these, some things are more important than other things, that instead of continuing with their old controversies they must prepare to deal with the avalanche that threatens them all. Moreover, they must be as quick to change their *modus operandi* as the usurper has been. This change cannot be accomplished without thorough preparation. Hence, in the months and even years when the threat of a fascist takeover is clearly visible, when, in fact, the democratic parties are themselves pointing out that the usurper intends to overthrow democracy, during these months and years the parties should believe their own propaganda, and instead of wasting time in deploying the old ins-

---

[21]Bracher, *op.cit.*, pp. 205-209.
[22]*Ibid.*, p. 208.

truments, they should prepare themselves for the new situation in which these instruments will be useless.

*A Preview*

The initial *coup* is an instructive episode: it gives us many clues about the character and techniques of the rule that is to follow. The principal technique will, as Angelo Tasca tells us in the case of Mussolini, continue to be the *fait accompli*, of "shooting first and talking later," of always going farther than any of the usurper's opponents—all "reasonable," conventional men!—think he ever will.

'Until he was convinced that the right moment had come Hitler would find a hundred excuses for procrastination. His hesitation in such cases was notorious. . . . Once he had made up his mind to move, however, he acted boldly, taking considerable risks. . . . Surprise was a favourite gambit of Hitler's, in politics, diplomacy and war: he gauged the psychological effect of sudden, unexpected blows in paralysing opposition. . . . In war the psychological effect of Blitzkrieg was just as important in Hitler's eyes as the strategic: it gave the impression that the German military machine was more than life size, that it possessed some virtue of invincibility, against which ordinary men could not defend themselves. . .'[23]

Moreover, the takeover and the first few months reveal the single most important characteristic—the hallmark—of such regimes. From now on the clique always and solely devotes itself to "the accurately chosen and ruthless application of all the physical and material power at its disposal. . . (And this) force is applied at all times for the one purpose of maintaining the (clique) in power—and (it is) applied ruthlessly, brutally and instantaneously. . .(for this sole purpose)."[24]

It is well to recall, thus, as the final lesson, the remark of Rauschning that was cited earlier: namely, that the takeover is just the beginning. Just as it would be foolish in the anxious months

---

[23]Alan Bullock, *Hitler: A Study of Tyranny*, Penguin, London, 1962.
[24]Rauschning, *op.cit.*, p. 142

that follow the first authoritarian grabs of the usurper for anyone to rely on the old instruments of an open polity, it would be ludicrous for anyone to think that as the fascist usurper is now firmly in the saddle, as he no longer has any reason to feel insecure, the regime will begin to ease up.

## II. Consolidation

Having executed the takeover with an ease that shocks its opponents and even surprises itself, the clique loses no time in consolidating its position. In the ensuing discussion we must bear in mind that the sole objective of the usurper and his clique is to maintain themselves in power. Thus, they move quickly to destroy all traces of pluralism in the polity. The process moves with the rapidity of machine-gun fire: "A recalcitrant parliament was suspended for seven decisive weeks and the stage was set for rule via emergency decree. On this pseudo legal basis, freedom of the press and opinion were sharply curtailed (February 4), Prussia was brought in line (February 6), basic rights were repealed (February 28) and the states that still resisted National Socialism after the elections of March 5 were subjugated. In each instance, political pressure and terror were used in combination with the dicta of Presidential Emergency Decrees. . . ."[25]

The Nazis, with their flair for euphemisms, called this policy *Gleichschaltung*, the policy of "coordination": all branches of government (the executive, the legislature, the judiciary), all levels of government (including the provincial and municipal governments) and all organizations (the trade unions, the party itself) were made the executive agencies of the usurper and his clique.

This part of the job is always done with the utmost thoroughness for the clique knows that it will be secure only when every activity (be it propaganda marches, or public meetings or anything else) and every organization is made into an instrument of domination. "Whatever it cannot dominate it must destroy, whatever it cannot absorb and master must go."[26] It also knows

[25]Bracher, *op.cit.*, p. 202.
[26]Rauschning, *op.cit.*, p. 88.

that to facilitate domination the citizenry must be reduced to an "atomized, structureless nation"²⁷ which is henceforth herded into officially sponsored and controlled organizations.

A lot of space will be required to detail the systematic manner in which this process was carried out in Germany and Italy. The reader will find an extensive treatment of it in Bracher, Fest, Shirer, Guerin, etc. By the end provincial governments were just, as Frick, the Minister as Interior said, "executive agencies" of the Fuhrer, political parties had disappeared, the courts, the trade unions etc., had all been "coordinated." Only two exmples can be cited briefly.

The judiciary was "coordinated" in three steps. First, its ambit was progressively reduced. The process started by assertions that lawmaking was the exclusive function of the Reichstag: "The making of laws is entirely removed from the judiciary; it is in the hands of the Reichstag, which in practice means in the hands of Hitler, Frank, Lammers, Bormann and a small circle of associates...."²⁸ Then came the assertions that, contrary to past notions, the legislative powers of the Reichstag were unlimited and, finally, that as the Reichstag—in practice, those who ordered it about— had exclusive and unlimited powers to make laws, it alone could furnish the correct interpretation of the laws.

Second, a larger and larger range of actions (e.g. those of the police) were put beyond the purview of the judiciary. Special courts were constituted ostensibly to provide "speedy justice" to the people. Thus from March 1933 Special Courts were set up in Germany (each consisting of three specially appointed, committed judges who were party members) to try cases of "insidious attacks against the government." From March 1935 "People's Courts" (consisting of 2 judges and 5 party officials, SS men and armed forces personnel) were set up to try cases of "treason"— the latter, of course, being defined comprehensively. Moreover, the executive was given the power to review all sentences—it could quash a sentence or "take merciless action" to enhance a

---

²⁷*Ibid.*, p. 139.

²⁸J.P. Stern, *Hitler, The Fuhrer and the People,* University of California, Berkeley, 1961, p. 123.

sentence that it thought was too light.[29]

Third, the judges were "coordinated" as individuals. The magic word was "commitment." In Germany the April 7, 1933 Civil Service Law was extended to cover the judges also: from now on a judge could be removed if, among other things, he, as the Law put it, "indicated that he was no longer prepared to intercede at all times for the National Socialist State." As Shirer notes, very few judges were actually expelled on this ground but the existence of the law—and, even more so, the general atmosphere—was a sufficient reminder to all of them of where their duty lay. The later (January 1937) Civil Service Law formalized the position even more unambiguously: judges, like other civil servants, could now be dismissed for "political unreliability."[30]

The most potent instrument for coordinating the judiciary, of course, was an entirely new concept of law. But more of this later. Here we need only to note the fate of the legislature in the name of whose sovereignty all the powers were usurped: "...The truly illegal nature of the emphatically stressed legality of the revolution is revealed by what followed." With the Enabling Act being stripped of yet another restriction, the state of emergency in fact became a permanent condition for now it was no longer possible to give the impression of the existence of a legal opposition and parliamentary controls. The Reichstag ceased to be even the one remaining sham institution whose existence was guaranteed by the Enabling Act; according to a joke then current, it became the most expensive glee club in the country. Its only function was to celebrate feasts of acclamation, listen to the Fuhrer's speeches, and extend the Enabling Act (1937 and 1939) if this was not done by Hitler himself (as was the case in 1943). National Socialist constitutional lawyers like Ernst Rudolf Huber consequently announced that the Reichstag "is neither an instrument of legislative powers nor a control organ of the Government. . . . It would be impossible for the Reichstag to propose and pass a law that did not originate with the Fuhrer or at least had not been approved by him beforehand." In short, the Reichastag "is an institution that expresses the political agreement of nation and

[29]On all these, see Shirer, *op.cit.*, pp. 269-270.
[30]*Ibid.*, p. 268.

*Symptoms* 65

Government." Like the plebiscites, it was to "document the unity of Fuhrer and nation." As in all modern dictatorships, the sole function of elections was "to confirm one-party voting lists or approve authoritarian decisions already reached. ..."[31]

The clique is quick to realize its total dependence on the armed apparatus—its own armed gangs (such as the SA squads), the paramilitary forces, the police and the army. So it moves swiftly to give those who man this apparatus a stake in the new arrangements: they are granted "the relative freedom of useful and willing henchmen. ..."[32] Increasingly their activities are placed outside the jurisdiction of courts etc.; that is, they are no longer subject to institutional review and scrutiny. Loyal party members too are given a stake by setting up organizations and offices that parallel the state bureaucracy. We shall see in a moment that this device—brought into being ostensibly to ensure that the bureaucracy "does not flout the wishes of the people" and that it "does not sabotage our programmes from within"—serves a basic organizational purpose of the ruler. Here it is enough to note that as far as the party functionary is concerned, it gives him direct access to the only coffers that are big enough to satisfy his voracious appetites—namely, the state's coffers.

The entire pattern and style of administration is completely transformed. It would take up too much space to detail all the changes and I can do no more than list two or three features.

Executive, as well as political, power is completely centralized. The customary devices are employed (the most important of which—the exaltation of the leader—will be examined in Section V). One of these is the familiar one of ruling by dividing:

> 'While he was in the Landsberg goal as long ago as 1924, Hitler had preserved his position in the party by allowing rivalries to develop among the other leaders and he continued to apply the same principle of "divide and rule" after he became Chancellor. There was always more than one office operating in any field. A dozen different agencies quarrelled over the direction of propaganda, of economic policy and the

[31] Bracher, *op.cit.*, p. 225.
[32] *Ibid.*, p. 217.

intelligence services. . . . The dualism of the party and State organizations, each with one or more divisions for the same function, was deliberate. In the end this reduced efficiency but it strengthened Hitler's position by allowing him to play off one department against another. For the same reason Hitler put an end to regular cabinet meetings and insisted on dealing with ministers individually so that they could not combine against him. . . .'[33]

He deliberately created 'an inextricable knot of interlocking authorities which Hitler alone, with virtually a Hapsburgian grasp of puppet mastery, could supervise, balance and dominate. . . This bureaucratic chaos was also one of the reasons (on account of which) the regime was inextricably bound up with the person of Hitler so that to the end there were no struggles over ideological questions, only over the Fuhrer's favour. . .'[34]

As a parallel with each state organization in Italy grew up an organ of the party: 'the fascist militia alongside the army, the Roman salute with the military salute, the special tribunals cutting across the ordinary law courts and the federal secretary at the side of each provincial prefect. . . Fascist law became the only effective law and the nationalisation of the fascist militia transferred an onerous burden from the shoulders of the rich party backers on to the taxpayer. Emblazoned on the State courts of arms was the party emblem of the lictor's fasces. The party secretary in the end assumed ministerial rank and attended cabinet meetings; he came to be a *de jure* member of the defence council and the board of education and was given precedence in ceremonial processions and court functions. . . . The *Gran Consiglio* of the party was made an organ of the State—a constitutional innovation of which Mussolini was particularly proud. Its secretary continued to be the secretary of the party. Mussolini alone could convene it and determine who would attend; he was its president by right, he could decide its agenda and use it as a check on the cabinet. . . .'[35]

[33] Bullock, *op.cit.*
[34] Fest, *op.cit.*, pp. 418-419.
[35] Greene, *op.cit.*, pp. 74, 76.

But does this not at least mean that the party will be independently powerful and that, even if they are destroyed outside, democracy, debate etc., will continue within the party? The answer to both questions is simple: "not in the least." The usurper's purpose in propping up the party is not that it should dominate or supervise the bureaucracy but that each of them should check mate the other.

'Unity was present only in the person of Hitler who continued to foster a multiplicity of divided authorities and who allowed the party only in a few special cases to assume governmental functions and carry through its totalitarian claims.'[36]

The party, like everything else, becomes nothing but an instrument for ensuring the dominance of the country by the clique and of the clique by the leader. Fest, Guerin, Rauschning etc., detail the transformation of the Nazi party. Mussolini's PNF fared no differently. It became nothing but a propaganda machine of the clique and the fascist *Gran Consiglio* became Mussolini's personal 'general staff.' In both cases the parties were depoliticised, in particular, the elements that continued to demand that the parties implement their radical promises were ruthlessly purged. Rohm's murder and that of his associates has already been mentioned. Mussolini too, remarking that 'the trouble is that the revolution having been made, the revolutionaries remain', completely restructured the party and made it into a depoliticised executive machine. It was no longer consulted on major decisions—be they the Conciliation with the Vatican, the Ethiopian war, or Italy's entry into the Second World War. Instead it was put to work, as Tannenbaum says, overseeing the local grocer to make sure that the prices were not raised 'illegally'. The more it was depoliticised, the more it was confined to inconsequential tasks, the more visible and audible it became.[37]

As for democracy, debate etc., surviving at least within the party, they were smothered as effectively within as they had

---

[36]Fest, *op.cit.*, p. 448.
[37]E.R. Tannenbaum, *The Fascist Experience*, Basic Books, New York, 1972, pp. 53-72.

been outside the party: "In order to turn the nation into a barracks fascism had to begin by being a barracks...."[38]

'...Another tendency was for the party itself to become increasingly centralized, and throughout 1923 there was a purge of its provincial directorates, as local fascist units were subordinated to the centre at Rome. Several times before 1922 the local *ras* had rebelled and overruled the leader, but never again for the next twenty-one years. After 1926, instead of the *Gran Consiglio* being elected at the annual party congress, nomination was introduced from the top—"supermen elect themselves" declared Mussolini. The *Gran Consiglio* then chose the party secretary, and the latter appointed the provincial secretaries who together made up the national council. These provincial secretaries then appointed the lesser officials of the local fasci....'[39]

The ordinary party official was as bound by the *Fuhrer Prinzip* —power from the top down. obedience from the bottom up— as the ordinary citizen. Perhaps a bit more so. Barely a few months after seizing power we find Hitler laying out his ideas about the party to the assembled *gauleiters*. Fest recalls Hitler's speech as reported in the minutes of the meeting:

'...The first Leader had been chosen by Destiny; the second must from the start have a loyal, sworn community behind him. No one may be selected who had a private power base. Only one man can be the Leader... An organization with such a hard core and strength will endure forever; nothing can overthrow it. The community within the movement must be incredibly loyal. There must not be any internecine struggles; we must never allow differences to be bared to outsiders. The people cannot trust us with blind faith if we ourselves destroy this trust. Even if wrong decisions are made, the effects can be mitigated by our unconditionally sticking together. We must never allow one authority to be played off against the other... Therefore: no superfluous discussions! Problems which the various headquarters have not yet clarified may

---

[38] Rossi, *op.cit.*, p. 230.
[39] Greene, *op.cit.*, p. 76.

under no circumstances be discussed in public, for that would entail involving the masses of the people in the decision-making process. That was the insanity of democracy, whereby the value of all leadership is lost....'[40]

Apart from transforming every single institution into an instrument of domination, the entire style of administration, the manner of state and party officials in dealing with the citizenry, is completely changed. Among the features that distinguish the new style is its increasing arbitrariness. This helps drill into the populace the notion that henceforth the will of the clique is "law," that there is no court of appeal. It helps keep the citizenry off balance, it sends everyone scurrying around to safeguard his own skin. It lets the lower functionaries of the regime experience for themselves the rewards that they can obtain from the new set-up and—through its random and wanton incidence—it teaches the public the penalties of not being on the right side of the regime.

Most important, this capriciousness helps create the total uncertainty that most frightens a citizenry—much more so than even doubly severe penalties for well-defined crimes would: a man can still race through a field if you lay out mines along well defined, clearly marked paths; but mere thorns will slow him down if they are scattered at random.

Throughout the period, the paraphernalia of "democracy" is studiously kept up. The reader will recall the National Socialist landslide of September 1930: as compared with the elections held two years earlier the number of votes it had received increased from 0.8 million to 6.4 million, the number of its Deputies had increased from 12 to 107. Later—for instance, when the Nazis launched their barrage of coordination decrees—it was to this landside that they used to point saying that the people themselves had given them the mandate for their ruthlessness. As they consolidated their hold over the State apparatus, managing "elections" and "plebiscites" became child's play. The "elections" and "plebiscites" invariably demonstrated that the people were behind every single measure that the fascists had decreed. In the 1933 "plebiscite" about Germany's withdrawal

[40]Fest, *op.cit.*, p. 454.

from the League of Nations, 39 million out of a total of 45 million were reported to have endorsed the Nazi party's "unity candidates." In the March, 1929, "plebiscite" held soon after the Lateran Accords, 90 per cent of the electorate in Italy voted and it was announced that 8, 519,559 had endorsed the regime's doing and only 135,761 (a mere 1.6 per cent) had expressed disapproval. Instances such as these, instances that can be multiplied, suggest two points that we should bear in mind about dictatorships and elections: there has scarcely been a dictator in modern times who has not decreed elections and there has not been a dictator who has lost an election decreed by him.

Much more can be said about the new machinery and the new pattern and style of operation but it is time to move on to other features.

### The Immoral Course

As this process of consolidation proceeds one feature becomes more and more apparent: "At the back of all National Socialist activities is a thoroughly marked preference for immoral methods. It is a fundamental principle of National Socialist tactics to strike fear by deliberate and pronounced incivility and violence and by making a show of readiness to go to any length, where the same purpose could be achieved without difficulty by milder means."[41]

This is not an accident. It is a deliberate tactic—for it confers many advantages upon the usurper and his clique.

'The immoral course is always more effective because it is more violent. The immoral course gives the illusion of strength and daring in persons who are merely underhand by choice.'[42]

It binds the individual member of the fascist clique, party or gang more effectively to the group—his culpability increases his dependence on the group and makes him that much more desperate to ensure that the clique will not be displaced. 'It

[41]Rauschning, *op.cit.*, p. 45.
[42]*Ibid.*

is important to remember, too, the unifying effect of violence and crime perpetrated in company... To commit crimes at top speed became a law, for one crime could only be washed out by another. The bond uniting the aggressors was not their own blood, which was seldom spilled, but the blood of their victims. Feeling that nothing could quench the hatred in which they were held, they went to all lengths, for they knew that once they hesitated, once their enemy was given a breathing space, they were lost...'[43]

But by far the most important consequence of immoral methods—and from the point of view of the clique the most useful and crucial consequence—is a different one: the deployment of these methods helps the usurper and his clique break down norms, standards, institutions. From the point of view of the usurpers these *must* be shattered for only then will the citizenry lose its bearings completely. A number of examples can be given. One or two will have to suffice. While in Hitler's case anti-Semitism was a pathological matter we should not overlook its conscious deployment as a vehicle for brutalising the police the SS, the party cadre, 'as a training ground for the coming social upheaval' as a way of making people 'flout all ideas of legality and the deep rooted conceptions of personal dignity, freedom and security'[44] as a means for 'the revolutionary unsettling of the nation, a means of destruction of past categories of thinking and valuation...'[45] Nor was this conscious objective limited to domestic affairs. Thus, to cite just one instance, '(Hitler's withdrawal from the League of Nations) and its manner were a frontal attack not just on the Versailles treaty but on the principles of legality and faith in treaties' in general.[46]

But does this habitual and conscious preference for immoral and violent methods not conflict with the regime's desire to maintain a facade of legality? We will see later how the issue is ultimately resolved by imposing a new conception of "law" and

[43]Rossi, *op.cit.*, pp. 180-181.
[44]Rauschning, *op.cit.*, pp. 91-92.
[45]*Ibid.*, p. 22.
[46]*Ibid.*, p. 233.

"morality" on the populace. For the present it is enough to note how it is resolved at the superficial level by insistent, unrelenting propaganda: "Its violent character is only superficially inconsistent with its practice of posing always as the champion of justice, denouncing wrongs that cry aloud to heaven. Everything it does is represented as done simply in defence of a sacred right and a moral mission... Every lie is adorned with a show of virtue. Always National Socialism is defending a right, always pursuing honour and faith. Moral indignation comes next after brutality in the National Socialist armory of effective propaganda."[47]

## The Public Enemies

But what if these immoral and violent methods—deployed solely for the preservation and aggrandisement of the usurpers—cause resentment among the populace? What if they become occasions for resistance?

'Should terrorism produce discontent there is always a public enemy to be discovered. Public indignation is poured over him from time to time so that collective outbursts may provide a diversion for accumulating private resentment....'[48] 'Early on Goebbels perceived that if he could conjure up dangers to the newly found security of most Germans then the regime could act as the national rallying point....'[49] And so Hitler, Goebbels and others continually screamed about conspiracies—from outside the country, from within, Jewish conspiracies, Bolshevik conspiracies, capitalist conspiracies—to destroy Germany. If the Jew did not exist, Hitler once remarked, 'we would have had to invent him. A visible enemy, and not just an invisible one, is what is needed.'[50] The smaller pretenders faithfully copied the master performers. Thus we find Quisling ranting away about 'a gigantic international plot by the Jews and moneylenders to destroy nationalism' and so on.[51]

---

[47]Rauschning, *op.cit.*, pp. 45-46.
[48]*Ibid.*, p. 46.
[49]Paul Hayes, *Fascism*, Free Press, New York, 1973, p. 169.
[50]Fest, *op.cit.*, p. 211.
[51]Hayes, *op.cit.*, p. 127.

## Symptoms

Of course, the regime does not just stop at conjuring up these "public enemies" in its rhetoric. It invariably takes the next step: "crimes are arranged and attributed to opponents."[52] It is compelled to do so by the inactivity of the alleged conspirators! The usurper works the people into a frenzy by screaming about dire conspiracies, he covers his tracks by concocting scare stories, and then, as no conspiracies had been planned by his opponents, nothing happens. He and his clique must, therefore, manufacture evidence, create incidents, provoke violence.

'On February 24 the police made a large scale raid on the Communist Party headquarters, Karl Liebknecht House... (The House) had long since been abandoned by the Communist Party leadership but the very next day the press and the radio reported sensational finds of "tons of treasonous materials." Subsequently these documents—which were never published—provided Nazi electioneering with atrocity stories of a projected Communist revolution...'[53]

'...One of the stratagems of legal revolution was not to openly crush the adversary, but instead to provoke him to acts of violence so that he himself provided the pretext for legal measures of repression. Goebbels described these tactics in a diary note dated January 31: "For the present we intend to refrain from direct countermeasures [against the Communists]. First the Bolshevist attempt at revolution must flare up. Then we will strike at the proper movement." This was Hitler's old dream: to be called in at the climax of a Communist uprising, and annihilate the great foe in a single dramatic clash. Then he would be hailed by the nation as the restorer of order and granted legitimacy and respect... He was worried, however, that the Communists might be in no position for a full-scale, vigorous act of rebellion. At various times he had expressed doubts of their revolutionary impetus —which, incidentally, Goebbels had also done early in 1932 when he said he could no longer see them as a danger. As a matter of fact, Nazi propaganda had to work hard to create the necessary bogey man....'[54]

[52]Rauschning, *op. cit.*, p. 47.
[53]Fest, *op. cit.*, p. 392.

Similarly, the question of whether the Nazis themselves perpetrated the Reichstag fire remains unresolved.

'...General Franz Halder, Chief of the German General Staff during the early part of World War II, recalled at Nuremberg how on one occasion Goering had boasted of his deed. 'At a luncheon on the birthday of the Fuhrer in 1942 the conversation turned to the topic of the Reichstag building and its artistic value. I heard with my own ears when Goering interrupted the conversation and shouted: "The only one who really knows about the Reichstag is I, because I set it on fire!" With that he slapped his thigh with the flat of his hand.' (Both in his interrogations and at his trial at Nuremberg, Goering denied to the last that he had had any part in setting fire to the Reichstag )[55]

'...considerable doubts remain, and the controversy has continued. We need not go into it ourselves, since the question of what individual set the fire is a criminological one, with only small bearing on our understanding of the political currents. By instantly taking advantage of the fire to further their plans for dictatorship, the Nazis made the deed their own and manifested their complicity in a sense that is independent of the "whodunit" question...'[56]

A number of other examples can be given. Two will have to suffice. The reader will recall that the Nazi takeover had been preceded by great propaganda about imminent Communist conspiracies to usurp Germany. Alleged Communist responsibility in the Reichstag fire was the main theme in Nazi accounts of the fire.

'...that night some 4,000 functionaries were arrested; most of them were members of the Communist Party, but included in the bag were some writers, doctors and lawyers whom the Nazis disliked... And although most of those arrested had to be fetched out of their beds, and the Reichstag faction leader

---

[54]*Ibid.*, p. 394.
[55]Shirer, *op. cit.*, p. 193.
[56]Fest, *op. cit.*, p. 396.

of the Communist Party, Ernest Togler, voluntarily surrendered to the police in order to demonstrate the untenability of the charges, the first official account—dated that very February 27!—stated: "The burning of the Reichstag was intended to be the signal for a bloody uprising and civil war. Large-scale pillaging in Berlin was planned for as early as four o'clock in the morning on Tuesday. It has been determined that starting today throughout Germany acts of terrorism were to begin against prominent individuals, against private property, against the lives and safety of the peaceful population, and general civil war was to be unleashed"...."[57]

The Rohm affair—in which Hitler had the plebian leaders of the SA, who had by now become an inconvenience to him, arrested and murdered—constitutes an excellent capsule illustration of this technique of the fascists.[58] The standard devices— forged documents, provoked violence, all figure prominently in the episode: "On June 25, 1934 an obviously forged secret order allegedly from Rohm calling the storm troops to arms was said to have come into the hands of the Counter-intelligence Department of the Defence Ministry. The forgery was inept; for the circulation list included the names of Himmler and Heydrich —Rohm's bitterest enemies! But it served its purpose."[59] By June 29 Hitler, Himmler etc., faced the minor inconvenience that no mutiny was taking place! And so, Himmler "set about producing the SA mutiny provided for in the plans which so far had failed to take place. Summoned by handwritten, anonymous notes units of the Munich SA suddenly appeared on the streets and marched about aimlessly. Their surprised leaders were called and (they) promptly ordered their men to go home; but Gauleiter Wagner of Munich could now report... the appearance of allegedly rebellious formations...."[60]

[57] *Ibid.*, p. 397.
[58] The reader should read an account of it, such as in Fest, *op.cit.*, Chapter 3, Book V.
[59] *Ibid.*, p. 461.
[60] *Ibid.*, p. 462.

## The Leader

Where is the leader while all this is happening? In these first few months he is little visible. He seems almost deliberately to withdraw from what is going on: "Hitler himself clung to his pose of the remote leader and arbiter outside and above everyday affairs, a tactic that allowed him to divorce himself from the risks inherent in his course. . . ."[61]; and when he appears his, as Bracher points out, is the voice of moderation, the voice that expresses pain at the fact that some excesses are being committed. All this is, of course, just a sham, a facade, a deliberate tactic. We find Hitler deliberately setting up his lieutenants as the truly brutal, reckless, head-strong ruffians so that he, by contrast, appears as the alternative of moderation, as the only one who can save the populace from the excesses of his lieutenants. Fest recalls how from the very beginning the notion ("so necessary for his good repute") was nurtured—"the deceptive notion of a moderate Hitler, the guardian of law and order, forever trying to subdue his radical followers. . . ."[62]

The truth of the matter, of course, was that he and his henchmen were one: "Only innocent souls soothed their consciences with the explanation that Hitler was surrounded by a clique of bad advisors, that he had no knowledge of what was actually going on, that he was the prisoner of his entourage and must be got out of their hands. . . ."[63] The truth was that Hitler was the most ruthless of them all, the most unscrupulous, the most afflicted by megalomania. And anyone who complained to Hitler received answers that should have dispelled the illusions:

> When Papen and others reproached Hitler after he had unleashed SS & SA on to the streets he countered by saying that, on the contrary, he admired 'the incredible discipline' of his SS & SA men; that indeed he had delayed stern action too long—'some day the judgement of history will not spare us a reproach because in a historic hour, ourselves perhaps sicklied over by the weaknesses and cowardice of our bourgeois

---

[61]Bracher, *op. cit.*, p. 188.
[62]Fest, *op. cit.*, p. 402.
[63]Rauschning, *op. cit.*, p. 78.

world, we proeceeded with kid gloves instead of with an iron fist,' and, hence, he told Papen 'most insistently' that henceforth he should not bring up any further complaints.[64]

When, later on, questions arose about the treatment that was being meted out to the Jews Hitler's response was characteristic; i.e., to take the offensive against his accusers. He blamed himself along with all other Germans for the half way measures, the compromises and the eschewing of a bloody surprise operation: 'Had we gone ahead as we should have, thousands would have been eliminated at that time... Only afterwards does one regret having been so good....'[65]

This deliberately perpetrated myth was an eminently serviceable one. Group after group was taken in by it. In supporting him and drawing hope from events such as the murder of Rohm etc., and the expulsion of Stenness, the Army, for instance, believed 'that Hitler was pursuing and was the guarantor of a course of moderation and cooperation, against the revolutionaries of his party....'[66] Party members, close associates were fooled just as effectively. 'Even party members were startled when in the spring of 1933, the practical steps taken by their leaders began to reveal the realities behind all the patriotic oratory—the unashamed pursuit of power and of key positions and a cynical resort to a brutality hitherto inconceivable.... This apparent change in the character of National Socialism (in reality it was no change but simply a revelation of the true character of the movement) was so striking that the suspicion arose among members of the party that it was the work of enemies within the party who were out to compromise the movement....'[67]

Although many more examples can be given, the sordid Rohm affair will have to serve as the final example. When the contest started shaping up between Rohm and his SS on the one side and the Army, Hitler decided to support the Army. From the beginning his strategy had been "to avoid conflict and rivalry

---

[64]Fest, *op. cit.*, p. 101.
[65]*Ibid.*, pp. 390-391.
[66]Bracher, *op. cit.*, p. 189.
[67]Rauschning, *op. cit.*, p. 16.

with the military or any act that might provoke calling out the Army against the party or SA. ...,"⁶⁸ for he knew that he and his clique could not withstand the Army. In this contest, moreover, there was an additional reason: Rohm and his crowd were by now a threat and an inconvenience to Hitler, what with their persistent demands that he let them loose, that he implement the party's progressive slogans. Hitler did little to disguise the fact that he would side with the Army. But Rohm continued to believe that Hitler "was, as always, playing some deep game and secretly agreed with him now as he supposedly had in the past. . . ."⁶⁹

Even as they were being arrested and murdered the SS officers just did not believe that Hitler was behind the arrests and executions. Most of them thought that someone had staged a *coup*, purging the entire leadership and many of them received their bullets with "Heil Hitler" on their lips.⁷⁰

In brief, the lesson is that the usurper and his henchmen are one. If the henchmen appear to be more ruthless, more unreasonable or more unscrupulous, it is so by the design of the usurper. And in part because of the usurper's superior talents at dissimulation. To believe more is to play the fool.

## III. *A Walk-over: Collaboration and Delusions*

One of the astonishing aspects of the seizure of power and its subsequent consolidation by usurpers like Mussolini and Hitler is that it all turns out to be much easier than anyone had predicted, in fact for easier than even they had themselves imagined it would be.

'The extraordinary thing is that Hitler had been able to carry through his policy of *Gleichschaltung* without serious opposition. The Reichstag, parties, trade unions, the federal states had all given way without a struggle. Hitler himself was surprised by the collapse of the opposition. The Nazis had shown great energy, determination and will power; unfortu-

---

⁶⁸Bracher, *op. cit.*, p. 189.
⁶⁹Fest, *op. cit.*, p. 453.
⁷⁰Cf. note 58 above.

nately, the moderate, reasonable, liberal elements had shown nothing comparable and even the Communists and Social Democrats, with their theoretical attachment to the idea of social revolution, had not dared to make a stand....'[71]

'Before Hitler came to power, an observer described what he considered the inevitable course of events: "Dictatorship, abolition of the parliament, crushing of all intellectual liberties, inflation, terror, civil war; for the opposition could not simply be made to disappear. A general strike would be called. The unions would provide the core for the bitterest kind of resistance; they would be joined by the Reichsbanner and by all those concerned about the future. And if Hitler won over even the Army and met the opposition with cannon —he would find millions of resolute antagonists." But there were no millions of resolute antagonists and consequently no need for a bloody *coup*....'[72]

Indeed, we have seen that one of the private worries of Hitler and his clique was that while they were assuming one dictatorial power after another by frightening the populace with scare stories about conspiracies of violent insurrections, murders, kidnappings which according to their propaganda the opposition was planning, no resistance seemed to be taking place; so complete was the collapse and surrender of the opposition that it strained the credibility of Hitler's hysterical propaganda!

How come? The basic factors that accounted for this collapse and the similar collapse in Italy would require a detailed examination of the concrete situation in each case: the stalemate among different classes, its manifestation in a political system that filtered ineffective and mediocre "leaders" to the top, the succession of parliamentary crises and weak governments that were unable to deal with the deteriorating objective situation (rising unemployment, the sense of humiliation and injustice following the 1914 war, etc.), the economic pressures on the middle class, its fright and that of the owners at the rising militancy of the working class, the political ignorance of the citizenry that kept it from seeing in these initial measures the seeds of a heinous state that would bring all to grief... and so on.

[71]T.L. Jarman in Greene, *op. cit.*, p. 124.
[72]Fest, *op. cit.*, p. 371.

As this essay deals only with symptoms, I will not examine these basic issues. Instead I will comment on two of the manifestations of these basic factors: first, collaboration by those who manned the state apparatus and, second, the many delusions by which so many hypnotized themselves and thus fell prey to the fascist usurpers. After a few remarks on each of these, I will illustrate the second aspect at somewhat greater length by recalling the conduct of the orthodox left in these crises.

*Collaboration*

The evil of the usurpers is done with our hands. This maxim is illustrated again and again by those who man the state apparatus at the time of the fascist takeover. Events in Germany as well as Italy showed conclusively that "fascism can do nothing without the help of the state and less than nothing as its enemy," and that "it is difficult for anti-fascism to win if it is simultaneously fighting the state and fascism in their entirety."[73] This is demonstrated by incident after incident that Tasca narrates: whenever the fascist gangs had the help of state functionaries (the civil servants and policemen who helped actively and the army men who shut their eyes to what was going on) they were invariably able to bash up the heads of their opponents; whenever they did not have this help, they rapidly retreated in disorder.[74]

In Germany's case too we have to contrast Hitler's ineffectual gesticulations of the 1920's with the terrible power of each of his whims and those of his clique once they had the state functionaries working for them. Therefore, these collaborators—without whose complicity the usurper would be nowhere—bear as heavy a responsibility for the ensuring events as the usurper and his clique.

The readiness with which these functionaries begin helping the fascists and serving the usurper once he is ensconced displays their middle class background: a class that is ever ready to make deals with whoever is in power, that—with its meager possessions—yearns for "security at all costs," that is being squeezed by economic developments and is finding it difficult to keep the

---

[73]Rossi, *op. cit.*, p. 346.
[74]For a few specific instances, see *ibid.*, pp. 144-145, 146, 242.

distance from the working classes that it thinks is decent, that —like the owners—is being frightened by the increasing (even if rhetorical) militance of the working class and is being inconvenienced by the occasional strikes etc., that the latter uses to register its distress. As the quintessence of this class, the civil servants act as its perfect representatives and guardians. The behaviour of these functionaries also illustrates the old maxim that the State is not an impartial referee but an instrument of the dominant class and its agents.

To these general factors are added the special ones that become so visible in the anxious months of the takeover and the consolidation. By his ruthlessness in dealing with opponents and his audacity in rewarding those who help him, the usurper at once signals that the personal costs of not collaborating will be severe while the rewards of collaboration will be on a scale that was unthinkable before. In this respect as in others the *coup* marks a decisive, qualitative break with the past: the usurper at once ups the ante to a level to which people are just not accustomed. This feature is clearly brought out by the autobiographical recollections of state functionaries who recall those anxious months in Italy and Germany when they acted as if stunned, when they suspended their mental processes and just carried out orders as if they were mere inert instruments.

(The situation in many ex-colonial territories is, of course, much worse to begin with. For the institutional memory of the civil service, the police, the army in these countries is that collaboration pays. Their peers and predecessors served the imperial power; they imprisoned, beat up and harassed their countrymen on behalf of the foreign rulers. And were they penalized for this collaboration? On the contrary. As soon as their imperial supervisors left these functionaries received accelerated promotions!)

Of course, state fuctionaries are not the only ones who collaborate and help the usurper. The professional—a Schact, a Speer—who lends his expertise to the machine, who lends his "respectibility" and reputation for "objectivity" to legitimizing the regime; the journalist who suddenly changes his tune and, with accustomed felicity, coins new aphorisms ("yes, there are excesses, but you cannot make an omelete without breaking eggs," "yes, a few people have got hurt, but in any comprehensive house-cleaning a few pieces of porcelain are bound to break," "yes, the new set-up does have a few undesirable features, but you must remember that we were in a rotten state before the *coup*; after all, even dirty water will do for putting out a fire. . ."); the lawyer or judge who uses his ingenuity to cover up the brutal character of the new set-up with sophistry and narrow legalisms—all these collaborate as much and are as useful to the usurper and his clique as the state functionary.

The complicity of all these in the new set-up is just as great as that of a Goering or a Himmler. Indeed, as has been remarked, if the Goerings and the Himmlers had been Hitler's only collaborators, he would have had a serious credibility problem *vis-a-vis* the people and the outside world. It is the "reasonable," "respectable" professionals who furnished his regime the legitimacy—and, of course, the acumen for day-to-day operations—that he so sorely needed.

The moral of all this is a very simple one: as the usurper succeeds by suddenly making functionaries realize that opposition, hesitation, reluctance will be costly, the only way a polity can protect itself is by teaching the functionaries that collaboration is costly. As one who has had some success in dealing with fascist regimes would say, the only answer to counter-revolutionary terror is revolutionary terror. The costs of collaboration must be made apparent to the collaborators at as early a stage as possible. Certainly when the regime is overthrown. It would be a fatal error for a polity that ultimately overthrows the usurper and his clique to think that the task is done once a Mussolini is hanged in a public square. If punishment is limited to the usurper and his clique the polity only reassures the collaborators. Similar penalties must be imposed on a sufficient number and a sufficiently wide range of collaborators so that the lesson—"collaboration is fatal"—is burnt into the consciousness of the polity for decades to come.

*Delusions*

The usurper and his clique employ lies, subterfuges, etc. But no one can take shelter behind the alibi that he did not resist in time because the usurper did things by stealth, that he took over the state "as a thief in the night." As Marx said in recounting the assault of Louis Boneparte on the French Republic: "It is not sufficient to say, as the Franch say, that their nation was taken by surprise. A nation and a woman are not forgiven for the unguarded hour in which the first available adventurer is able to violate them...." Far from being a thief in the night, the usurper and his clique warn the polity again and again about their objectives.

> Even as Hitler took the 'legality oath,' 'he left no doubt that once he had won his legal victory "heads would roll" '[75] and, while affirming that he would abide by the Constitution, he openly told the court that 'the Constitution only maps out the arena of battle, not the goal. We enter the legal agencies and in that way will make our party the determining factor. However, once we possess the constitutional power, we will mould the state into the shape we hold to be suitable....'[76]
> Nor was this candour confined to the leader. Again and again the leading functionaries warned the populace of their objectives and their diabolic determination to have their way: 'My measures,' Goering boasted, 'will not be sicklied o'er by any legal scruples. My measures will not be sicklied o'er by any bureaucracy. It is not my business to do justice; it is my business to annihilate and exterminate, that's all.'[77] Or, as Wilhelm Murr told the 'victory celebration' upon the Nazis' taking over Wurttemberg: 'The Government will brutally beat down all who oppose it. We do not say an eye for an eye, a tooth for a tooth. No, he who knocks out one of our eyes will get his head chopped off, and he who knocks one of our teeth will get his jaws bashed in.'[78]

Statements such as these were far more numerous than the apparently conciliatory tone of some of the Fuhrer's speeches and of his private and public expressions of regret at some "excesses." Even if a few statements were falsified to mislead, the deeds were unambiguous. Thus, there is little substance in the alibi of those who say that they did not know what the usurpers were up to.

[75] Bracher, *op. cit*, p. 186.
[76] *Ibid.*, p. 193.
[77] Fest, *op. cit.*, p. 392.
[78] Bracher, *op. cit,*, p. 209.

The real explanation is that the would-be opponents were "blind and deaf by choice." They trembled at taking the personal risks that—now that the usurper had suddenly raised the ante—were suddenly much graver. And, thus, they deliberately took to hallucinogens. Here we can recount no more than two brands of self-deception.

Many hoped that someone else would do their work for them: that the good Lord would intervene in the guise of natural calamities; that foreign powers would sense the danger to themselves and act in time; that an assassin would end it all with a single well-placed bullet; that "events" would of their own accord "open people's eyes"; that—how much more pathetic could they get—the usurper himself would help them out, that by assuming office he would "expose his mediocrity and incompetence," that he would entangle himself in the intricate web of the constitution, that—in an incarnation which at least acknowledged the usurper's prowess!—he would save the citizenry from his diabolic colleagues.

'Rudolf Breitscheid, chairman of the Social Democratic Party faction in the Reichstag, clapped his hands with pleasure when he heard the news of Hitler's appointment as Chancellor. Now at last the man would ruin by himself, he said. Breischeid ultimately died in the Buchenwald concentration camp. Other parliamentarians added up the votes to prove that Hitler would never be able to achieve the two-thirds majority necessary to alter the Constitution. Julius Leber, another leading Social Democrat, remarked sardonically that he was waiting like everybody else in hope of at last "finding out the intellectual foundations of this movement".'[79]

'According to the sneering commentaries published at the time of his accession to office, he would not survive as Chancellor for very long. Illusions were the order of the day; from the Center all the way to the Social Democratic and the Communist parties, he was widely regarded as a "prisoner" of Hugenberg. Skeptical predictions were legion. He would run afoul of the power of his conservative partners in the coali-

---

[79] Fest, *op.cit.*, p. 384.

# Symptoms

tion, of Hindenburg and the army, of the resistance of the masses, of the multiplicity and difficulty of the country's economic problems. Or else there would be foreign intervention. Or his amateurishness would be exposed at last....'[80]

Things were no different in Italy:

'Most of the anti-fascists did not realise how serious things were. People's nerves had been on edge for too long and the first impression was of relief and resignation. They mostly thought, "on the whole things are better so. They cannot last two months." In Montecitorio, a group of deputies was speculating about the future. Amendola was optimistic: "there is nothing to be frightened of. Mussolini too will get caught in the constitutional coils and finally we shall have a government." A socialist deputy replied "that is an illusion; the fun is only just beginning and you will be eliminated in your time"....'[81]

General Badoglio was certain that the fascists would never reach Rome: 'After five minutes under fire fascism will collapse.'[82]

When Hitler murdered Rohm, Heinz and other old associates "....some people hoped that Hitler's action would at last open German eyes. This, however, was a complete error. People said instead: 'leave me in peace with your terror stories. I don't want to know them...Hitler saved us from a far worse civil war' "[83] Worse still on this specific occasion and often in general, "the public mind interpreted the terror as an expression of a ruthlessly operating energy for which it had looked all too long in vain...."[84]

'The Nazis were convinced that evil doing in our time has a morbid force of attraction...The attraction of evil and crime for the mob mentality is nothing new. It has always

---

[80] Ibid., p. 387.
[81] Rossi, op. cit., pp. 321-322.
[82] Iibd., p. 258.
[83] Jarman in Greene, op. cit., p. 131.
[84] Fest, op. cit., p. 374.

been true that the mob will greet deeds of violence with the admiring remark: "it may be mean but it is very clever".'[85]

While these groups prayed for others to do their work for them, many were full of confidence in their ability to "tame" the usurpers:

When Hitler joined the coalition (which was composed of only three National Socialists and eight Conservatives who in addition to the Vice Chancellorship held such important ministries as Defence, Economics and Foreign Affairs) Papen, the Vice Chancellor, exclaimed, 'We have engaged him' and remonstrated with a conservative critic, 'What do you want? I have Hindenberg's confidence. Within two months we will have pushed Hitler so far into a corner that he'll squeak.'[86]

Fest, Shirer and others describe the fatal delusions and miscalculations of Hugenberg, Papen, etc.[87] The following passage depicts the general flavour:

'Papen saw it (the coalition) as a brilliantly conceived splendid combination, which, moreover, placed that troublesome Herr Hitler at the service of employers and big landowners and of Papen's own plans for an authoritarian new state. His own unfortunate fling at the chancellorship seemed to have taught that a modern industrial nation shaken by crisis could not be openly governed by the dismissed representatives of an outmoded epoch. By harnessing the slighly unsavory manipulator of the masses to his own wagon, Papen seemed to be solving the ancient problem of conservatism: that it did not enjoy the support of the people. In this sense, using the vocabulary of a political impressario, Papen complacently replied to all warnings: "No danger at all. We've hired him for our act".'[88]

[85]Hannah Arendt, *The Origins of Totalitarianism*, Harcourt Brace Jovanovich, New York, 1973, p. 307.
[86]Bracher, *op. cit.*, p. 195.
[87]See Fest, *op. cit.*, Chapter 4, Book IV., also Shirer, *op.cit.*, Chapter 6.
[88]Fest, *op. cit.*, p. 366.

## Symptoms

Nor were these illusions confined to individuals; entire classes and groups duped themselves. The old elite thought that they would be the new elite too in an elitist, hierarchical Nazi state.[89] The Army was confident that, as it had the guns, it could rein Hitler in whenever it felt that he had gone too far and that mere cleverness (e.g., in sowing seeds of discord between Rohm and Hitler) would make Hitler more dependent on it.[90] The businessmen who thought they had "bought" Hitler because of their financial support to him were smug in their belief that Hitler would continue to need them; they—as their counterparts in Italy had done earlier—took the usurper's moves against labour (the ban on strikes, measures to paralyse the unions) as overtures to themselves, as clear evidence not just of the fact that Hitler was dependent on them but also of the fact that he knew he was dependent on them and was, therefore, eager to please them.

This self-confidence, unmatched as it was by any energetic resistance, proved to be as thin a reed as the prayers of others that someone else would do their work.

> While the army exulted at the murder of the SA leaders, confident that now Hitler was entirely at its mercy, 'Hitler with his intuition for power relationships had realised that if the army would stand for the murder of armymen, he had achieved the break-through to ultimate control. . . .'[91] And subsequent events proved him right. 'If the public order was actually threatened by rebels and conspirators, as von Blomberg later represented the situation, then the army probably had the duty to intervene. If that were not the case, then it should have called a halt to the killing. Instead it had waited, had made weapons available, and in the end its leaders had congratulated themselves on their acuteness at emerging with clean hands and nevertheless as victors. They succumbed not to the "nemesis of power," as the English historian John W. Wheeler-Bennett has asserted, but to their failure to recognize how short-lived this victory would be. At the height of the killing former State Secretary Planck urged General von

---

[89] Rauschning, *op. cit*, p. 30.
[90] Fest, *op. cit*, pp. 471, 497.
[91] *Ibid*., p. 471.

Fritsch to intervene. The commander in chief of the army replied that he had no orders to do so. Planck warned him: "If you, General, stand by idly watching, sooner or later you will suffer the same fate." Three and a half years later, Fritsch, together with Blomberg, was dismissed under a dishonoring cloud. The charge, as in the cases of Schleicher and Bredow, was based on forged documents, and now it was the turn of the SA to rejoice over the "revenge for June 30" *Les institutions perissent par leur victories.* This aphorism was totally borne out by subsequent events. . . .

'It is true that June 30 dealt a fatal blow to the SA. Its formerly rebellious self-assertive profile henceforth almost vanished behind petty bourgeois features. Brass knuckles and rubber truncheons gave way to collection boxes. But the army did not assume the place vacated by the storm troopers. Three weeks later Hitler coolly took advantage of the manifest weakness of the army leadership. On July 20, 1934, he freed the SS "in view of its great services. . . especially in connection with the events of June 30" from its subordination to the SA and raised it to the rank of an independent organization directly subordinate to himself. At the same time it was allowed to rival the army in maintaining armed forces—at first of only one division.'[92]

While businessmen thought that Hitler was their agent and that his acts of ending strikes, guaranteeing markets, that his frequent promises of a tremendous expansion of the national economic base, that these showed him to be a reliable and eager agent, Hitler's assessment was the opposite and, as it turned out, the more perceptive one. These acts were just 'Hitler's way of providing himself with henchmen. Among his intimates he justified this course with some cynicism and acuteness: he had not the slightest intention, he declared, of killing off the propertied class, as had been done in Russia. Rather, he would force it in every conceivable way to use its abilities to build the economy. Businessmen, that much was sure, would be glad if their lives and property were spared, and in this way they would become true dependents. Why

---

[92]*Ibid.*

should he change this advantageous relationship when to do so would only mean he would afterwards have to thrash everything out with Old Fighters and overzealous party comrades who would be forever reminding him of all they had done for the party? Formal title to means of production was only a question of detail, was it not? How much landed property or how many factories people owned did not matter when they had consented to a master they could no longer overthrow. "The decisive factor is that the State through the party controls them whether they are owners or workers. Do you understand, all this no longer means anything. Our socialism reaches much deeper. It does not change the external order of things, but it orders solely the relationship of man to the State.... Then what does property and income count for? Why should we need to socialize the banks and the factories? We are socializing the people"....'[93]

Many other delusions can be listed apart from these two. Some put their hopes in the expectation that as soon as the usurper was secure, he would allow things to relax; others expected that factional fights within the clique would paralize it. And so on. A little reflection would have shown that there was not the slightest basis for any of these self-deceptions. One must conclude that those who fell for them were, as Tasca would say, blind and deaf by choice; that they just did not want to shoulder the risks inherent in any resistance to the usurper and, hence, took refuge in these soporifics. Goebbels used to say that people will believe any lie if only it is big enough. It is equally true that people will refuse to believe any truth—howsoever obvious it is—if only it is inconvenient enough.

It will be clear also that the success of the usurper is due as much to his own acumen and single-minded determination as to the total bankruptcy of his opponents: "thus (the usurper) is nothing without his opponents, his *betes noires*, the democracies, the 'respectable' people, quiet and orderly but comfort seeking and irresolute. It is these elements which (make) him...."[94]

---

[93]*Ibid.*, p. 432.
[94]Rauschning, *op.cit.*, pp. 270-272.

## The Orthodox Left

Even though the role of self-invoked delusions may be obvious by now, I would like to press the point further by listing a few of the delusions and characteristic habits by which the orthodox left paralyzed itself in the face of the fascist onslaught. The reader should remember that this is the group that had proclaimed its faith in revolutions, that had an analytical frame which could have enabled it to interpret the events correctly, that had been marching up and down Europe warning everyone of the dangers—and, even more, of the inevitability—of fascism, this is the group that had been the target of the most venomous rhetoric in Germany and the most brutal physical attacks in Italy.

Yet, it had done nothing to prepare itself for the avalanche it had been prophesying. The elaborate rationalizations it put out for not acting, the intricate theories it took refuge in, the heated internal debates about "tactics" and about "strategy"—all these were a despicable cover-up for having been caught unprepared.

The orthodox left consisted of the usual hues: the "maximalists," the "revolution or nothing" brand—and others displaying varying degrees of moderation.

The orthodox Communist Party in Germany—the KPD—was wedded to its textbook formulations and it was beholden to Moscow. It—as its counterpart in Italy—had convinced itself that the fascist assault was "the final crisis of monopoly capitalism," and that, by definition, capitalism itself would crumble during the crisis. Indeed, it reasoned, the fascist assault would by itself "sharpen the contradictions within the system," that it would by itself open people's eyes, that it would remind them about the acuity of the Communist's analysis and the accuracy of their forecasts and that, on being reminded thus by events, the people would turn to Communism. Hence, the leadership prescribed a four-fold strategy: (*a*) Listen to Moscow; (*b*) snigger in private and make-believe that—in a real sense—things are going your way; therefore, let things worsen; (*c*) in the meantime lie low, survive, ensure that your organizations are not persecuted or banned; be patient, in fact make placating gestures "whatever the cost, no provocation"; (*d*) finally, as social democrats are an even greater menace than fascists (the former, so the textbook says, obscure the contradictions) do not cooperate with them; to the extent possible, use the crisis to embarrass them.

The moderate socialists, on the other hand, were never quite able to make up their minds as to who was the worse enemy—the fascists or the Communists—and, therefore, they allied with neither. In addition, having memorized some of the same textbooks, they too had convinced themselves that the fascist *coup* was the last card of reaction which, by definition, was bound to fail. In the meantime they decided that by pursuing conciliatory tactics they could compel the government to be moderate. A few of them went on issuing useless calls to resistance; useless, as no organization had been built up for insurrection before the *coup*.

The passages that detail this sorry tale are so numerous that they cannot all be reproduced here. And they are so fascinating that they should be read in the original accounts—accounts such as those of Guerin, Tasca and others. Here I can do more than reproduce a small sample.

'...The rapidity with which the political Left was overwhelmed, to the astonishment even of the new rulers, also was connected with deception and self-delusion. The reasons were manifold. Because of their refusal to take hold of the reins of government in 1930 and their capitulation before Papen's coup in Prussia, the Social Democrats found themselves excluded from the political arena even before 1933. And the Communists had not passed up any opportunity to stir up civil strife and weaken the democratic defenses. Contrary to the claims of present-day East German historians, it is an indisputable fact that the KPD's main attack was directed against "social fascist" Social Democracy. The Communist leadership, despite the antifasicst propaganda campaigns, co-operated in the overthrow of the Social Democratic Government of Prussia, and on many occasions made common cause with the National Socialists against the Republic: in parliamentary votes of no confidence, in the Prussian plebiscite of 1931, during the Berlin transport workers' strike of November, 1932.

'This incongruous yet typical cooperation was based on the

calculation that with the overthrow of the Republic, Germany would become ripe for a Communist revolution. Moscow, which sanctioned this policy, obviously did not count on the survival of the National Socialist dictatorship, but saw it merely as the executor of a preparatory function. This explains why Stalin immediately initiated efforts to establish friendly relations with Hitler, and even to continue the cooperation between the Reichswehr and the Red Army. In return, he was willing to accept without protest the persecution of Communists; one of the first international acts of recognition of the Third Reich (in April, 1933) was the renewal of a German-Russian trade agreement that had expired in 1931....Moscow's strategy was based on a monumental misjudgement of the nature of the National Socialist takeover. By denying it the character of a true revolution and maintaining that it was simply a manifestation of the final crisis of monopoly capitalism, it served to paralyze and fragment the forces of resistance and steer them onto a false course....'[95]

'...Moscow held back its support (to resistance) for reasons of foreign policy; it was interested not in conflict with the new regime but rather in the preservation of German-Soviet relations, and indeed, the Berlin Treaty of 1926 was reaffirmed in May, 1933. And so the Soviet Union, by treating the fate of the KPD as a German domestic problem and concentrating its concerns on its missions and the unhindered conduct of their affairs, became the first foreign power to grant diplomatic recognition to the Hitler regime; this grotesque fact was outdone only by the Realpolitik of the Hitler-Stalin pact of 1939....'[96]

'...Hitler feared a general strike, but the SPD and the unions showed a touching faith in legality; their primary task, they thought, was to keep their organizations from being outlawed; to keep them intact for the moment when the new regime would collapse (a matter of months!). Contrary to all expectations, the SPD confined itself to legal opposition, and

---

[9 5]Bracher, *op. cit.*, p. 198.
[6] *id.*, p. 220.

thus, it, too, fell victim to the legality strategy. This miscalculation was intensified by yet another move of the Socialist leadership. Immediately after January 30, 1933, they announced that the fight against the reactionary capitalists, that is, against the Hugenburg camp, was the paramount issue. Apparently, Hitler's accomplices were held to be more powerful and dangerous. Thus, in its own way, the Left became the victim of the Marxist thesis of Nazism as mere counter-revolution and of the deceptive slogan of a national revolution. Real resistance began to form only after it was too late.[97].

'...The SPD's demonstrative adherence to the path of legality was able to prolong its existence for only some months.... Standing pat, saving the organization by steering a middle course, faith in the historically inevitable collapse of Fascism—those were the slogans, and not calls to open resistance against a supposedly short-lived mass movement. Paralyzed by legalistic stand-by tactics, weakened by persecution, flight, and organizational disintegration, this largest of the democratic parties increasingly lost touch with its membership. The death of the unions and differences with the exiled SPD leadership as well as within socialist resistance groups were followed by a last-ditch effort of tactical accomodation: a vote in the Reichstag on May 17, 1933, for Hitler's foreign policy statement on his peaceful intentions. It was the final delusion of the pursuit of legal methods by which a Social Democratic leadership too deeply committed to its own traditions thought it might preserve its substance even in the face of Goering's confiscation on May 10 of all its assets—buildings, newspapers, and party treasury.

'At this last meeting of a multiparty Reichstag, Hitler was able to demonstrate to the world the legality of his rule. Its numbers cut in half, the SPD Reichstag delegation capitulated to pressure as well as out of concern for its jailed comrades in voting for the resolution jointly offered by the NSDAP, DNVP, the Centre Party, and the BVP on May 17. Yet despite this vote, the decimated SPD was held responsible for

[97] *Ibid.,* p. 198.

the increasing activity of exiled SPD leaders. On June 22, after a period of growing terror, the last blowt fell: the outlawing of the SPD as a party "hostile to the nation and state," its expulsion from the Reichstag, more arrests, and ruthless persecution of all oppositional activities. . . .'[98]

'Among the most important phenomena was the absence of any unity among the left. . . . In Germany no popular front was ever secured. Mutual distrust between the SPD and the KPD was deeper than their common fear of NSDP. The directives of Stalin aimed at the KPD in any event condemned the possibility of cooperation with the "social fascists." The KPD forgot that the task of a revolutionary party was to see to the task of promoting a national revolution and became instead the agent of a foreign power. The antics of the leadership of the KPD split the working class movement and at the same time rendered the task of the SPD. . . virtually impossible. . . . As Clark observed so bitterly: ". . . Its one positive deed was to stab German democracy in the back and paralyze its resistance to counter-revolution. The monstrous imaginings of National Socialism deceive only those who want to be deceived; Hitler had no better allies and no one knew that better than Hitler himself". . . .'[99]

'In this system there is no room for the fatal illusion, long held by the communists, that fascism might do some good by destroying "democratic illusions." The Italian communists actually announced in May 1921 that: "It is true that White reaction is celebrating a few ephemeral victories over an enemy which is paying dear for its unpreparedness, but it is destroying the democratic and liberal illusion and breaking down the influence of social democracy among the masses." And in the resolution of the Presidium of the Communist International, published in January 1934, the following statement concerning Germany may be read: "The establishment of an undisguised fascist dictatorship, by dispelling the democratic illusions of the masses and liberating them from the influence of social democracy, is accelerating Germany's

---

[98] *Ibid.* p. 220-221.
[99] Hayes, *op. cit.*, pp. 165-166.

advance towards the proletarian revolution." This is not the place for a detailed criticism of this conception, which the Communist International has never abandoned in spite of all its changes of front, and we need only record that fascism suppresses not only "democratic illusions," but the workers' and socialist movement which is subject to them. Fascism is like a completely sucessful operation: the patient dies and all his illusions are removed.'[100]

'The Nazis then turned upon the unions, which had already exposed their dismay and weakness during the early March days. They seemed to think that they could buy off the impending doom by a series of placating gestures. Although the arrests and harassment of leading union members was steadily increasing throughout the Reich and the SA was staging a series of raids on local union offices, on March 20 the Labour Federation's Executive Committee addressed a kind of declaration of loyalty to Hitler. It spoke of the purely social tasks of trade unions "no matter what the nature of the political regime"....'[101]

'...The population everywhere stood by, surprised but passive, while these decisive events were taking place. There were a few incidents here and there, such as took place every Sunday in Italian towns and countryside. Barricades were set up in Parma; in Rome shots were fired in the suburb of San Lorenzo, through which the black-shirts of the Bottai column passed on their way to the centre of the town. That was all. The fascist squads, on the other hand, took advantage of their mobilization in almost every district to occupy newspaper offices, set fire to Chambers of Labour, ransack private apartments and turn out such socialist councils as had survived previous offensive....The so-called leaders of the working class lost no opportunity of showing their incapacity, right up to the last moment. The communists, although persuaded that no defence is possible against such overwhelmingly powerful forces, suggested that the Alliance of Labour should be immediately reconstructed and a general strike proclaimed. They were quite aware that

---

[100] Rossi, *op. cit.*, p. 65.
[101] Fest, *op. cit.*, p. 413.

nothing could come of this, but their own reaction to the tragic events which had sealed the fate of the Italian people was to suggest this feeble manoeuvre, which would give them a chance to do nothing and cry "treason" at the General Confederation of Labour. The leaders of the Confederation very properly denounced this as a piece of communist provocativeness, but did so in a statement which contained this shameful passage: "The General Confederation of Labour feels that it is its duty when political passions are running high and forces alien to the workers' syndicates are disputing the power of the state, to warn the workers against the speculations and incitements of political parties and groups which would drag the proletariat into a struggle in which it must take absolutely no part"...'[102]

'...How did the labour movement defend itself against the fascist gangs during this first phase? In the beginning, the bold military tactics of the Black Shirts or Brown shirts took the workers by surprise, and their reply was feeble. But they would have quickly adapted themselves, spontaneously, to their adversary's tactics if their own leaders, afraid of direct action, had not systematically put a brake on their militancy.... Let us be careful not to reply to fascist violence, the reformist leaders said in both Italy and Germany; we would arouse public opinion against us. Above all, let us avoid forming combat groups and semi-military bodies, for we would risk antagonizing the public authorities, who, we are confident, will dissolve the semi-military groups of fascism! Let us not borrow the weapons of fascism, for on that ground we are beaten in advance...These legalistic and defeatist tactics tended to profoundly demoralize the working class, at the same time as they increased the enemy's audacity, self-confidence, and feeling of invincibility....In the province of Rovigo, union leader Matteotti and the labor exchanges gave the word: "Stay home: do not respond to provocations. Even silence, even cowardice, are sometimes heroic." As they possessed contacts in the state apparatus, the socialists on several occasions were offered arms to protect themselves from the

---

[102]Rossi, *op. cit.*, p. 321.

fascists. But they rejected these offers, saying that it was the duty of the state to protect the citizen against the armed attacks of other citizens. They relied on the bourgeois state to defend them against the fascist bands....

'After a punitive expedition the antifascists abstained from reprisals, respected the fascists' residences, and launched no counterattacks. They were satisfied with proclaiming general protest strikes. But these strikes, intended to force the authorities to protect labour organizations against the fascist terror, resulted only in ridiculous parleys with the authorities, who were in reality the accomplices of fascism.... Meanwhile, a number of union organizations had themselves formed defense groups, either in the shops where they had members or among the unemployed. But the Labour Federation considered the situation not sufficiently grave to justify the workers preparing for a struggle to defend their rights. Far from centralizing and generalizing these preventive measures, it considered them superfluous....

'When the Storm Troops announced their intention of parading on January 22, 1933, in front of the Karl Leibknecht House, the party leaders begged the Ministry of the Interior to forbid the Nazi demonstration. The Communist Party, they stated to the press, holds the authorities responsible for what will happen in the Buelow Platz.... "Send letters of protest to the Chief of Police": such was the instruction given to the workers. Furthermore, combat groups which were ready to counterattack, received formal orders not to intervene and had to obey, rage in their hearts....'[103]

'...The Italian Socialists were suffering from parliamentary cretinism: because fascism received only a limited number of votes in the elections and had only thirty-five representatives in parliament, they did not consider it dangerous and even periodically announced its decline and decay. On the very eve of the March on Rome, the party leaders laughed when anybody spoke of possible danger.... As for the Communists, they forced themselves to deny the fascist danger by asserting that all forms of bourgeois domination were identical, whether

---

[103]Guerin, *op. cit.*, pp. 108-109, 111-113.

wearing the democratic or fascist label. Thus in 1922, at the second congress of the Communist Party in Rome, Bordiga rejected the hypothesis of fascism's taking power and believed a compromise among all the bourgeois parties was inevitable. When the mobilization of the Black Shirts began on October 28, the party secretariat sent a communication to all the branches stating that the March on Rome will never take place....The German Socialists and Communists similarly refused to believe in the triumph of National Socialism. More than that, they periodically announced its rout. The Socialists uttered shouts of victory on every occasion: in August, 1932, because President Hindenburg refused Hitler's demands; and after the election of November 6, because the votes for the Nazis showed a falling off. On that date Vorwaerts said: "Ten years ago we predicted the bankruptcy of National Socialism; it is written in black and white in our paper!" And just before Hitler's accession to power, one of their leaders, Schiffrin, wrote: "We no longer perceive anything but the odor of a rotting corpse. Fascism is definitely dead; it will never arise again".[104]

'...As for the Communists, in spite of their revolutionary verbiage, they took refuge behind the excuse that the reformists would do nothing—and so did nothing themselves....'[105]

'...Instead the left shirked its task. It lurked in the background all through the post-war crisis. This desertion is the sole explanation of the fascist success. Society, even more than nature, abhors a vacuum, and the forces of barbarism are ever ready to rush in and fill it....The Italian socialists waited for the middle class to die off naturally, without considering whether its death struggle, as they assumed it to be, if unduly prolonged, might not generate seeds of decay which would infect the whole nation, the socialist movement included. They behaved like the sole heir to an estate who prefers not to turn up till the last minute, just before the will is read. While they waited they confined their activities to "separating

[104] *Ibil.*, pp. 119-120.
[105] *Ibid.*, p. 122.

their own responsibilities from those of the ruling classes.'' This separation was, up to a point, justified and even necessary. But responsibility for evil committed is always shared by those who have failed to prevent it; and we have no right to connive at others' actions unless we are prepared to step in at the right moment and succeed where they have failed. It is all the easier to separate our own responsibilities from those of the ruling classes if we are able and willing to shoulder our own responsibilities on behalf of an entire nation. If not, it is quite simple to avoid "legal" responsibilities by pleading a kind of alibi, the last resort of all scoundrels.... Useless, then, to say "we were not there." The masses who have lost all, will want to know why not.... The policy of the Italian communists and maximalists was to let things get as bad as possible. A policy which depends on aggravating a situation the better to control and direct it is justifiable so long as one is ready and willing to intervene at the right moment and restore order in the chaos that follows. Such tactics, which must be employed with the utmost precision, become too easily a game of chance, depending as they do on the blindest and least reversible of forces....

'The Italian maximalists and communists had no idea of tactics: theirs was a state of mind that combined demagogy with inactivity and was quite devoid of the prophetic passion which calls down evil in order that virtue may triumph more brilliantly, and of the creative spirit which is capable of bringing about a vigorous transition from lowest to highest... such failings always imply a lack of humanity: the syndicate, section, party or class remains hidebound by its own limitations, and instead of regarding them as such, ends by making a fetish of them and loses that power of transcending them, which is the supreme necessity and spirit of socialism....The deadlock might have been ended by a firm policy uniting all the national resources to end the depression and assure at all events a minimum living wage to all workers. But who could have carried out such a policy? Not the socialists who had been explaining for two years that this was a crisis of the capitalist system, that it was actually the final crisis of this system, and that the bourgeoisie must be left to sift for itself. Still less the ruling classes, whose one aim and obsession was the political and industrial enslavement of the workers. Fascism was there to simplify their task. . . .

'Consequently the slump which the socialists had reckoned as an asset, proved their undoing. For every slump starts a process of social disintegration, with results that cannot be foretold, dependent as they are upon uncertain human reactions. An exasperated desire to "put an end to things" somehow may lead to despondency and panic unless it is directed towards some concrete aim, and allowed a glimpse of a new order. The slump crushes those who cannot thus look ahead and are therefore without hope. Its value as a revolutionary factor lies in the forces of order it sets in motion; if these are not the forces of a new order it only serves to consolidate the old. . . .'[106]

These passages can be multiplied many times over. But the few that have been cited will acquaint the reader with the standard alibis that were put forward to cover up the lack of preparation. Indeed there is no greater betrayal of the toilers than to goad them on by militant rhetoric and then, when the issue is joined, to leave them in the lurch, to coin clever phrases to explain away the lack of preparation. For, as we have seen, rhetorical militance and occasional harassment frightens the owners and the middle class, they alert them, they make them turn towards the fascist elements within their classes. On the other side, they embolden the toilers to stake their fortunes, to take up advanced positions which they cannot then defend, to even be reckless. The leaders—of the trade unions, of the left political parties— often get away quite lightly. Some of them even join the regime, telling their followers all the time they will "reform" (or, depending upon the audience, "sabotage") the regime from within. But the labourers are left defenceless and disheartened and ultimately they are crushed.

[106] Rossi, *op. cit.*, pp. 325-332.

## A Lesson

The reader who has persevered thus far will be able to draw many inferences. So as not to make this longer I will confine myself to one inference: the usurper and his clique will not stop short of the final step. The regime will not stop till it has brought every section, every organization, every community, every area under its domination. It is foolish for anyone to take heart merely from the fact that such and such an area or such and such a section has been spared thus far: just as it was foolish for some to draw heart from the fact that Bavaria had not been "coordinated" in the first round, just as it was foolish of the Poles to feel that they would be spared when the Reich Citizenship Law gave them a chance to become citizens even though they were in the despised category of "Slavs."[107]

Unless the base (an area, a group) that has been left undisturbed in the first round is actually being used to mount active resistance, it should constitute no grounds for hope. The usurper will get around to the area or group soon enough. *A fortiori* it would be even more foolish for one area or group to rejoice at the discomfiture of another area or group—the rejoicer's fate will be the fate of the army generals who were happy at the execution of the SA leaders.

Thus instead of deluding ourselves we must know that the fascist regime will not rest till it has reduced the society to an "atomised, structureless nation," that by the end it would have made every region, every section suffer, that mere cleverness, that appeasement will not induce it to abandon its course and, finally, that things will not reverse themselves on their own. "The temptation of our day is to accept the intolerable for fear of still worse to come. But before considering what will convert an intolerable situation into a better one (before succumbing to this temptation) we have to face another question—the crucial question of what must inevitably be the end of a process if it is left to itself and its logical outcome...."[108]

The counsel that the citizenry must sit back and await a

---

[107]G. Mosse, *Nazi Culture*, Grosset and Dunlap, New York, 1968, p. 320.
[108]Rauschning, *op. cit.*, p. xi.

catastrophe that will dislocate the regime ignores the tremendous destruction that the regime will heap upon the country in the interim. The reader familiar with Plutarch will recall the maxim that he attributes to Cicero: that when the character of a would-be usurper is sufficiently established in his youth for a valid prediction to be made about the harm he will do to the republic, he should be dealt with appropriately before and not after he has wrought the mischief. This maxim is as valid for their regimes as it is for the usurpers considered as individuals.

## IV. *Programmes as Scraps of Paper*

The unexpected ease with which the usurper is able to seize power leads people to assume that he is operating from a master plan, from a detailed blue-print that spells out how to seize power and what to do with it once it has been seized. Neither supposition is correct.

We have the evidence of one of the participants that the policy of 'coordination' which so stunned everyone, which seemed to be the essence of masterly planning, was 'very much a hand to mouth affair';[109] one step made way for and, in most cases, necessitated the next; the only order in them was chronological—in that one step followed another—and the only reason they seemed so masterly was the total absence of resistance from the opponents.

As for knowing what to do with power once it had been gained, 'Hitler had no specific programme. At the Cabinet meeting of March 15, he for the first time admitted his dilemma, saying that it was necessary to employ demontrations, pomp and a show of activity "to direct attention to the purely political affairs because the economic decisions will have to be postponed for a while"....As Rauschning saw it, Hitler took power with virtually no other guideline than his total confidence in his own ability to deal with things on the primitive but effective maxim: give an order and it will get done, more or less roughly, perhaps, but for a while some-

---

[109]*Ibid.*, p. 89.

thing will be moving, and meanwhile we'll look around for the next step...."[110]

The usurper now begins to act on two fronts: first, he liberates himself from his past slogans and programmes and, second, he overwhelms the populace with a barrage of so-called "programmes" which are make-shift affairs without any integrating principle.

From time to time the National Socialists had adopted many a progressive platform. Their 1920 manifesto had demanded that the major industries and combines be nationalized, that unearned income be abolished, that profiteering and speculation be ended, that equal opportunities be provided for all in education and employment, that workers' shops be instituted and that the right to work be guaranteed. They had proposed a reduction in the capital value of agrarian debts and a reduction in the interest rates to about 2%.[111] They had proposed that "the bank and money market princes" and the "Eastern Jews" be expropriated, that the commercial banks be nationalized and that mortgage, credit and stock policies be strictly regulated in the communal interest.[112]

So Hitler's first task was to liberate himself from these past resolutions. He did so by familiar devices: "even while he insisted on the unalterability of the party programme, he was filled with that lively instinct of the born tactician not to commit himself. Thus he forbade the press in the first few months to publish unauthorized quotations from *Mein Kampf*. Even republications of one of the 25 points of the party programme was banned on the ground that "henceforth what mattered would not be programmes but practical work...."[113]

All the rhetoric urging immediate reforms was suddenly abandoned. In July 1933, having just staged his *coup*, Hitler warned everyone that "the revolution is not a permanent state of affairs and it must not be allowed to develop into such a state. The stream of revolution released must be guided into the safe

---

[110]Fest, *op. cit*, pp. 429-430.
[111]Hayes, *op cit*., pp. 66, 130.
[112]Bracher, *op. cit*., p. 186.
[113]Fest, *op. cit*., p. 430.

channel of evolution." A week later he told the assembled Gauleiters, "political power we had to conquer rapidly and in one blow; in the economic sphere, other principles must govern our action...." And on July 7, 1933, Hess issued an edict prescribing that disciplinary action should be taken against those who failed to follow the Fuhrer's evolutionary path.[114] Later when some of his plebian associates continued to insist—among other things—that he implement the party programme, that he "continue the revolution," Hitler, as we have seen, purged them.

Mussolini's case was no different. The reader will recall that when the fascist nuclei first met in 1919 in Milan, its manifesto had included demands for workers' participation in the management of industry, partial expropriation of wealth by means of special taxes, confiscation of assets belonging to religious establishments, the almost total seizure of the profits of war, a heavy capital levy, and handing over of uncultivated land to peasants' cooperatives.[115] Indeed in 1920-21, the fascists had so successfully used the slogan "land to him who tills it" that they had outdone the socialists.[116]

Soon after gaining power, of course, as we have seen, Mussolini complained that "the trouble is that the revolution having been accomplished, the revolutionaries continue." Thus, he often harked back to his statements of 1922 that "to go back to the beginning—i.e., to get back to the 1919 programme—is to give proof of childishness and senility." As Tasca was to say later, "(Mussolini's) versatility and complete lack of scruple proved an invaluable asset to fascism...."

Having liberated himself in this manner, the usurper hurls upon the population one programme after another, each of which "is a mere make-shift, concocted to meet the needs of immediate political strategy."[117] This style has been accurately characterized as "permanent improvization,"[118] as "incessant activity...embarking on anything so long as it keeps things

---

[114]Hayes, *op. cit.*, p. 131.

[115]S. J. Woolf (ed.), *The Nature of Fascism*, Random House, New York, 1968, pp. 119-151, 229.

[116]Rossi, *op. cit.*, pp. 101-102.

[117]Rauschning, *op. cit.*, pp. 352-353.

[118]Fest, *op. cit.*, p. 430.

moving...(a) dynamics in vacuo."[119] In this hectic, feverish atmosphere, programmes—such as Hitler's 25 points or Mussolini's 30 points "Charter of Labour"—succeed one another. Elements are grafted one upon another as the rush to power proceeds, anything that is handy is incorporated, anything that has become a liability is jettisoned or, more often, just forgotten.[120] "I am always on the watch," said Mussolini with his characteristic candour, "when a changing wind fills the sails of the ship of fortune...."[121]

It is hardly surprising then that such programmes as are put out are mere "rhetoric and blather"...(just) "vapid aphorisms,"[122] "all too plainly a mixture of inconsistencies and simple nonsense...."[123] One should not be surprised at this feature nor, as we shall see later, waste much time in pointing out the inconsistencies, shortcomings, etc., of the programmes: "It (the doctrine, the programme) is not a whole. It is of functional importance only, a means and nothing more. It is (just) the main element in propaganda. The question to be asked is not its meaning but its purpose...."[124]

And this purpose is unambiguous: like everything else, the programmes too are just instruments of domination, instruments to dislocate the population, to keep it off balance, to give all those who are desperately looking for rationalizations, for reasons to continue hoping, the reasons they seek, instruments for giving contrary signals so that each section sees an opportunity for itself.

As these programmes are instruments of domination, they are invoked incessantly as the rationale for overriding the rights of individuals and groups, for putting scruples and standards aside. Moreover, an element or two of them—the element that figures most conspicuously in the subsequent events—is such that its implementation necessarily entails that rights of individuals and

---

[119] Rauschning, *op. cit.*, p. 23.

[120] *Ibid.*, pp. 19, 21, 49-50; Greene, *op.cit.*, p. 85; Rossi, *op.cit.*, pp. 141-142, 146, 172, 234.

[121] *Ibid.*, p. 141.

[122] Denis Mack Smith, *Italy, A Modern History*, University of Michigan Press, Ann Arbor, 1959.

[123] Rauschning, *op. cit.*, p. 112.

[124] *Ibid.*, p. 52.

groups be violated. The objective of the usurper in pursuing that element is not to combat the problem that the element ostensibly deals with, but to accustom the populace to the notion that once "a higher good" has been proclaimed, personal rights, notions of law, etc., can be trampled upon. The usurper strives—as in the persecution and humiliation of Jews—to make the people themselves participate in violating the rights, norms and standards to which they have thus far been accustomed.

Remember always that from the point of view of the usurper the fate of the individual programme—or the element in the programme—is not important. What is important is to accustom the populace to the idea that its rights, etc., can be overridden at will. Indeed, it is to the usurper's advantage that one programme should not be pursued for long, that one should be replaced by another in quick succession. For, the notion that the usurper wants to drive home is not that the rights of the populace can be overridden for *this* particular programme, but that he can override them whenever he will; not that scruples, standards, norms, etc., do not apply when the implemetation of *this* particular programme is in question, but that they do not apply in general.

In this specific way—as well as in the ways noted above—the various programmes and their numbered points serve a purpose. But they are never enough. For deep down the usurper and his cohorts—all of whom know how hollow their aphorisms and programmes are—fear that the populace too will at some stage see through their 25-point programmes and 30-point Charters of Labour, that soon enough it, too, will begin to view them with the same cynicism with which they themselves view the programmes. Hence, the usurper and his cohorts begin to sense that articulation and thought are the real threats, the true saboteurs, from whom they must protect themselves.

*Four Themes*

Subsequent propaganda, therefore, presses four themes.

First, it exhorts the faithful to stop thinking: "*credere, obbedire, combattere*" went the fascist chant—"believe, obey, fight." This new chant was issued by the same Mussolini who, in his socialist incarnation, had said, ". . .to love an idea it is necessary to understand it. To love socialism it is not enough to issue a superficial profession of faith...to love socialism it is necessary to understand it, study it, pursue its practical manifestations and its doctrinal commitments...to believe out of sentiment means to have religious faith. To believe as a consequence of a determination of will and reason is to have the faith of free spirits, the conscious faith that does not delude itself....It is necesary to make socialism a reasoned faith....To believe is not enough; it is necessary to reason. To those who cry 'Believe,' we reply 'Demonstrate'...."[125] But now the same Mussolini exalts fascism as "a religious conception." "If fascism were not a faith," he asks, "how could it give its adherents stoicism and courage?" "Nothing great can be accomplished except in a state of loving passion, of religious mysticism." To "reason" is now opposed "intuition." Fascism proclaims itself as the enemy of reason, as "a movement...an intuition summed up in a vision and a faith...." It is "a myth," asserts Mussolini and adds, "...it is not necessary for it to be reality...."[125]

The second task is to stress "action" and to ridicule those who talk of "paper programmes." The same Mussolini who in a factional fight had insisted in August 1922 that the party must have a clear and specific programme[127] now goes back to his early rejection of uncomfortable doctrines and arguments as "the verbal constructions of sterile and solitary intellectuals" and opts for a "philosophy of action, a pragmatic philosophy."[128]

He now tells us that "fascism is not the nursling of a doctrine worked out before hand with detailed elaboration; it was born of the need for action and it was itself from the beginning practical rather than theoretical...a living movement."[129] Fascists, he tells us, are "problemists" and realists: "We fascists have no preconceived doctrine; our doctrine is based on facts...."[130] "Action,"

---

[125] A. James Gregor, *The Ideology of Fascism*, Free Press, New York, 1969.
[126] Guerin, *op. cit.*, pp. 65, 169-170.
[127] Rossi, *op. cit.*, pp. 178-179.
[128] Gregor, *op. cit.*, p. 121.
[129] See the extracts from his article in the Italian Encyclopedia, in Greene, *op. cit.*
[130] Rossi, *op. cit.*, p. 37.

he says on the train to Rome as he travels to form a government at the King's invitation, "action has dug a grave for philosophy."[131] His favourite expression became "actualism," and "pragmatic realism." In actual fact, of course, this "realism" in his case and that of Hitler was just an euphemism for "unscrupulousness."[132]

Third, even though its own programmes are, as we have seen, essentially that much "talk and blather" fascism "effects to despise speeches and talk."[133] Thus, we have Mussolini screaming in his harangues against "talkative articulation." Now, the point to remember is not that this ranting against articulation and talkativeness shows any genuine preference for action over speech, but that this is the usurper's way of bottling up a genuine threat to his set-up—namely, the threat that people will examine what he is saying, that they will compare his deeds with his professions and then talk among themselves about the contrast between the two.

But even this is not enough. And so, sensing the real root of the trouble, the fascist usurper takes the offensive and begins to ridicule thinking itself. The "blatant anti-intellectualism"[134] of the regimes of Hitler and Mussolini was notorious. They made it into a boast, a fetish.

And so we have Mussolini exclaiming, "the century of fascism will see the end of intellectualising and of those sterile intellectuals who are a threat to the nation. . . ."[135] and we have Hitler proclaiming that cogitation is really a parasitic activity, that those who think are "queen bees living off worker bees."[136] Quite obviously, the reason for this ridicule is not that thinking or thinkers are a hindrance to the country's progress; but that they, even when they can do little to remove him from office, are a threat to the usurper, like that single stray hair which will ultimately wear down the strongest rider. The usurper—with his characteristic identification of his personal fortunes with the fortunes of the country—reads and presents the threat to himself

---

[131]*Ibid.*, p. 353.
[132]Rauschning, *op. cit.*, p. 100.
[133]Greene, *op. cit.*, p. 85.
[134]Fest, *op. cit.*, p. 427.
[135]Guerin, *op. cit.*, p. 170.
[136]*Ibid.*, p. 171.

as a threat to the country.

> 'The introduction of intellectual processes of criticism and analysis marked the intrusion of hostile elements which disturbed the exercise of (his) power. Hence Hitler's hatred of the intellectual: "in the masses instinct is supreme and from instinct comes faith. . .while the healthy common folk instinctively close their ranks to form a community of the people, the intellectuals run this way and that, like hens in a poultry yard. With them it is impossible to make history, they cannot be used as elements supporting a community". . . .'[137]

Hence, again and again the fascist regime decries the habit of thought, again and again it ridicules thinkers, again and again it admonishes them not to be so presumptuous as to examine and judge the programmes, etc., of the regime, over and over again it tells them that, indeed, they are congenitally incapable of grasping the genius of the Leader.

> Thus we have Gentile, the intellectual who took upon himself the task of rationalising Mussolini's blather, telling us that, 'Often the Duce, with his profound intuition of fascist psychology, has told us the truth, that we all participate in a sort of mystic sentiment. In such a mystic state of mind we do not form clear and distinct ideas, nor can we put into precise words the things we believe in, but it is in those mystic moments, when our soul is enveloped in the penumbra of a new world being born that creative faith germinates in our hearts. . .the fascist spirit is will, not intellect. . . .Intellectual fascists must not be intellectuals. . .' Intellectuals were told not to try and examine the Duce's words because between them and the latter was a 'simply astronomical gap' and that they should desist from throwing 'the cold water of prose on the enthusiasm of poetry.'[138]

But is this utter lack of programmes not a severe handicap? It certainly is to the nation: valuable time is lost, the miseries of a

---

[137]Bullock, *op. cit.*
[138]Greene, *op. cit.*, pp. 97-98.

people are prolonged, the citizenry loses its freedom and all this to no purpose. But it imposes no disadvantages upon the usurper and his clique. Quite the contrary.

First, it enables them to effectively "(avoid) the dangerous ground of principle, as well as the difficulties of being coherent."[139] It leaves them free to manoeuvre, to wheel and deal. Second, the eclectic, opportunist, open-ended character of their programmes attracts all sorts of sections to them each of whom thinks that it can strike a deal to its own advantage. In particular, it provides yet another occasion for many so-called intellectuals to persuade themselves that the regime is malleable, that they can "reform it from within."

> '...(other intellectuals) felt it their mission to strengthen the affirmative forces within the "great idealistic popular movement" called National Socialism. They meant to take those honest but primitive Nazi ruffians under their wings, to sublimate those unthinking energies, to refine "the well meant but clumsy ideas" of Adolf Hitler, "the man of the people".... This was the hope, so frequently found in revolutionary eras of averting something worse, oddly coupled with the notion that under the banner of the new fraternity idealism could be introduced into "dirty politics." Cowardice and conformism were certainly present and widespread; but (so were these) intellectual illusions....'[140]

Secondly, the total control over the state apparatus gives them the instrument for reconciling the inconsistencies of their rapidly obsolescent programmes: "absolute power alone enables (the regime) to overcome its inherent inconsistencies and to maintain its advance; the spoils can be used to satisfy the most varied appetites, the prestige of victory to attract supporters and the power of the State to crush its enemies into submission for a long while...."[141]

---

[139]Rossi, *op. cit.*, p. 36.
[140]Fest, *op. cit.*, p. 427.
[141]Rossi, *op. cit.*, p. 345.

## Symptoms

### Two Inferences

A number of inferences can be drawn from the preceding account. I will confine myself to two.

First, it is foolish to indulge oneself in the fantasy that fascist regimes can be "reformed from within." To delude oneself in this way is to ignore the class basis of the regime and to shut one's eyes to the constraints that this and the singleminded and exclusive devotion to domination impose on what the regime will and will not do. Moreover, it is to make the even more elementary error of over-looking the fact that the nihilists and vandals who head such regimes don't care two hoots for their own programmes or their so-called ideology, and, thus, one cannot accomplish anything by improving these programmes. And they know perfectly well what they are up to; thus one cannot hope to improve matters by educating them to the "true consequences" or the "unintended effects" of their programmes and policies.

> '...there has scarcely been a single old National Socialist who attached any importance to the programme and the programme literature of the party....And the National Socialist "Bible," that remarkable book which is now accorded the sanctity of verbal inspiration, was far from playing its present part among the...old members of the party; they paid no particular attention to it. Nobody took it seriously; nobody could, for nobody could make head or tail of it....The movement has no fixed aims, either economic or political, either in home or foreign affairs. Hitler was out, even in 1932, to liberate himself from all party doctrines in economic policy and he did the same in all other fields; and this "realist" attitude was adopted, and still is, not only by the leader but by every member holding any official position in the party or admitted at all into its confidence. The only objective was the victory of the party and even favourite doctrines were abandoned for this sake....'[142]

'It would be a great mistake to suppose that so cunning an

---

[142] Rauschning, *op. cit.*, pp. 20-21.

individual as the German Minister of Propaganda is not perfectly well aware that the atrocity propaganda against the Jews, including the "Protocols of the Elders of Zion," is preposterous nonsense, that he does not see through the racial swindle just as clearly as those compatriots of his whom it has driven out of their country. It would be simply foolish to imagine that any member of the (clique) truly and sincerely believes in the bases of the "philosophy." They have been deliberately concocted for their demagogic effectiveness and for the furtherance of the party's political aims....'[143]

Is it not foolish for some so-called intellectuals to delude themselves into thinking that they can "reform" this cynical bunch "from within"? Would it not be foolish of them to think that the clique is seriously interested in what they have to say when, as it often does, it asks them for their views or lets them engage in some debates?

'The government permitted the expression of all sorts of heterodox ideas as long as these ideas did not challenge the regime itself, but it ignored them completely in formulating its own policies....Indeed these polemics served as an ideal safety valve for powerless fascist intellectuals and idealistic fascist students....'[144]

The second inference is allied to the first: no one should draw comfort from the latest round of progressive promises, no one should believe that because such and such an item has been included in the latest programme, the character of the regime is going to change. The moment it is confronted with yet another round of progressive promises, the reflex action of the populace should not be to rejoice, but to remind itself that Hitler's party was called the National *Socialist* Party; instead of taking the new or dusted promises at face value, the reflex action should be to recall the many progressive slogans that figured so conspicuously in the programmes of Mussolini, Hitler and Chiang Kai-Shek.

Instead of being taken in by the new promises, the populace

[143]*Ibid.*, p. 53.
[144]Tannenbaum, *op. cit.*, p. 77.

should look behind the facade: what is the class basis of the regime; if the promises were not implemented before, now that the Enabling Act has been passed, now that the press has been "coordinated," now that all traces of pluralism in the polity have been banished, are the compulsions for implementing the promises more or less? True that the regime proclaims much solicitude for the poor but when there is an engagement (between the landlords and the landless labourers in Chiang's China, for instance), when such an engagement takes place, on whose side is the state apparatus brought to bear, on the side of the labourers or on the side of the landlords? Instead of wasting its time following one programme after another, these are the questions that the populace should be asking itself.

## V. A Myth in Five Parts

With the takeover and consolidation complete, the usurper has the country prostrate, he has the "power" he has sought, but he still does not have any notion of what to do with it. The usurper and his clique must now create a myth to legitimize their absolutist rule, their arbitrariness, their violence and lack of scruples. Hence, "like a parvenu...suddenly discovering his noble quarterings," the fascist rulers set about devising an "ideology." History, as Tasca says, is ransacked in a frantic search for precedents. The "national character" is reinterpreted to suggest that throughout history the populace has yearned for "the strong man" who will lead it by the scruff of its neck.

The myths they will discover in their vandal expeditions into history are entirely predictable. All we have to do is to remember three features that are implicit in the preceding account. First, the usurper and his clique have captured the state apparatus: this is their singular possession. Second, they have done so by bludgeoning their opponents, by violating the spirit and the letter of Constitutions, by bulldozing institutions, by casting aside all their promises, by deliberately using violent, unscrupulous methods. Third, their sole purpose is to perpetuate themselves in power and for this purpose they are busy putting together a machinery of domination.

## Statolatory

To begin with, the regime mounts an hysterical campaign to exalt the "State" or, as in the German case, the *Volk* and the "State" as an instrument of it. The turnaround is indeed dramatic. The same Mussolini who had earlier written editorial after editoral about the individual's duty to take his stand on his conscience, who had spoken unequivocally of the supremacy of the individual, ("...outside the individual no other human reality exists... we have rent every revealed truth, we have spat upon every dogma, rejected every paradise, turned away every charlatan—white, red, or black—who has put in circulation miraculous drugs which promise 'happiness' to mankind. We do not believe in programs, schemes, saints or apostles; above all we do not believe in felicity, salvation, the promised land. We do not believe in a unique solution—be it economic or political or moral—a unilinear solution to the problems of life because... life is not linear....We return to the individual. We support everything that exalts and amplifies the individual, that increases his liberty, well-being, and latitude of life. We oppose everything that oppresses and mortifies the individual.... The state is a tremendous machine that swallows living men and regurgitates dead ciphers... This, this is the great malediction that struck mankind during the uncertain beginnings of its history: to create, over the centuries, the state, to find itself overcome, annihilated! ...Down with the state in all its forms and incarnations. The state of yesterday, today, and tomorrow...."[145]) the same Mussolini now issues the slogan "everything for the State, nothing against the State, no one outside the State." The same Mussolini now asserts that the State is the sole arbiter, "the sole and ultimate source of imperative sanction...."[146] The same Mussolini—with his characteristic obsession for labelling not the year or the decade but the century itself—tells us that the twentieth century will be "the century of collectivism and hence the century of the State." The same Mussolini now tells us that "for fascism the State is the absolute before which individuals and groups are only relative....The State has become the true

---

[145]Gregor, *op. cit.*, pp. 156-157.
[146]*Ibid.*, pp. 188-189.

reality of the individual..." and one of the legitimizers now asserts that "the individual liberty is only a concession granted by the State to the individual...."[147]

All over the country bill-boards now proclaim the slogan from the 1913 programme of the "futurists." "The word ITALY must loom larger than the word LIBERTY."[148] Things are no different in Germany: "What is primordial for us," the *thug* Goering declares, "is not the individual...there is only one thing that counts: the National Socialist State must be placed above everything else."[149]

The old assertions about the individual are now covered up by new obfuscations. Giovani Gentile is once again the chief obfuscator: "The only freedom that can be taken seriously is that of the State and of the individual within the State"—a brilliant philosophical riddle that, as Vitta-Finzi says, becomes the cornerstone of Fascist theory.[150]

Elaborating the conundrum on another occasion Gentile tells us that, "The Duce discussed whether action should be by force or consent, and concluded that the authority of the State and the liberty of the subject are counterparts and inseparable...Fascism does not oppose authority to liberty, but sets a system of real and concrete freedom against an abstract and false parody.... Even in the nineteenth century people were beginning to think that a strong was necessary in the interests of liberty itself.... One can even say that the new Corporative State, by stressing the identification of liberty with authority, and through a system of representation which corresponds better with reality, is actually more liberal than the old."[151]

Now, the reader who has followed the discussion thus far should have no difficulty in discerning the purpose, as well as the import, of this "statolatory." The usurper and his clique know that in practical terms the "State" means the clique that controls the state apparatus—namely, them. Hence, by exalting the

---

[147]Guerin, *op. cit.*, p. 175.
[148]Woolf, *op. cit.*, p. 230. For a shrill paean to the State the reader should read his "The Political and Social Doctrine of Fascism"; an extract is included in Greene, *op.cit.*, pp. 39-45.
[149]Guerin, *op. cit.*, p. 175.
[150]Woolf, *op. cit.*, p. 232.
[151]Greene, *op. cit.*, p. 98.

"State" they are only laying the propaganda basis for their own dominance.

Once this aspect of the myth has been drilled into the populace, three consequences follow immediately.

*Three Consequences*

First, the State—which means the clique—now has the exclusive right to provide final judgments on everything. No other standards, reference points, matter.

Second, from now on the ordinary citizens who are seeking protection against injustice and arbitrariness, who are trying to remind the State of its duty, and not the usurpers who have mauled institutions, violated Constitutions, etc.—from now on, by definition, the former and not the latter are the outlaws.[152] All notions of the "rights" of individuals or groups become obsolete. The right to life, liberty, to seek the protection of courts? None of these is now a "right"—it is a concession granted by the State (i.e., the clique) which can be taken away at will. And they are in fact taken away in succession—taken away before the very eyes of the usurper's would-be opponents, by the very hands of the legislatures and courts who were supposedly the guardians of values, rights, Constitutions.

At each new turn of the screw these personages accept the new "law" or "decree" saying that it is no more than "an extension of past trends" or that it is no more than "a formalisation of current practice." And each turn gives the usurper and his henchmen further license.

'The decisive factor was that the conservatives made no effort to preserve the rights of habeas corpus. This "fearful gap" meant that henceforth there was no limit to outrages by the state. The police could arbitrarily arrest and extend the period of detention indefinitely. They could leave relatives without any news concerning the reasons for the arrest and the fate of the person arrested. They could prevent a lawyer or other persons from visiting him or examining the files on the case.... They could crush their prisoner with work, give him the vilest food

---

[152]Rauschning, *op. cit.*, p. 221.

and shelter, force him to repeat hated slogans or sing songs. They could torture him...No court would ever find the case in its files. No court had the right to interfere, even if a judge unofficially obtained knowledge of the circumstances....'[153]

Third, all talk of class suddenly becomes impermissible, it is swallowed up by the rhetoric of "nation." Thus, e.g., efforts to remind the workers of their class interests, to tell them how these are being violated, to organize them to defend these interests—such efforts suddenly become impermissible. Hitler uses the slogan of *Volksgemeinschaft*—the "united nation"—to bury all talk of organizing the poor or awakening them to their interests. In a statement the like of which is to be repeated again and again he says that

> 'the slogan, "the dictatorship of the bourgeoise must make way for the dictatorship of the proletariat," is simply a question of a change from the dictatorship of one class to that of another, while we wish for the dictatorship of the nation, that is, the dictatorship of the whole community. Only then will we be able to restore to the millions of our people the conviction that the State does not represent the interests of a single group or class and that the government is there to manage the concerns of the entire community....'[154]

In his socialist incarnation Mussolini had vehemently opposed all moves to involve Italy in the war of 1914. He had said at that time that war is to be opposed as it "requires the most insistent class collaboration" within a country when the task of the workers is to join hands with workers of other countries in a class war to throw off all exploiters. The logic of class obligation, even though it may appear "heretical, pardoxical, sacreligious," he said, requires that everyone must "reject the Fatherland...the proletariat must never spill its precious blood for the Moloch of patriotism. ...The national flag for us is but a rag to be planted on the dunghill. There are only two nations

---

[153]Fest, *op. cit.*, pp. 397-398.
[154]Greene, *op. cit.*, p. 238.
[155]Gregor. *op. cit.*, pp. 129-136.

in the world: that of the exploited and that of the exploiters...."[156]

Now that the working class must be overwhelmed, a new rhetoric is evident. We are told that the trouble with the concept of a class cutting across national boundaries is that "the unit of loyalty is too large;" that the concept of nation must supersede that of the class: "class is based on a community of interests but the nation is a history of sentiments, of traditions, of language, of culture, of race...," that for the fascists there are only two "sustaining realities": production and the nation; that production is "the supreme commmandment of the hour," that production in turn requires "strict class collaboration" and discipline; and, finally, that, as people are not liable to discipline themselves, society must be organized along hierarchical lines.[156] "Productivity" and "discipline" become the catchwords in Italy just as the term *"Leistung"* is exploited by the Nazis.[157]

In accordance with these notions strikes, etc., were

'outlawed by being declared inimical to the "German concepts of social conscience and honour." Under these concepts...the interests of the workers and employers are alike subsumed in their "high purpose of creating a true national community"....' (Stern, pp. 133-34)

In the name of production, all reins are lifted from private enterprise. In May 1921 Mussolini insists that there should be no further experiments in State socialism. "The State," he says, "must be deprived of all economic functions" and be brought in line with "Manchester School Economics"; "we must abolish the collectivist State that the war forced on us and return to the Manchesterian State...."[158]

With production and nation as the two "sustaining realities" Mussolini is now able to proclaim: "We want to strip the state of all its economic functions. Enough of the state which acts as railway owner, postman, insurance company. Enough of the state which functions at the taxpayers' expense and exhausts the

---

[156]*Ibid.*, pp. 137-180.
[157]Woolf, *op. cit.*, p. 128.
[158]Rossi, *op. cit.*, pp. 122-134.

finances of Italy. With the police, the education of the rising generation, the army to ensure the integrity of the fatherland, with foreign policy, no one can say that the state thus restricted is diminished in stature. No; it is still very great, retaining all its spiritual realm and renouncing the material one."[159]

Now, the thing to remember is that all this screaming about the nation is just rhetorical nationalism. Subsequent events are to show, both in Italy as well as Germany, that even when they have led their countries into bloody and humiliating defeats, even when it is entirely clear that continuing the war can only amount to more death and humiliation for their countries, the regimes insist on continuing the wars. Does this demonstrate much attachment to the nation? Incidentally, the regimes' attachment to youth is equally vociferous. "(The youth) are found in all of Hitler's harangues from 1921 to 1923: 'We appeal above all to the powerful army of our German youth...the young Germans will some day be the architects of a new racist state. Later, Goebbels lyrically exclaimed, 'The revolution we have made...has been almost entirely the work of the German youth.' 'In Germany, it is the youth that governs'...."[160] And the attachment is equally shallow: the same cliques that were shouting these cliches sacrificed the youth of the two countries like fodder and continued to do so till they were themselves eliminated.

Thus, in the case of fascist regimes, the new rhetoric about the "nation" is not to be viewed as evidence of a sudden dedication to the nation's interests; rather it is to be seen for what it really is—another instrument of domination, an instrument that is deployed to overwhelm one mass sentiment—that of the working class—by another one.

## The Leader

In an effort that parallels the exaltation of the "State," the Leader is exalted to an almost divine position.

'The (usurper) is then..."promoted to the rank of a demi-

---

[159]*Ibid.*, p. 249.
[160]Guerin, *op. cit.*, p. 70.

god." He is proclaimed infallible and omniscient. "Mussolini is always right," we read in the *Decalogue of the Militia Man.* And in the *Credo of the Balilla,* "I believe in the genius of Mussolini." "Adolf Hitler is a personality of universal genius," asserts Wilhelm Kube. "There is unquestionably no domain of human activity that the Fuhrer does not supremely dominate." Goering said to a representative of the *Morning Post* "Just as Catholics consider the Pope infallible in all questions of religion and morality, we believe with the same profound conviction that the Fuhrer is infallible in all matters concerning the moral and social interests of the people". "One person is above all criticism, the Fuhrer," exclaimed Rudolf Hess. "Everybody knows that he has always been right and that he always will be right." From this to worship, there is only a step, and it is quickly taken. In Italy, the official publication, *Milizia Fascista* offers this instruction: "Remember to love God, but do not forget that Italy's God is the Duce." Gentizon, Rome correspondent of the *Temps*, relates: "Peasants and their wives knelt on perceiving on a distant hill the tower where the Duce had just arrived for a brief stay.... Already a halo of idealism and poetry envelops him. For some he has become a legendary figure. When he appears at a demonstration, the faces of many spectators seem to be illuminated." In Germany, Goebbels made himself the high priest of the new cult. "Faith in the Fuhrer," he said, "is surrounded one almost might say, with a mysterious and enigmatic mysticism!" He addresses Hitler in the style of a Father of the Church: "In our profound despair, we found in you the one who showed the road of faith....You were for us the fulfillment of a mysterious desire. You addressed to our anguish words of deliverance. You forged our confidence in the miracle to come." When "his" Fuhrer had become master of Germany, he went still further and spoke to him as to God himself. On April 20, 1930, Hitler's birthday, he sent him this prayer over the radio: "Today *Thou* must know that behind *Thee*, and if necessary before *Thee*, stands a compact army of fighters who at any moment are ready to sacrifice themselves for *Thee* and *Thy* idea....We promise *Thee* solemnly that *Thou* wilt always be for us what *Thou* art today: *Our* Hitler!" Roehm called him a "New redeemer". Hess affirmed that "this man will lead the German people without concerning himself with earthly influences" "His will is in fact the will of God," wrote a panegyrist.'[161]

There is nothing but nothing that the Leader's life and blather cannot illumine. Here is a typical admonition. The subject is "On the National Responsibility of Publishers" and, among other things, they are told that

'...the great master of the education of his people, Adolf Hitler, has in a few years transformed our souls and has also sharpened in the whole book publishing trade the feeling that it bears a tremendous responsibility....Thus the great distance that separates the present-day conception of the publisher's calling from yesterday's becomes quite clear: instead of an inwardly uninvolved cultural-mirror, he is a cultural-politician imbued with his task. The servant of the writer has been changed into a deputy of the state....Thus today it is not enough for the publisher to master his craft and to be as cultured as possible; he must be thoroughly imbued with the idea of the state leadership of Adolf Hitler and in this idea he will find the guidelines for his own work. No one will be able to say that he is no position to do this. The countless great speeches of the Fuhrer, along with his book, afford an exhaustive exposition of the state idea that he has created and espoused, down to the smallest details of personal life. Anyone who fully absorbs, over and over again, the lavish fullness of this brilliant mind which literally runneth over and his example of a truly great life will know what he has to do....'[162]

The chorus ascends ever higher. The party leader Joseph Wagner calls Hitler "the greatest artist of all time," the labour leader, Robert Ley, tells us that he is "the only man in history who never errs." Hess affirms that he is "pure reason in human form," and Himmler gives us his reading of history: "from its earliest beginnings Aryan humanity has not produced anything

---
[161]*Ibid.*, pp. 66-67.
[162]Mosse, *op. cit.*, pp. 160-161.

to compare with him."[163]

The leader—by his speeches, his visits to churches and what not—himself does what he can to promote this identity with—or at least his proximity to—the Divine. In *Mein Kampf,* Hitler had written, "by defending myself against the Jew, I am fighting for the work of the Lord".[164] In March 1936, he proclaims, "I go the way that Providence dictates with the assurance of a sleep walker. . . ."

And by 1937, he tells the audience to believe that the good Lord is helping him along: "However weak the individual may be when compared with the omnipotence and will of Providence, yet at the moment when he acts as Providence would have him act he becomes immeasurably strong. Then there streams down upon him that force which has marked all greatness in the world's history. And when I look back only on the five years which lie behind us, then I feel that I am justified in saying: That has not been the work of man alone."[165]

And thus he enters the pantheon; he becomes an incarnation: a Thuringian church warden proclaims to the world that "Christ has come to us through Adolf Hitler."[166]

*The Leader is the State*

Having exalted the State on the one hand and the Leader on the other, the next step is easily taken: the Leader is now declared to be the State. On February 25, 1934, Rudolf Hess makes the leaders of the Hitler Youth and the Labour Service take the oath:

'Adolf Hitler is Germany and Germany is Adolf Hitler. He who pledges himself to Hitler pledges himself to Germany.'[167]

From now on the oath of the armed forces too is altered; it becomes a personal oath to Hitler:

---

[163]Stern, *op. cit.*, p. 111.
[164]Fest, *op.cit.*, p. 209.
[165]Greene, *op. cit.*, p. 218.
[166]Fest, *op. cit.*, p. 444.
[167]*Ibid.*, p. 445.

## Symptoms

> 'I swear by God this holy oath that I will give unlimited obedience to the Fuhrer of the German Reich, Adolf Hitler.'[168]

In Italy the Duce is conceived as "the living and active incarnation of the nation" and the rule of his whim is elevated into being "the charismatic theory of national society."[169]

### Four Consequences

Even though two aspects of the new mythology are yet to be enumerated, let us pause for a moment and consider some consequences of the three aspects that have been listed above.

First, the rationalizations for the complete centralization of power are now complete: the state is now to be run by an apparatus, the apparatus by the clique and the clique by the Leader. As the Leader personifies the people, the State, God and everything else, everyone, every institution must from now on function merely as executors of his will; if they do not they flout (not the usurper, the individual Hitler or Mussolini) but the people, the State, God.

Second, there is no longer any reason for the usurper to explain his conduct. He does not have to do so because (as Article 47 of the Statute of the Forlange Esparola Tradicionalista y de las Jons put it), he "is responsible to God and history."[170] After the Rohm murders Hitler tells the nation:

> 'If anyone reproaches me and asks me why I did not resort to the regular courts of justice, then all I can say to him is this: in this hour I was responsible for the fate of the German people and thereby I became the supreme justiciar of the German people.... And everyone must know for all future time that if anyone raises his hand to strike at the State, then certain death is his lot....'[171]

'The moment the faithful *believe*, nothing is easier than to

---

[168]Greene, *op. cit.*, p. 131.
[169]Gregor, *op. cit.*, p. 444.
[170]Woolf, *op. cit.*, p. 48.
[171]Fest, *op. cit.*, p. 469.

play with truth and logic. They will notice nothing. And if by chance, they open their eyes, there will be no difficulty in closing them immediately with the argument: it is so because the Leader says so!'[172]

An Italian compulsory reader issued for eight year olds in 1936 tells its impressionable readers:

'A child who, even while not refusing to obey, asks' "why?" is like a bayonet made of milk. . . . "You must obey because you must," says Mussolini, when explaining the reasons for obedience.'[173]

Nor, because of their proximity to the personification of the people, State and God, do his clique or his designated henchmen. From now on the secret police acted on the simple, official rule that "as long as the police carries out the will of the Fuhrer it is acting legally." Therefore, all acts of the Gestapo were placed beyond the purview of the courts.[174]

Third, the way is now clear for a new concept of "Law."

Goering tells the Prussian prosecutors: "the Law and the will of the Fuhrer are one."[175]

'Dr. Hans Frank, Commissioner of Justice and Reich Law Leader, told the jurists in 1936, "The National Socialist ideology is the foundation of all basic laws, especially as explained in the party program and in the speeches of the Furher." Dr. Frank went on to explain what he meant: "There is no independenee of law against National Socialism. Say to yourselves at every decision which you make: 'How would the Fuhrer decide in my place?' In every decision ask yourselves: 'Is this decision compatible with the National Socialist conscience of the German people? Then you will have a firm iron foundation which, allied with the unity of the National Socialist People's State and with your recognition of the eter-

---

[172]Guerin, *op.cit.*, p. 63.
[173]Greene, *op.cit.*, pp. 109-110.
[174]Stern, *op.cit.*, p. 125.
[175]Shirer, *op.cit.*, p. 268.

nal nature of the will of Adolf Hitler, will endow your own sphere of decision with the authority of the Third Reich, and this for all time".'[176]

'Our Constitution,' said Dr. Hans Frank on another occasion, 'is the will of the Fuhrer.'[177]

'There is no authority and ultimate source of law other than the conscience of the Nation itself, writes Roland Freisler in his commentary on the Nuremberg laws, echoing Hans Frank who, in 1929, as Hitler's defending counsel, informed a court of law that "justice must be that which makes the whole Nation prosper, injustice must be that which harms the whole Nation"; and since the Fuhrer is the keeper of the Nation's conscience, his word is law. "It is the first time in the history of the People," Hans Frank tells the assembled members of Munich University, "that love of the Fuhrer has become a concept in law." And in June 1938, now holding the splendid title of Reichsiechtsfuhrer, Frank proclaims: "Whether the Fuhrer does or does not govern according to a formal written constitution is not a fundamental legal issue. Only the question whether the Fuhrer through his activity safeguards the life of the Nation is the fundamental legal issue of our time." This sovereignty of the "Fuhrer's Will" is confirmed in the law of 26 April 1942, which consists entirely of a verbatim passage from Hitler's address to the Reichstag, and specifically mentions that he is not "bound by existing legal regulations".'[178]

The fourth consequence—the last that we will list here—is that as the Leader personifies the people, there is now no longer any rationale for representative democracy: "The new and decisive aspect of the Fuhrer constitution," we learn, "is that it goes beyond the democratic distinction between rulers and ruled to create a unity in which the Leader and the following have merged. . . ."Hence, "though there exists a considerable fascist literature about the shaping of the state, in the last resort

---

[176]*Ibid.*
[177]Greene, *op. cit.*, p. 235.
[178]Stern, *op. cit.*, pp. 122-123.

it was secondary. For if all members of *Volk* and nation shared a common myth, a common soul, then their participation in government need only be symbolized by the Leader who has activated their shared human natures through his own activism, his heroic will."[179]

The mould is now set for plebiscitory dictatorship. The usurper and his clique rule unhindered, but from time to time they pose complicated questions to the people. All the devices are deployed on behalf of the rulers—propaganda, blandishments, threats, admonitions, intimidation. And the results invariably show the people approving by massive majorities what has already been decided. And a Hitler can proclaim, as he did in the election campaign which followed the denunciation of the Locarno Pact and the reoccupation of the Rhineland: "In Germany bayonets do not terrorize a people. Here a government is supported by the confidence of the entire people. I care for the people. In fifteen years I have slowly worked my way up together with this movement. I have not been imposed by anyone upon the people. From the people I have grown up, in the people I have remained, to the people I return. My pride is that I know no statesman in the world who with greater right than I can say that he is the representative of his people. . . ."[180]

The massive success of each dictator in the plebiscites he has held only shows how easy it is to arrange victories for oneself once you have established absolute domination.

*The Elitist State*

Now all that remains is to "justify" the special position of the clique, of the chosen henchmen, and to "justify" the violent, unscrupulous means of the regime. Hence, the fourth and fifth aspects of the myth.

At first in private gatherings and then more openly, the word is put out that the people cannot govern themselves, that they need to be led. Passages from Spengler, Hegel, Sorel, Maurras are recalled, passages that forecast, urge, look forward to the coming Caesars. Mussolini who had written paens to the people

---

[179]Woolf, *op. cit.*, p. 9.
[180]Greene, *op. cit.*, p. 236.

now exalts audacious minorities and insists that history has only been made by such minorities. The *Handbook of the Italian Fascist* tells everyone that "you must believe in the aristocracy of minorities" and that this minority must impose its will upon the people, even if it is necessary "to make them yield by force."

The audacious minority is now presented as the stern parent who must discipline his wayward child. Rocco affirms that the masses "tend to do what a few dominating elements desire" and Malaparte assures us that "the people need tyrants." In Germany Nietzsche is invoked for the exalts "the terrible and enchanting counter-war cry of the prerogative of the few." Hitler follows him and gives us yet another of his inferences from history; this time we are told that "everything extraordinary accomplished since the world was a world has been accomplished by minorities."[181]

Beneath all this lies a supreme contempt for the people. They view the people as a "stupid, tractable, manipulable mass whose needs (can) be satisfied with the classical method of *panem et circenses*."[181] All the talk about remoulding society, about forging a new man is just a device for making people put up with privation, injustice, cruelty in the present by asserting that it is all necessary for insuring a glorious future. Forging a new man or a new just and humane society is farthest from their objectives. They identify the worst instincts of individuals and groups—jealousy, envy, hatred for others, a morbid fascination for brutality when it is inflicted upon others, anxiety to protect their own skin, a willingness to go to any length, to suffer every humiliation, to put up with every injustice so long as it seems to promise protection for oneself, a boundless ability to go on hoping for something to turn up—this is what they see in individuals and groups and then they set about using these traits to their own purposes.

They follow the cynical policy of "taking men as they are and pandering to their weakness and their bestiality...."[183] As the candid Mussolini said, "the masses are so much cattle, the prey

---

[181]Guerin, *op. cit.*, pp. 173-174.
[182]Bracher, *op. cit.*, p. 181.
[183]Rauschning, *op. cit.*, p. 46.

of spasmodic, fluctuating and irresponsible forces; inert matter, without volition and without future. We must overthrow, therefore, the altars raised by demos to their Holiness the Masses...." Thus, he proclaimed, "the century of democracy is over. The ideals of democracy are exploded beginning with that of 'progress.' Ours is an 'aristocratic' century which followed the old democratic one. The state of all will end by becoming the state of a few. The new generations are not going to let the corpse of democracy block their way into the future."[184]

All this, the reader will recall, comes from the very "leaders" who but a short while before were deifying the masses in their harangues, who were saying that the will of the people is supreme, who had assumed power, so they said, to save the people from chaos.

These new proclamations at once constitute the rationale for an hierarchical state in which power flows from the top down and obedience alone must travel from the bottom up. Moreover, given its special position in this new theology, the clique and the chosen henchmen are freed from all restraints, as, by definition, they are distinct from that inert mass—the people. As they embody the "dynamic will" they can no longer be shackled by rules, regulations, programmes, or even ideology. Soon enough this freedom from all restraints is indeed what comes to mark every member of the elite.

> 'That which is intended for the masses is not applicable to the elite. Programmes and official philosophy, allegiance and faith, are for the mass. Nothing commits the elite—no philosophy, no ethical standard. It has but one obligation, that of absolute loyalty to comrades, to fellow members of the initiated elite....'[185]

Free from all restraints, the clique and their henchmen who usurped power to save the republic from chaos, who usurped it "to serve the people"—their character is now at last in full view.

---

[184]Rossi, *op. cit.*, pp. 237-238.
[185]Rauschning, *op. cit.*, p. 20.
[186]*Ibid.*, p. 31.

'...the secret of the union of the elite is their lack of doctrine. No allegiance to any sort of philosophy merited membership in the actual elite, but the simple fact of having fought for its power.... The actual participants in power... are a ruling minority of super careerists. This cream of the elite use the power they have seized to feather their own nests....'[186]

## Unscrupulousness as a Virtue

Only one task remains and that is to "justify" the violent, immoral methods that the regime habitually employs. This is accomplished in a characteristic way—by assertions, by incessant, shrill assertions. Three sets of assertions are employed.

First, the power lust of the usurper is glorified. The State itself is now defined—we are using Mussolini's words once again—as "the will to power and domination."[187]

Second, violence, cunning, lack of scruples are elevated to being the highest principles of nature.

'Mussolini, in Sorelian style, proclaims the "value of the violent deed." "Violence," he states, "is perfectly moral." "Almost all my life I have been the apologist of violence." "Struggle is at the origin of everything... Struggle will always be in the depths of human nature like a supreme fatality. Moreover, it is good that this should be so. The day when struggle ceases will be a day of melancholy, end and ruin." Man reveals his true self only "in bloody effort." "War makes all human energy sublime and sets the seal of nobility on the people who have the courage to accept it..." Hitler likewise hails the "Victorious efficacy of violence": "Humanity has grown up in eternal combat; in eternal peace, humanity would waste away... Nature annihilates the weak to give their place to the strong." He glorifies the right of the strongest as the "right which in nature is the only one possible, the only one reasonable." He boasts of "utilizing all weapons, even the most brutal." Thus a cultivated social class, proud of its "respectability," personified by an elderly gentleman honored by an entire nation, arrives

---

[187]Rossi, *op. cit.*, p. 354.

at the point of entrusting state power to the most sinister gangsters known to all history.'[188]

The keystone is placed by the final assertion: power *per se* is morality, and violence is the only guarantor of progress. "Right," declares Hitler in *Mein Kampf*, "abides in strength alone... the sole earthly criterion of whether an enterprise is right or wrong is its success...." Nature, he tells us, "Nature... puts living creatures on this globe and watches the free play of forces. She then confers the masters' right on her favourite child, the strongest in courage and industry.... Only the born weakling can view this as cruel, but he after all is only a weak and limited man; for if this law did not prevail, any conceivable higher development of organic living beings would be unthinkable.... In the end, only the urge for self-preservation can conquer. Beneath its so-called humanity, the expression of a mixture of stupidity, cowardice, and know-it-all conceit, will melt like snow in the March sun. Mankind has grown great in eternal struggle, and only in eternal peace does it perish."[189] On the other hand, conscience, he says, is "a Jewish invention... a blemish, like circumcision...."

At last the structure is complete. Everything the usurper and the clique do is now fully justified. When they massacre Jews, they are "doing God's work," when they bulldoze other nations to rubble, they are only fulfilling nature's design of progress, when they pillage the state's coffers, they do not more than what is "legal" (for they are the "Law"), when they bludgeon their opponents they do so for "reasons of State" (as they are the "State," their reasons are "reasons of State"). Their "power"—which is morality—entitles them to adopt the swagger of Mussolini's fascists: *mene frego*, I don't give a damn.

Hence are all standards, all norms, all notions of justice, humaneness, propriety, responsibility, hence are all institutions pulverized.

Once again, many inferences can be drawn. I must confine myself to the most obvious one: the phenomenon is an integrated whole. Once a regime embarks on this course, it will go the

[188]Guerin, *op. cit.*, p. 188.
[189]Fest, *op. cit.*, p. 208.

entire distance unless it is overwhelmed by active resistance. It will not stop or relax on its own. Nothing can be more foolish than to suppose that by working from within we can prevent it from taking steps "y" and "z" even though we are not able to prevent it from taking the initial twenty-four. Nor, when a regime with the features that have been listed here comes into being, should we reconcile ourselves to the set-up in the belief that the worst excesses of Hitler and Mussolini are not yet evident. The harm that Hitler and Mussolini did was not confined to, it was not contingent upon the worst excesses. Nor should we lull ourselves by thinking that "the time to wake up is not yet; very few have been asked to do something positively immoral; for most of us life goes on more or less as before." Even under Hitler and Mussolini very few were actually involved in immoral and violent action, (incidentally, almost none of them was of a congenitally criminal nature)[190] and for most life did continue more or less as it had been.[191] And yet the countries—and the peoples—were brought to such grief.

## VI. Applause and Partial Results

Fascist regimes have little difficulty in rattling off impressive statistics about prices, production, employment, the balance of payments. In the case of Germany national output doubled between 1932 and 1937, the number of registered unemployed fell from 6 million to less than 1 million between February 1933 and the spring of 1937, the share of investment in national income rose from 9 per cent in 1932 to 23 per cent in 1937. In Italy the index of industrial production increased by 40 per cent between 1934 and mid-1935. These indices can be multiplied manifold.[192]

And these partial results occasioned much applause. Hitler was widely acclaimed "as the strong man who alone (is) capable of reestablishing order in Europe and saving the continent from Bolshevism."[193] With his eye on Germany, General Smuts,

---

[190] Greene, *op. cit.*, pp. 204-206.
[191] Eg., Hayes, *op. cit.*, pp. 169-170.
[192] Woolf, *op. cit.*, pp. 10, 223; Shirer, *op. cit.*, pp. 258-289.
[193] Guerin, *op. cit.*, p. 12.

presiding over the Assembly of the League at Geneva in 1933, "praised the new national discipline which some nations (are) imposing on themselves."[194] Lord Rothermere let it be known in 1928 that Mussolini is "the greatest figure of our age" and Cardinal O'Connell of Boston intoned that "Mussolini is a genius in the field of government given to Italy by God to help the nation continue her rapid ascent towards the most glorious destiny."[195] These were not exceptional comments. In his meticulous book[196] Diggins shows how uniform and unambiguous the applause was.

Nor was the applause confined to ill-informed foreigners. Within the countries too Hitler and Mussolini were able to win acclaim on the basis of the partial results and their aggressive, unrelenting propaganda. Among the persons who worked hardest to find attenuating features in the new set-up were many who had at first espoused liberal values, who knew what was going on, but who were now desperate to find justifications for their own inaction.

'...It was at this time, in the late summer of 1934, that I came to live and work in the Third Reich....The overwhelming majority of Germans did not seem to mind that their personal freedom had been taken away, that so much of their culture had been destroyed and replaced with a mindless barbarism, or that their life and work had become regimented to a degree never before experienced even by a people accustomed for generations to a great deal of regimentation....

'In the background, to be sure, there lurked the terror of the Gestapo and the fear of the concentration camp for those who got out of line or who had been Communist or Socialist or too liberal or too pacifist, or who were Jews. The Blood Purge of June 30, 1934, was a warning of how ruthless the new leaders could be. Yet the Nazi terror in the early years affected the lives of relatively few Germans and a newly arrived observer was somewhat surprised to see that the people of this country

---

[194]Rauschning, *op. cit.*, p. 232.
[195]Hayes, *op. cit.*, p. 37.
[196]John P. Diggins, *Mussolini and Fascism: The View from America*, Princeton University Press, Princeton, 1972.

did not seem to feel that they were being cowed and held down by an unscrupulous and brutal dictatorship. On the contrary, they supported it with genuine enthusiasm. Somehow it imbued them with a new hope and a new confidence and an astonishing faith in the future of their country....

'Hitler was liquidating the past, with all its frustrations and disappointments. Step by step, and rapidly... he was freeing Germany from the shackles of Versailles, confounding the victorious Allies and making Germany militarily strong again. This was what most Germans wanted and they were willing to make the sacrifices which the Leader demanded of them to get it: the loss of personal freedom, a Spartan diet ("Guns before Butter") and hard work....'[197]

'...But, however varied their ends, there was one thing which every social and political group that voted Hitler into power as well as some that opposed him, chief among them the Communists, were prepared to forgo, and that was political liberty under the law; one thing that every group (except the Jehovah's Witnesses) was ready to sacrifice, and that was freedom of individual conscience. Hitler himself knew how to exploit this defective concern.... So complete was the absence of any strong feelings on the subject of civil liberties that even today, in a very different situation, few if any historians of the Third Reich remark on it.... It is surely noteworthy that in the thirties such feelings were absent not only among the ideologists of the regime and its fellow-travellers on the Right, but also among its opponents....'[198]

'...It can hardly be doubted that Hitler was genuinely popular in Germany. If his party failed to win outright in any free and competitive election it seems likely nonetheless that at virtually any time between 1936 and 1939 Hitler would have won an overwhelming vote of support from the German people. Until disasters began to occur (after 1936) it seems probable that this would have been true of Mussolini too.... Both Hitler and Mussolini had enjoyed some success in coping with the difficult economic problems of the decade and it seems un-

---

[197] Shirer, *op. cit.*, p. 231.
[198] Stern, *op. cit.*, pp. 98-99.

likely that Italians and Germans would have neglected this fact in giving any verdict on the regimes. . . .'[199]

By 1936 unemployment had beens harply reduced and 'the regime's stubborn, wide ranging wooing of the workers had its effect, especially since many of them saw the difference between present and past "less in lost rights than in regard to full employment". . . .'[200]

In retrospect we can see how short-sighted and self-serving this applause and enthusiasm were.

Many of the claims of the regimes had no basis in fact *at all*. "The question still remains how such immense dynamic power could proceed from petty and contemptible source. It is characteristic of the present time that an appearance of gigantic achievements can be created with no basis in fact. The technical and organising resources available enable any sort of phantasmagoria to be given for a time the semblance of reality. Politics is bound up today with the appearance of a specialised "machinery". . . ."[201]

One of the advantages that works in the usurper's favour is precisely that he is presiding over a transition from an open to a closed polity. People—even in the matter, for instance, of believing or not believing figures of achievements that are put out—operate as if things had not changed or had not changed much. Thus, the usurper will proclaim that 95 per cent, 110 per cent and 120 per cent of targets x, y and z have been fulfilled. The citizen is liable to respond by telling himself—"well, you can't say that nothing is being done; even if the fellow is exaggerating and we do not take his figures at face value, the targets may have been fulfilled 80 per cent or 75 per cent; but, surely, even that is a lot." Knowing this the usurper puts out a complete lie confident that even if they discount it a bit, the people will believe its substance.

Goebbels correctly articulated the position when he confidently asserted that the bigger a lie the more liable people are to believe it. Subsequent events alone show how rotten the claims

---

[199]Hayes, *op. cit.*, p. 144.
[200]Guerin, *op. cit.*, p. 434.
[201]Rauschning, *op. cit.*, p. 37.

were: the splendid successes that were claimed by Mussolini in his "battle for wheat," in his "battle for the Lira," the claims that were issued by Chiang Kai-Shek about the results of his "extermination campaigns," the claims that were issued more recently by the Thieus, the Kys and their mentors about the number of Vietcong and North Vietnamese killed.

Other claims, while true, were only a part of the picture. Production did increase but the gross indices that people cited did not indicate what goods were being produced, they did not indicate the extent to which the recovery was dependent on rearmament, they did not indicate how the economy was being converted into a war economy.

But the main problem with these indices that were the basis of applause was a different one: they were indices about trivial matters. Even if all the claims had been valid they should not have occasioned applause. The fate of peoples is not determined by balances of payments, or the rate of inflation that Schacht stemmed, or production or unemployment. But by the more fundamental factors to which we have drawn attention: the relationship of different classes, the assumption of arms on behalf of one class or another, the relationship of individuals to the State, the norms, standards and institutions that are being built up or destroyed, the values that are being inculcated in the ruling groups and, by example, among the people.... Events that followed the applause and approval in Germany, Italy and, more recently, in regimes such as those of Ayub showed the true consequences of these regimes.

These events alone were to demonstrate the truth of Fuller's dictum that we must never judge a whole from its parts, rather we must judge the parts from the whole. "...German Conservatives and Nationalists defended their capitulation to National Socialism by saying that there was much that was open to objection in National Socialism, its methods were reprehensible, non-moral as one minister expressed it, but on the whole the National Socialist course was the right one for Germany. The truth is almost the opposite: National Socialism has some splendid achievements to its credit, and even much of its work in foreign policy cannot be seriously objected to from the national stand-point, having in view the difficulties with which Germany has had to contend; but its general course is mistaken, unfruitful, and in the long run infinitely disastrous. . . ."[202]

## VII. The Real Consequences

The cynicism of the usurper and his clique, their exclusive devotion to their own interests, the conduct of the regime, the *ambience*, breeds cynicism in the populace at large. All these bring out its worst instincts. The process begins with the chosen henchmen and ultimately infects every section of society.

> '...The lower elite, the Storm Troops, S.S. men, Hitler Youth and Werkscharen or National Socialist factory groups, have also passed through a process worth attention—the development of tactics of their own and of a new style of living. It is not surprising that the political methods and the style of living of the upper section of the elite have had an influence on the lower elite. The secret National Socialist doctrine of total nihilism, in the crudest of forms, has made unmistakable progress in the party formations. No one who has secured even a superficial insight into German conditions can have failed to realise the almost incredible deterioration of moral standards in the party formations. The unscrupulousness that has developed in the ranks of the S.A. and S.S. must sooner or later have the most fatal reactions on the general membership. Behind a few well-worn cliches about loyalty to the Leader and about the German nation there is concealed an outlook of undiluted materialism and a lust for every sort of violence, which will never be drilled out of the Storm Troops again. The simplicity and the crude conceit with which these men flaunt their brutality, as though it were something to be proud of, show the results of their education by example... (The society comes to be dominated by) a totally anti-social body of men, (who are) likely to infect the youth of the nation with the miasma of their unscrupulous readiness for anything. . . .'[203]

---

[202] *Ibid.*, p. 274.
[203] *Ibid.*, pp. 76-77.

'...Nobody will be so naive as to imagine that consistent training in brutality and unscrupulousness could produce a spirit of decency or that the systematic flouting and rejection of every principle of civilised law and order could produce a loyal citizen....'[204]

The values of the populace are transformed in this way by the example of rulers, by the nature and conduct of the regime. It would take too long to recount all the relevant factors once again. We must confine ourselves to one aspect of this education by example: corruption.

Corruption and immorality are not an accidental feature of such regimes. They are an inherent characteristic—they are an essential way by which the usurper gives a vested interest to and acquires the power of blackmail over his henchmen.

'...Lack of morals in civic life is not frowned upon: it is no ground for suspicion of a member of National Socialist orthodoxy. National Socialism demands, indeed, of its sworn elite that all personal scruples shall be over-ridden by the needs of the party. Anyone who reveals that he is allowing himself the luxury of guidance by his own conscience has no place in the elite and will be expelled. It is not surprising to find that absence of moral scruples in the private life of a member of the elite is dealt with very gently by the party authorities. It is impossible to demand scrupulous correctness in a member's private life when any crime may be required of him in the interest of the party. Demands have actually been made of individuals in order to have a future hold over them, or to test their readiness to obey. In Danzig the Senator for Public Health was required, against clear medical evidence, to declare in the case of the death of a National Socialist "militant" that the man had been killed by a blow struck by a political opponent. The Senator refused to make an official declaration in conflict with the truth; he was deprived of his office and his senatorship. This is one instance of a method pursued deliberately in order to make the elite a following sworn to blind obedience, a company from which every

[204]*Ibid.*

member's escape is cut off, because he has been incriminated...."[205]

The reader will recall how Chiang would pillage the State coffers to pay the warlords even when he knew perfectly well that the money was going straight into their pockets and not to fight "the bandits." The conduct of the rulers, the ubiquitous corruption carries the gangrene to the populace. The citizen experiences it in his daily existence and thus is continually reminded of how his rulers are conducting themselves. This process robs the populace of all scruples, all idealism and justifies in its mind the most crass pursuit of immediate, private gains.

But does the regime not at least introduce discipline and order in a populace? And are these not desirable? The truth of the matter is the direct opposite. As Rauschning was at pains to point out, beneath the surface discipline and order, all elements of order in the nation—institutions, norms, standards, values—are ruthlessly destroyed [206] and this process is continued "until at last people no longer (know) whether the system (is) acting justly or unjustly and (can) no longer decide between loyalty and opposition...."[207] Nor—as the regimes are nihilist, as they are concerned about nothing but their own dominance—are the institutions, values etc., replaced by anything that would be of any value to the nation.

If not order, do they not at least introduce efficiency and dispatch? Once again, the surface signs are completely misleading. For all their bombast, such regimes are notoriously inefficient. The atmosphere in which administration must be conducted, the bitter and frequently fatal in-fighting, the jostling for the Fuhrer's favour, the fear and insecurity, the deliberate duplication of responsibilities by which the usurper maintains his hold—all of these factors take an enormous toll.

Moreover, a regime of this sort filters a particular brand of persons to the top—mediocre, weak men strutting around as strong, quick to make deals with any adventurer, cynical,

---

[205] *Ibid.*, pp. 144-145.
[206] *Ibid.*, p. xi.
[207] Fest, *op. cit.*, p. 390.

devoid of all principle. Quite apart from the filtering process of the regime's structure, the personal security of the usurper requires that only such persons reach the top.[208] It would be an odd analyst who could deduce that personnel such as these will usher in an era of efficiency.

But will the regimes not at least make the country strong militarily? Will they not equip it to better defend itself against hostile neighbours? This is indeed the most frequently touted rationale of fascist regimes and, as we have seen, they work feverishly to conjure up external and internal enemies. Nothing can legitimize repression at home as much as war hysteria.

'... Certainly the prospect of checking by a war the process of radicalisation within the revolution will be one of the main considerations that will make the idea of war attractive to the old elite (of the party)....'[209]

And the armament programmes of such regimes create the illusion that the country is being strengthened. Once again, the facts of the matter are very different from these initial suppositions. They are shown up best in the cases of Chiang and Mussolini: they are only a bit obscured by the massive armaments build up and the initial pusillanimity of his opponents in Hitler's case.

The record of these regimes shows that, fearing those who command the armed forces, they disable them by deploying the same means by which they have earlier disabled the civilian and political leadership. They factionalize the forces, pitting war-lord against war-lord in China, pitting general against general in Germany and Italy.[210] They go out of their way to furnish opportunities for corruption to the commanders so that the latter acquire a stake in the new set up, so that they are more easily brought to heel—Chiang's conduct vis-a-vis the war-lords is well-documented, to say nothing of the latter day Thieus and Kys; the situation in Germany and Italy was no different, it just could not be.[211] This progressive corrup-

---

[208] Rauschning, *op. cit.*, pp. 24-25; Fest, *op. cit.*, p. 77.
[209] Rauschning, *op. cit.*, p. 61.
[210] *Ibid.*, p. 152.
[211] *Ibid.*, pp. 152-153.

tion of the armed personnel buys time for the ruling clique but it makes the armed forces less able to resist aggression or to wage successfully the wars that these regimes provoke. It also increases the distance between the people and the professional armed forces—a factor whose utmost importance is well illustrated by Chiang's China and by recent events in South East Asia.

Moreover, as the regime is consolidated, as the personality cult of the usurper is built up, as terror and insecurity take hold and begin to paralyze even the upper reaches of the clique, no one dares convey the facts to the ruler—a factor that certainly diminishes his military capacity.[212] Finally, the general climate of opportunism, and cynicism is not, as we have noted earlier, the most fertile ground for loyalty to take root in the populace at large.

The most important consequence, the one that will determine much else, is the complete cessation of political life. Reflecting upon the Italian experience, Tasca tells us:

'...Wherever fascism is established the most important consequence, on which all the others depend, is the elimination of the people from all share in political activity. "Constitutional reform," the suppression of parliament, and the totalitarian character of the regime cannot be judged by themselves, but only in relation to their aims and their results. Fascism is not merely the substitution of one political regime for another; it is the disappearance of political life itself, since this becomes a state function and monopoly. Political doctrines circulate, are abandoned or modified, but the people have nothing to do with their adoption or their fluctuations. Even when syndicates, or even a party continues to exist, they are mere instruments, subordinate branches of the state. By becoming part of the machinery of state their nature does not undergo any change; they merely become instruments in the second degree, the instruments of instruments. With the removal of all freedom and independence from their institutions, the people are reduced to a malleable raw material whose properties of resistance and yield can be calculated and controlled. They still take part in parades and demonstrations,

---

[212] *Ibid.*, pp. 143-144, 146, 156.

and may be kept in a constant state of alertness and tension, but this is simply part of the drill and never approaches the level of political consciousness....'[213]

It would be a grave error to think that this feature affected only the voluble politician of the old set-up or the intellectuals and journalists. Quite the contrary. These sections are well able to protect themselves—by switching to the new masters, by changing professions, by emigrating. The poor masses are the ones who have no recourse now against the class tyranny of the rulers. It is that much more difficult to organize and awaken them under a fascist regime through which, as we saw in the beginning, the ruling classes have taken up arms precisely to prevent such organisation and awakening.

## The Final Inferences

There is much more to be said and many inferences that can be drawn. But the reader must already have been tired by this long account of events that happened many years ago in other countries. Hence I will, once again, leave the numerous inferences as exercises for the reader and confine myself to just stating three.

Fist, it should by now be obvious that no good can come from regimes of the kind we have been discussing.

Second, the regimes will not go away of their own accord. Nor can their character be altered by cleverness, appeasement or attempts to reform from within. The only way to change them is to overthrow them.

Third, overthrowing them involves protracted struggles. By their nature these struggles cannot proceed along a straight line, marching from success to success. Setbacks are inevitable. Even a rotten tree will withstand many a storm. But the fact that the fascist regime can resist all efforts to reform it from within, that a Chiang is able to defuse dozens of armed rebellions, that he and his regime are able to thwart all gentle efforts from without their system to make them change their course—all this is not as unambiguous an evidence of their invincibility as may seem

[213] Rossi, *op. cit*.

at first sight. Indeed, it is a precondition for the eventual collapse of the entire structure—the ruler, his clique, their henchmen. If Chiang and his cohorts had been successfully persuaded to keep "reforming" their regimes, to keep making marginal adjustments, they may well have lasted longer. The fact that they were so "successful" in warding off these gentle pressures was the guarantor of their complete annihilation.


## SELECT BIBLIOGRAPHY

The material on the subject is so vast that I can do no more then list a few of the titles that have been directly helpful to me in preparing the essay.

Hannah Arendt, *The Origins of Totalitarianism*, Harcourt Brace Jovanovich, New York, 1973.
Karl Dietrich Bracher, *The German Dictatorship*, Praeger, 1970.
Alan Bullock, *Hitler: A Study in Tyranny*, Penguin, London, 1962.
John P. Diggins, *Mussolini and Fascism: The View from America*, Princeton University Press, Princeton, 1972.
L. Eastman, *The Abortive Revolution*, Harvard University Press, Cambridge, 1974.
Joachim C. Fest, *Hitler*, Harcourt Brace Jovanovich, New York, 1973.
E. Fraenkel, *The Dual State*, New York, 1941.
Nathanael Greene, *Fascism, An Anthology*, Thomas Crowell, New York, 1968.
A. James Gregor, *The Ideology of Fascism*, Free Press, New York, 1969.
Daniel Guerin, *Fascism and Big Business*, Pathfinder Books, New York, 1973.
Paul Hayes, *Fascism*, Free Press, New York, 1973.
G. Mosse, *The Crisis of German Ideology: Intellectual Origins of the Third Reich*, Grosset and Dunlap, New York, 1964.
——*Nazi Culture*, Grosset and Dunlap, New York, 1968.
E. Nolte, *Three Faces of Fascism*, Holt Rinehart and Winston, New York, 1963.
N. Poulantzas, *Fascism and Dictatorship, The Third International and the Problem of Fascism*, Western Printing Press, Bristol, 1974.
H. Rauschning, *The Revolution of Nihilism*, Longmans, Green, New York, 1939.
A. Rossi, (pseud. A. Tasca), *The Rise of Italian Fascism, 1918-22*, Howard Fertig, New York, 1966.
W. Shirer, *The Rise and Fall of the Third Reich*, Simon and Schuster, New York, 1960.

Denis Mack Smith,, *Italy, A Modern History*, University of Michigan Press, Ann Arbor, 1959.
A. Speer, *Inside the Third Reich*, Macmillan, New York, 1970.
F. Stern, *The Politics of Cultural Despair*, University of California, Berkeley, 1961.
J.P. Stern, *Hitler, The Fuhrer and the People*, University of California, Berkeley, 1975.
E. R. Tannenbaum, *The Fascist Experience*, Basic Books, New York, 1972.
P. Togliatti, *Lectures on Fascism*, International Publishers, New York, 1976.
H. A. Turner, (ed), *Reappraisals of Fascism*, Franklin Watts, New York, 1975.
S. J. Woolf, (ed), *The Nature of Fascism*, Random House, New York, 1968.
E. B. Wheaton, *Prelude to Calamity: The Nazi Revolution 1933-35*, Doubleday, New York, 1968.
Elizabeth Wiskemann, *Fascism in Italy, Its Development and Influence*, St Martin's Press; New York, 1969.

# 4  The Role of Popular Movements: A Gandhian Perspective*

Gandhiji's life and teaching affirm that rulers do not have a divine right to their office or to the allegiance of the ruled. When they betray the trust of the people the latter have a right and a duty to drive the rulers out. He felt that if the ordinary citizen is somnolent the powerful will invariably abuse their office. But that—and he laid equal stress on this proposition—the rulers can abuse their position only so long as the citizenry puts up with misrule. He felt that the citizenry does not take the steps that would bring the rulers to book because it does not realize the "immutable maxim" that the hegemony of the rulers depends solely on the subservience, the tacit and active cooperation of the ruled and that, therefore, the people can bring misrule to an end at any time by withdrawing from the oppressors, the rulers, their cooperation in every detail. The people do not take the steps also because they are weighed down by fear, by feelings of helplessness and impotence *vis-a-vis* their rulers, their exploiters.

So as to set people free from fear, so as to make them realize their strength *vis-a-vis* their rulers, Gandhiji led the people in a series of tactical engagements—a number of *satyagrahas*—that,

*August 1975

ostensibly, had specific, limited aims, but which were, in fact, intended to drive the fear of their rulers from the minds of the people and to teach them that once they are prepared to accept hardship, to make sacrifices, they can bend the regime to their will. His experience and his teaching affirm that in the end popular movements conducted along the lines he suggested are bound to prevail over the might of the rulers: it is in the logic of such movements that as they unfold the rulers are compelled to adopt a more and more unreasonable stance, to reveal more and more their brute, authoritarian hand while the formerly somnolent, timid citizens learn the value of organized action as well as the importance of fundamental principles—an importance that they do not suspect at the beginning.

Gandhiji's experience affirms that as the fundamental task is to change the people's attitudes, the principal—though not the only—focus of such movements must be the broad, dispossessed masses. And that participation in electoral politics, fighting cases in courts and the like—in short, combating the rulers in forums and along avenues that the rulers have themselves prescribed—is a diversion, an error, a waste of time. The principal vehicle for changing the people's attitudes must be to engage them in direct action, to pit them directly against their rulers, their oppressors. For a variety of reasons he felt that such action must be non-violent. The movement for independence that he led—a movement spread over many decades, a movement marked by many ups and downs—taught him that people's attitudes cannot be changed overnight. The struggle to change people's attitudes—to awaken them to the true nature of their rulers, to their strength relative to that of their rulers—such a struggle has to be a protracted one. It does not ascend along a straight, unbroken line. Rather, it proceeds with the motion of successive waves battering a rock.

Finally, and this is perhaps the most important lesson that Gandhiji's teaching and example hold out for us, the *sine qua non* of such movements is not the single leader, the Messiah, but the band of individuals who are prepared to forsake all for the cause of the people, the country, for justice.

Much of Gandhiji's writing and all of his life was devoted to affirming the right and the duty of the people to demand excellence from their rulers to throw the leaders out in case they palter with the people or with the interests of the country. He was unequivocal on this point.

Once a government has become autocratic and corrupt, violent and unjust, once it has begun to "prostitute its own laws," once it has stopped listening to the ordinary citizen, once its conduct is keeping the country and the people back, the citizens, he affirmed, have "the inherent right" to withdraw their cooperation from the regime and to bring it to a halt, that "a citizen who barters with such a State shares its corruption or lawlessness," that he cannot surrender his "birthright" to resist such a State without surrendering his self-respect. Disloyalty to such a regime, he used to say, becomes a duty, sedition a religion, obedience to its laws a sin and disobedience a virtue.

Moreover, the people must evaluate the regime as a whole. A regime cannot lay claim to the people's allegiance by an occasional good deed, by one or two reforms. These do not change the essential character of the regime. At one point, Gandhiji tells us, "I said to myself there is no State run by Nero or Mussolini which has not good points about it, but we have to reject the whole once we decide to non-cooperate with the system. There are in our country grand public roads and palatial educational institutions, I said to myself, but they are part of a system which crushes the nation. I should not have anything to do with them. They are like the fabled snake with a brilliant jewel on its head but which has fangs of poison." Indeed, an occasional progressive measure is but a ruse—a device to trap the people in "a delusion of reprieve."

For Gandhiji the right and the duty of each citizen to judge the regime for himself was an absolute one.

He subordinated the dictates of all authority, secular, religious, scriptural, to the individual's conscience. He often emphasized, for instance, that he would disregard even the scriptures, otherwise so dear to him, if the text did not accord with his conscience. He insisted that the right he was reaffirming was a "birthright," that the right—as well as the efficay—of *satyagraha* was universal: that the individual had the right to resort to it under all circumstances and in his dealings with all persons and institutions, be they family members or others, employers or governments, foreign governments or governments he had elected himself and that—if the goals were not selfish—

he would find the weapon equally effective in all cases. "Satyagraha to be genuine," he wrote, "may be offered against parents, against one's wife or one's children, against rulers, against fellow citizens, even against the whole world. Such a universal force necessarily makes no distinction between kinsmen and strangers, young and old, man and woman, friend and foe...."

In particular, we should not believe for a moment that the right to take a stand on one's conscience and to withdraw one's cooperation from a regime that is harming the interests of the country is limited to occasions when the government is a foreign imperial power. He emphasized repeatedly that he was opposing the British government not just because, not even primarily because, it was British but because it had "brought about the moral, material, cultural and spiritual ruination of this great country." And he repeatedly affirmed that "if I am a social reformer in the true sense of the term...I must be watchful whether it is the foreign government that is in power or the indigenous."

This attitude is well revealed in the counsel he gave to two members of the Assam Legislative Assembly who visited him in December 1946. N.K. Bose recalls that they had reservations about a constitutional provision and yet were being counseled not to press these as by doing so "they would be helping the (Muslim) League... (that) Assam could not be allowed to stand in the way of the progress of the rest of India and so on." Gandhiji said that he did not need a single moment to reach a decision. He urged them to protest, retire from the Constituent Assembly and, in this way, offer a kind of *satyagraha* against the Congress. If their stand was right, he said, both the Congress and the country would benefit from their refusal to go along.

Far from limiting the right and duty to the special circumstance when foreigners rule a people, his view was that after independence, precisely because the regime would be our own, the people would have a right to expect that it would work for their welfare, precisely because it would be manned by individuals in whose promises the people would have placed their trust, the latter would have a duty to ensure that the so-called leaders do not let the country down.

It is idle, he said, to raise questions about the legality or otherwise of this right and duty. Law in the ultimate analysis, specially law as decreed, interpreted, altered, mutilated by the authorities, is, he said, but the convenience of the powerful. In any case, what does "legality" mean when "laws" are being changed every day? Is the country bound to accept, say, the Rowlatt Act (an Act that seems such a mild one in retrospect) just because some persons who have arrogated the mantle of the State to themselves have decreed it, just because it has been printed on government stationery or notified in the government's gazettes?

It is even less relevant, he would say, to chastise the citizen for adopting non parliamentary methods. Parliamentary methods, he said as long ago as 1920, should indeed be used but the *satyagrahi* is not to wait forever, he must not just sit back and wait for officials and leaders to heed his petitions, to see the error of their ways. "It is a superstition and an ugly thing," Gandhiji said, "to believe that an act of the majority binds a minority. Many examples can be given in which acts of majorities will be found to have been wrong and those of minorities to have been right. All reforms owe their origin to the initiative of minorities in opposition to the majorities. If among a band of robbers, a knowledge of robbery is obligatory, is a pious man to accept the obligation?" "So long as the superstition that men should obey unjust laws exists," he concluded, "so long will their slavery exist." When his attention was drawn to this passage many years later, he reaffirmed his belief that the passage "appears to me to propound a great truth often overlooked" and continued to say that "I am so jealous of the rights and wishes of the minorities if only because I have been always, in the beginning at least, in a minority."

But if his assertion of this fundamental right of the citizenry were to be accepted, "would not," he was asked, "ordered government be impossible?" His answer was straight-forward: "Ordered government cannot be impossible if totally inoffensive people break the laws. But I would certainly make government impossible if I found it had taken leave of its senses." Misrule, he was to affirm repeatedly, is worse than no rule for it spells ruin and stagnation for the country. Obviously no one willingly opts for chaos, but a government that is holding back a country and a people cannot charge the *satyagrahis* with fomenting chaos and disorder.

If the regime is setting itself up as a roadblock and is refusing to mend its ways, if an intermediate stage of disorder is the unavoidable consequence of efforts to teach the rulers a lesson, then the *satyagrahi* must gladly opt for such disorder rather than countenance a regime that is holding his people and his country back. The responsibility for such disorder as may follow rests on the regime that has betrayed the trust of the people, that by its obduracy has refused to mend its ways, that has clung to office, to so-called "power," by petty machinations and police methods and which has left the *satyagrahi* no choice but to resort to direct action.

A political system can thrive only if ordinary people have the opportunity as well as the self-confidence to bring their governors to account. Mahatma Gandhi often emphasized that *swaraj* would not come when a few acquired authority from the British but when all acquired the capacity to resist authority when it was abused; that independence would be real only if it meant independence of the people and not just of their rulers; that the mere withdrawal of the British would not spell freedom, that freedom would come only when the average villager became conscious of the fact that he was the maker of his destiny and when he began to act as such.

As the years have passed, as memories of Gandhiji and the independence struggle have faded away, as each individual, acting alone, has begun to feel a dwarf in front of an enormous and pervasive State apparatus—an apparatus camouflaged behind intricate rules, regulations, procedures which he barely comprehends—a feeling of helplessness has overwhelmed the citizen. Just as the leaders have viewed "power" in a narrow sense, the citizen too has begun to feel that indeed power rests with those who occupy office. Therefore, he has withdrawn from the political arena and when he has dealt with the State apparatus he has done so as a supplicant.

As under the guise of socialism, patronage has been centralized in governmental institutions, the citizen has come to see himself as one dependent on those who occupy office—much as the landless labourer will feel dependent on the landlord. This feeling of dependence has left him sullen and resentful of those who hold the reins of patronage. But it has also reinforced his feeling of helplessness *vis-a-vis* the State apparatus as a whole. The result has been precisely what Gandhiji had forecast it would be: if people leave everything to the government, if they withdraw from active participation in political affairs and in the affairs of their community, he used to say, we would end up with pupilage and not *swaraj*.

Gandhiji used to stress that, if the people relax their vigil, almost everyone elected or appointed to office will abuse it. On the other hand, if the people are vigilant, if they are politically conscious, alert and active, almost everyone elected or appointed to office could be made to work to keep the people's trust. The sloth of a populace, he warned, is all the license that rulers need. The rulers and the ruled would then corrupt each other. As circumstances grind people's expectations out, the leaders will obtain the license they need to indulge themselves. Wrong doing by leaders will lead people to wonder why, if their social and political leaders are behaving in questionable ways, each of them should not look after his own interests in the same manner. As each citizen begins to cut corners, he will further embolden his leaders: an entire system will come into being in which those who can outdo others in low level cunning, petty intrigue and questionable resourcefulness are the ones who will rise to the top.

The ancient adage—*yatha raja tatha praja*—Gandhiji would say, is only half the truth. Its converse, *yatha praja tatha raja*, is just as true. "Where the subjects are watchful a prince is entirely dependent on them for his status. Where the subjects are overtaken by sleepy indifference, there is every possibility that the prince will cease to function as a protector and become our oppressor instead. Those who are not wide awake have no right to blame their prince. . . ."

Thus, Gandhiji affirmed not just the "birthright" and duty of every citizen to judge his rulers and to bring down a regime that had become a force for evil, he also taught us the "immutable maxim" that a people can be governed in a particular way only so long as they—consciously or unconsciously—consent to be so governed, that "no man loses his freedom except through his own weaknesses," that "no government can exist for a single moment without the cooperation of the people, willing or forced, and (that) if people suddenly withdraw their cooperation in every detail, the government will come to a standstill."

Far from being invulnerable as the ordinary citizen now assumes it to be, a regime is vulnerable to each act of conscience. Even very small groups can inconvenience it a great deal. If, for instance, just the top 100 persons in each profession were to decide that they would have nothing to do with a regime as it had come to manifest evil, it would be greatly inconvenienced. It isn't just that it would lose their services but, even more important, non-cooperation of this kind would damage the regime's standing, its *iqbal;* and, in the ultimate analysis, regimes are able to hold countries in their thrall because of their *iqbal*, because of the esteem in which people hold them and not because they have the army and the police at their command.

Even as Gandhiji launched his *satyagrahas* in Champaran, Kheda, Dandi and other places, the sceptics asked: Has the people's lot improved since the previous agitation was concluded? Even in that district have things not more or less subsided to what they were before the agitation? What, after all, will be gained even if the enquiry he is asking for is instituted? Even if the recommendations of the enquiry committee are implemented would the effects not be confined to just that particular district— nay, that particular *taluka*? What would the people of the country as a whole gain? In any case, what is so great about getting the land revenue collections suspended for a season or improving the conditions of a few thousand tenants growing one, minor crop in a remote district?

Those who asked these questions were, in fact, missing the point. It is true that the ostensible objectives of the *satyagrahas* were extremely limited: the removal of inequitous conditions for the cultivation of indigo in one case, the suspension of land revenue collections because of extensive crop damage in another, the revision of a land revenue assessment in the third, the withdrawal of the tax on a necessity in the fourth and so on. The ostensible objectives of each of the 40 odd local *satyagrahas* that were launched between 1916 and 1948 were even more limited and few will be able to recall them today. Can we recall, for instance, what were the demands of the Mulshipeta or Midnapore *satyagrahas* in 1920/21? Each of these *satyagrahas*, I am thinking now of the local *satyagrahas* and not those of the nation-wide movements of 1921, 1930, 1932, 1940 and 1942, was a very localized affair, involving often no more than a district or even a *taluka*. While each of those *satyagrahas* was in progress, one could say that the major proportion of the population of the region was standing aloof, that only the minutest, in fact, an almost negligible, proportion of the population of the country as a whole was actively participating in them.

In each case after the immediate, announced objective was achieved—in fact, often after the government just agreed to appoint a commission of sorts to examine the matter—the *satyagraha* was called off. And once the agitations were called off the *status quo ante*, to all intents and purposes, slid back into place. The reader will search in vain for records of any dramatic political movements in Champaran, Kheda, Bardoli, etc., in the years that followed the initial *satyagrahas*.

Nor could it be said of any of these *satyagrahas* that they solved the particular problem they addressed for the country as a whole or for the decades to come. The 1919 agitations against the Rowlatt Act were followed by even more pernicious acts and ordinances—for example, the decrees of 1930-32 and those of 1942. But would we, in retrospect, say that for this reason the 1919 agitation against the Rowlatt Act was a failure?

The point is that even though at the time each of these movements seemed to be a localized affair, the doing, as the British commissioner said at the time of the Kheda *satyagraha*, of just a few "professional agitators and outsiders," a minor agitation for a very limited objective, in retrospect they correctly stand out as milestones in the country's progress towards independence. The reason for this is obvious in retrospect: the immediate, limited demands were never the principal objectives of the *satyagrahas*. And the fulfilment of the immediate demand was never their principal effect. For Gandhiji the inequitous conditions of indigo cultivation, the postponement or cancellation of land revenue payments for a year, the revision of a land revenue assessment, the removal of a tax on a necessity—these were but the occasions for teaching people basic lessons, precisely the lessons that have been listed above: that they and not the government was powerful, that their salvation depended on their own efforts, that there was a method of protest—nonviolent noncooperation—by which they could neutralize such power as the government derived from its command over the police apparatus and so on.

Gandhiji was very clear in his mind about this matter. Hundreds of examples can be given to document this fact. One or two will have to suffice.

N. K. Bose records a press statement that Gandhiji issued in April 1918 at the time of the Kheda *satyagraha*. In it Gandhiji declares that "the ryots do not need to be literate to appreciate their rights and duties. They have but to realize their invulnerable power and no government, however strong, can stand against their will. The Kheda ryots are solving an imperial problem of the first magnitude in India. They will show that it is impossible to govern men without their consent.... This struggle is not for suspension of land revenue only but it involves the interests of thirty crores of people.... This is a struggle for self-government." Later, in recounting the *satyagraha* in his autobiography, he was to say that "the main thing was to rid the agriculturists of their fear by making them realize that the officials were not the masters but the servants of the people inasmuch as they received their salaries from the taxpayers." And in pronouncing the campaign a success Gandhiji was not thinking of the fact that the government had agreed to suspend the collection of revenues (in fact, he expressed disappointment at the form of the settlement and the surreptitious way in which the government had conceded the point). Rather, "the end of a *satyagraha* campaign can be described as worthy only when it leaves the *satyagrahis* stronger and more spirited than they were in the beginning," and that "the Kheda *sataygraha* marks the beginning of an awakening among the peasants of Gujarat, the beginning of their true political, education.... The *patidar* peasant came to the unforgettable consciousness of his strength. The lesson was indelibly imprinted on the public mind that the salvation of the people depends upon themselves, upon their capacity for suffering and sacrifice."

The *satyagraha*s were, as they were intended to be, the open universities in which people learnt basic lesson— that they need not fear their rulers, that they could be subjected to misrule only so long as they countenanced it.

Moreover, Gandhiji pointed out that even if the limited,

ostensible objective of the *satyagraha* is not attained, the *satyagraha* if properly conducted by men of conscience cannot but help in attaining the larger objectives. It is, he pointed out at the time of the Kheda *satyagraha*, in the logic of things that as the movement unfolds governments are driven to fight for their "prestige" and the people are driven to fight for principles which at first they scarcely understood. One can best discern the manner in which this principle works itself out by recalling the way in which a specific engagement between the regime and the people unfolds. Consider the Kheda and Bardoli *satyagrahas* as an instance.

The initial position in both instances was a very simple one. The crops in the Kheda area had been greatly damaged by an assortment of calamities. The local officials had surveyed the crops and had declared that while the crops had been greatly damaged, the proportion that could be salvaged was greater than four annas in a rupee and, hence, the area must pay its land revenue dues. The people felt that this crop was less than one fourth the normal yield and they persuaded leaders like Sardar Patel and Gandhiji to take up their cause. In Bardoli the assessment officials had revised the assessment upwards after a perfunctory survey of the area. The peasants felt that the extent of the enhancement was not justified.

In both cases, when they initially entered the fray, the leaders did not even demand that the collection of land revenue be completely suspended in one case or that the old assessment be immediately restored in the other. All they said was that the government should have the matter re-examined by independent groups. However, once the issue was joined, the government in each case could not view it as just a simple matter of collecting or not collecting the revenue from a particular area in one year or confirming the assessment of one official. It convinced itself that much more was at stake.

From the government's point of view the demand for an impartial enquiry really amounted to the following questions. Should the government believe the word of "outside agitators" about the value of standing crops and the returns to cultivation or should it believe the word of its officials? Once government officials have assessed the state of the crop or the normal returns from a tract of land, should the government agree to review the assessment each time some "professional agitators" start demanding that it do so? If the government gives in on this point and on this occasion, would it not be compelled to give in on issues of much greater importance also? Will the concession not set a precedent? Will it not give a signal to the people that the government was weak-kneed and irresolute? Did the government not have the sole right to determine the amount of revenue that must be paid? Does the government not act through its functionaries and, therefore, by implication do they not have the sole right—on behalf of the government—to exercise the government's exclusive powers for determining the amount of revenues to be collected?

From these questions it was but a step for the government to be pushed into the position of defending each act of each one of its functionaries. During the Kheda movement, for instance, after the village officials resigned and when the government felt that it must cow down the villagers by a show of force, it brought in policemen from another region—some Pathans—to do the attachment work and to frighten the people by their swagger. It so happened that some of these Pathans were high-handed in their behaviour. They roughed up some villagers, struck or abused some women and maltreated the animals of the villagers.

Now, by itself this is a common-place and unimportant occurrence. However, when Gandhiji and the villagers complained about the high-handedness of the Pathans the government was put on the defensive, it rushed to proclaim that the Pathans were entirely loyal, that they were motivated by a sense of justice and fairplay. How could it not proclaim all this without inviting blame on itself? After all, it had brought the Pathans to the areas on its own initiative. Moreover, the Commissioner and others felt that unless they stood by their men, they could not expect the men to serve them with the degree of loyalty that the delicate situation demanded.

Just as the logic of the situation pushes the government into taking unreasonable and rigid stands, so also it pushes the people into fighting for principles. At first the demand that is uppermost in the people's mind is the specific issue for which the movement has been organized—be this the suspension of the land revenue collection, the revision of the land revenue assessment, the removal of a minister or the dissolution of a legislature. But as the movement unfolds the people begin to perceive that their difficulties stem from the fact that the government has violated fundamental principles. They also begin to perceive the importance of abstract notions such as the rights to free speech and free association. They begin to see that, if these notions are violated, they will have no recourse left at all. In this way they are pushed into fighting for these general principles—principles whose importance they had only dimly perceived at the beginning of the struggle.

Experiences such as these convinced Gandhiji that regimes are not as powerful as they seem at first sight. The instruments on which they rely—their control over the armed apparatus of the State, their ability to direct and manipulate media, their access to money, their legislative majorities and the like—these instruments cannot be pitted against an aroused citizenry, a citizenry that is prepared for hardship and sacrifice.

Thus, a regime secures an initial advantage because of its access to—licit and illicit—money. Eventually this very access smears it in the public's mind. The regime is able to keep people in line by centralizing patronage and then coopting the ring leaders so that the latter keep their followers in line. The machine seems invulnerable for a while. Yet, soon enough, the arrangement brings disrepute on the ring leaders: the people see through the fact that their leaders have been bought over and so the pillars on which the regime rests suddenly give way.

One year the regime seems unassailable because of its overwhelming legislative majority. But the very size of the majority makes it complacent and arrogant. As difficulties outside the legislative assembly cannot assail it within the building, it ignores them, declares them to be non-existent, the imaginings of *agents provocateur*. But this just turns the people away from the legislative assemblies themselves and in the end the regime's hold on its flock in the legislature leaves it no stronger in dealing with the situation.

One day people feel helpless because the regime controls all the media in the country. Soon enough people stop believing what they hear over the radio or read in the papers. The fact, for instance, that the British regime could make the media assert that adequate help is being sent to the drought stricken in Bihar or to the Bengal of 1943, that no one is dying of starvation, this power does not actually fill the bellies of the hungry. When they and their children are hungry, when they have seen bodies dead of starvation, people do not postpone believing the facts just because these have been denied by the radio or because they have not been certified by the newspapers. When they see the corrupt flourish, when they have to shell out favours to get even the smallest things done, when they see grain enter a ration shop and then disappear, they do not dismiss what they have seen just because the media assert that there is no corruption, that the rationing system is working well.

And so, soon enough, the regime becomes unable to use its control over the media to make people believe what it wants them to believe. Soon enough it is unable to even ensure the much narrower task of keeping leaders of the people from spreading their ideas. The facts speak for themselves. Moreover, the people learn that even when they are denied the truth about developments in the country as a whole they can help cleanse the place by just finding out the truth about their immediate neighbourhood—a truth they can discover with their own eyes. And, finally, they soon learn that they do not need the newspapers and the radio to even broadcast their views: they learn that the pen can be, as Gandhiji would say, their foundry and the hands of willing copyists their printing machine.

But what if the regime incarcerates writers, editors, copyists? Here is Gandhiji's assessment:

'I believe that an editor (and, we may add, a writer, a copyist, anyone, in fact) who has anything worth saying and who commands a clientele cannot be easily hushed so long as his body is left free. He has delivered his finished message as soon as he is put under duress. The Lokamanya spoke more eloquently from the Mandalay fortress than through the columns of the printed *Kesari*. His influence was multiplied a thousandfold by his incarceration and his speech and his pen had acquired much greater power after he was discharged than before his imprisonment. By his death he is editing his paper without pen and speech through the sacred resolution of the people to realize his life's dream. He could not possibly have done more if he were today in the flesh preaching his *Mantra*. Critics like me would perhaps be still finding fault with this expression of his or that. Today all criticism is hushed and his *Mantra* alone rules millions of hearts which are determined to raise a permanent living memorial by the fulfilment of his *Mantra* in their lives.'

Initially, the regime's control over the police apparatus of the State seems to fortify it. But, as the regime begins to deploy the apparatus against the people, the latter learn that the regime will much rather use its police apparatus to suppress them than alter the system that now serves it and the interests it represents. Nor can the regime deploy the police apparatus against the people beyond narrow limits. Even during the British days most of the armed apparatus consisted of Indians. And it became clear to the regime over the years that this apparatus could not be insulated from the people for long: recruits who manned it could not be kept happy and obedient in hermetically sealed incubators even as their families and neighbours suffered privation and injustice.

For reasons such as these Gandhiji affirmed that a citizenry that is willing to put up a fight for its rights, for justice, cannot but triumph, that it would successfully melt away every instrument that an oppressive regime may deploy against it.

In the Gandhian doctrine, to be begin with, direct action and popular movements are an integral part of democracy. They are an insurance against tyranny and abuse. He did not feel it necessary to lay down hard and fast rules about their frequency and extent. These depend on the state of affairs: if the rulers are working for the interests of the people there will be no reason to initiate such movements, but whenever misconduct has become the order of the day, when the behaviour of rulers has shown that they are beyond the reach of parliamentary institutions and electoral processes, it would be the right and duty of citizens to launch such movements, to launch them ten times a year if necessary, to continue them for decades if necessary.

Gandhiji knew from his own experience that the enormous sacrifices that these movements entail will themselves ensure that the people will not resort to them lightly. They shall do so only after they have exhausted parliamentary and electoral means. If misrule persists then the churning and shaking up that these movements entail will indeed be the things that the country needs.

*Second*, his protracted attempts at changing people's attitudes and the limited success that attended them taught him that the attitudes of an entire people, their perceptions about themselves, about their governors, about their strength, these cannot be changed in a few months or in a year or two. The withdrawal, resignation, compromise that had brought the country to its knees by the end of the nineteenth century (and that have brought us to our present state) after all, were not (and are not) just a day or two old. They had marked (and they have marked) decades of our national and personal lives. Therefore, reconstruction of a polity is a protracted task.

Gandhiji knew that his movements must touch all aspects of our national life and all regions of the country. Only then would they lead us to re-examine fundamentals and—what is even more difficult and takes even longer—only then would they lead each one of us as an individual to re-examine and alter his own social conduct. Moreover, the rapidity with which the Indian people have lapsed back into somnolence, fear, feelings of helplessness that held them in their thrall before Gandhiji took hold of the national movement, this relapse itself shows that the struggles have to be waged again and again.

*Third*, it was Gandhiji's firm conviction that legislatures, courts and the like—in short, the institutions and avenues set up by the rulers—cannot be the principal means for transforming a polity. Even if one bunch of individuals were to be replaced by another through on election, a court judgement or a coup, things would revert the *status quo ante* within a year or two. For the election or the coup by itself would have done little to ensure the precondition of good governance—an alert and active citizenry conscious of its strength.

Gandhiji's attitude to, say, the courts—one of the institutions on which his predecessors and colleagues had been relying—rests on this insight. When Gandhiji reached Champaran he discovered that the local leaders had been filing cases on behalf of indigo growers in sundry courts. The local leaders were well intentioned, of course, and, as they were lawyers, this was the only way they knew of helping the growers. But Gandhiji counselled them to abandon this approach. He told them that "having studied these cases I have come to the conclusion that we should stop going to law courts. Taking such cases to the courts does little good. Where the ryots are so crushed and fear stricken law courts are useless. The relief for them," he said, "is to be free from fear."

Hence he counselled his associates to stop wasting their time in courts and to help him mobilize the tenants in a programme of direct action. Gandhiji repeated this counsel in many contexts. For example, in commenting on the prosecution of the editor of *Navkal* he said he wished the editor "had not thrown away good money in counsel's fees. Law courts like every other government institution are designed to protect the government in time of need. We have had practical experience of this time without number. They are necessarily so. Only we do not realize it when popular liberty and the government run in the same direction. When, however, popular liberty has to be defended in spite of government opposition, law courts are poor guardians thereof. The less we have to do with them the better for us."

Gandhiji's view was that when the people were pitted against an oppressive regime, when they had decided that the regime was evil, then two deductions followed immediately: that, as the regime was an oppressive one, the people should know in advance that it will not hesitate to use every weapon in its armoury to keep itself in power; and, second, that in such circumstances it is futile to hope that we can outwit the regime by mere cleverness in the forums it has prescribed—legislatures, courts, the newspapers it controls, etc. As soon as our clamour becomes too loud, as soon as our pressure begins to really inconvenience it, the regime will not hesitate to change the rules of the game.

Thus, for instance, when the Press Act was passed in 1920 (a very mild act in retrospect) Gandhiji's advice to the editors was that rather than see them publish a censored report he "would rather see a complete stoppage of a newspaper if the editor cannot, without fear of the consequence, freely express his sentiments or publish those which he approves." To publish a censored piece, he felt, is much the worst alternative. The mere appearance of a censored paper gives the most disheartening signal at a time of crisis: the signal that things are nine-tenths normal.

Thus, he said,

'non-cooperation while it gladly avails itself of the assistance that may be rendered by the press, it is—has to be—by its very nature independent of the press. There can be no doubt that every thought we print is being printed on sufferance. As soon as its circulation takes effect, the Government, for the sake of its existence, will try to prohibit it. We may not expect this or any Government to commit suicide. It must either reform or repress. In the ordinary course repression must precede reform under a despotic Government such as ours. The stoppage of the circulation of potent ideas that may destroy the Government or compel repentance will be the least among the weapons in its repressive armoury. We must therefore devise methods of circulating our ideas unless and until the whole press becomes fearless, defies consequences and publishes ideas, even when it is in disagreement with them just for the purpose of securing its freedom. An editor with an original idea or an effective prescription for India's ills can easily write them out, a hundred hands can copy them, many more can read them out to thousands of listeners. I do hope, therefore, that non-cooperation editors, at any rate, will not refrain from expressing their thoughts for fear of the Press Act. They should regard it as sinful to keep their thoughts secret—a waste of energy to conduct a newspaper that cramps their thoughts. It is a negation of one's calling for an editor to have to suppress his best thoughts.'

Thus, his counsel to citizens was, first, that they must withdraw their cooperation from the regime *in every detail*—to abide by the rules of an oppressive regime regarding the procedures to be followed in courts and legislatures, regarding what could or could not be printed or broadcast, to abide by these rules was to cooperate with the regime, to play its game, to coquet with evil. Second, that instead of wasting their time in trying to outwit the regime by mere cleverness the people should devise alternative forums, alternative means for getting their voice heard.

*Fourth*, Gandhiji realized that the fundamental task is to change the attitudes of the broad, unpropertied and unorganized masses, to awaken and organize them. Hence, they—and not the rulers or the elite—should be the principal focus of the reformers' efforts. These masses constitute the class who, to pluck a phrase from Marx, have no interests to protect except what all humans need. They have no assets to preserve or aggrandize except their bare humanity. Hence, while the furtherance of any other class may end up being the furtherance of that class alone, the emancipation of the unpropertied, unorganized masses will mean the emancipation of the citizenry as a whole. From this insight flowed Gandhiji's efforts to help groups like the Harijans.

Most of Gandhiji's predecessors had been blaming the British government for the country's state and also looking up to it for bringing about changes. They were busy sending petitions, memoranda, resolutions to the government in the conviction that once the government was persuaded about the desirability of change, things would indeed change. After all, was it not the government that had the ultimate power to change things? Gandhiji questioned the faith of his predecessors and associates both in the capacity and the willingness of the government to alter the state of affairs.

The view that attributed the dismal state of affairs to the British government was, he said, a superficial one. The root causes lay in the values, attitudes and conduct of the Indians; fear, these values, attitudes, conduct were what enabled the British government to hold such a vast and numerous country in its thrall with just a handful of men. Thus, he often emphasized, even if the British were to give formal independence on a platter, true *swaraj* would elude the country; for the root causes that had brought the country to its knees would not be removed by a British decree. True *swaraj* would dawn only when our people changed their values, attitudes and conduct.

Moreover, he said, the British government was behaving in the only way that was natural to it—that is, in the way in which it thought it could best protect British interests in India. A few petitions were not going to persuade it to abandon interests that it perceived to be vital. Thus, change would not come by persuading the government but by awakening the people. Once the people awoke, once they saw through the ruses of their rulers, once they realized their strength *vis-a-vis* their rulers, the latter would not be able to preserve the system for a day. Hence, he counselled, stop wasting your time in addressing petitions to the government, start talking to the people.

This insight and conviction explain, for instance, Gandhiji's insistence that participants in political meetings must speak in

Hindi or in the provincial language. Until he came upon the scene most leaders used to speak and write in English in the fond belief that only when they did so would they be adequately reported in the English language press, that only when they were adequately reported in the English language press would their views reach the government. And, after all, the important thing was to convince the government. Was it not the government that had the ultimate power to take decisions for the constitutional changes that the movement wanted? What was the point in wasting time convincing the street hawker? *He* could not decree constitutional changes.

Gandhiji turned all this around at the 1917 convention of the Gujarat Sabha at Godhara—the first such convention over which he presided. Even though a number of non-Gujarati delegates, ranging from Tilak to Jinnah, had come for the convention, he insisted that all delegates must speak either in Gujarati or Hindi. Even the fastidious Jinnah had to declaim in his broken Gujarati. Gandhiji's objective was to turn the sights of the delegates away from the government, from the English press and its readers, to the people. Beneath all this was the insight that the ultimate outcome would depend on the people and not on the formal decisions and decrees of the government and that, therefore, the so-called leaders must turn their sights away from the rulers and towards the broad masses.

While the dispossessed masses must be the principal focus of the movement's attention, Gandhiji realized and stressed that reformers must make sure that their message reaches other sections also. In particular, it must reach those who man the State apparatus—the bureaucracy, the police and the armed forces. If these individuals remained uneducated in the broad political sense then they would be unthinking instruments that could be unleashed against the people at any time. Even though in the long-run these functionaries would realize that they were propping up an oppressive regime, a great deal of harm would be done in the meanwhile. It was for this reason that leaders during the national movement took care to get their message across to functionaries of the regime and, on occasion, to address direct appeals to them.

*Fifth*, Gandhiji wanted the people to focus on the system that was holding them down. He knew that in India we tend to lose ourselves in following, adulating or condemning individuals and so he wanted us to look beyond individuals.

This standpoint—of shifting the focus from the individual leader or subaltern to the system, of viewing leaders as just the representatives of the system—does not dilute the responsibility of the leaders for what is going on. Quite the contrary. As an individual, a Viceroy, say, or a provincial satrap can evade responsibility for, say, the torture of political prisoners or police firings by asserting that he did not know what was going on, by asking how he, sitting in the provincial capital or in Delhi, could possibly keep track of what was going on in the jurisdiction of each police *chowki* or in each wretched prison. But as the principal representatives of the system in which such firings and tortures occur the leaders cannot talk away their culpability.

Nor, of course, does this standpoint of looking beyond the individual leader mean that his ouster, his punishment should not be an objective of popular movements, or that agitations should not be directed against his particular misdeeds. Quite the contrary. Gandhiji was in the forefront of efforts to expose the responsibility of General Dyer and others for the Jalianwala Bagh massacre. He knew that one of the principal tasks before his movement was to remind people of their strength *vis-a-vis* their leaders.

As individual leaders loom large in the consciousness of the people, as people believe that just because these individuals occupy office they are powerful, their ouster from time to time, their censure, is an important objective. These ousters and censures acquaint the people with their power *vis-a-vis* their rulers and the State apparatus. Moreover, focussing on the misdeeds of a high functionary of the system helps to concretize an abstract issue for the people—much as a stone idol will help to focus on an abstract quality.

His point merely was that the ouster and censure of individuals, the dissolution of assemblies, etc., are just interim objectives; they are signposts by which the movement and the people keep track of their progress. Once they learn to focus on the system and outgrow their fetish for individuals, the people will be able to work towards transforming the system without dissipating their legitimate anger in the form of hatred or malice towards individuals. They will no longer be fooled by stories about the captivating "private face" of this or that leader, by stories about his personal kindness to colleagues, friends, or even, occasionally, to a destitute stranger. Most important, they will not be fooled by the *pro forma* replacement of one individual by another.

His hope was that once they begin to see past individual leaders the people will also begin to look beyond groupings such as individual political parties. His experience had taught him that most so-called leaders, whether they formally belonged to one political grouping or another, came from the same pool of charlatans. And so, the people should not relapse into "sleepy indifference" just because they had managed through elections or the courts or through violent means to replace one set by another. Their ceaseless vigilance and their unremitting efforts at transforming the system itself were the only guarantees of good government.

Gandhiji's wanderings around the country and his intimate contact with people taught him that, just as at the national level the people are apt to focus on one or two leaders, each of us as an individual is apt to view his particular difficulties as having their origin in his particular circumstances, as being caused by the unreasonableness of his particular employer, the rapacity of his particular landlord. He felt that through praxis, through actual confrontations with representatives of the system, popular movements must teach each of us that his particular difficulties have common causes that have to do with the fundamental nature of the system itself.

Finally, Gandhiji believed that the movements must remain non-violent. For him, of course, *ahimsa* was a religious principle. He commended non-violent *satyagraha* partly on the grounds that if the *satyagrahi* happened to be wrong, then, by adopting a method of persuasion that imposed suffering only on himself, he would be certain not to injure his adversaries in any way. He also believed that the *satyagrahi* must believe in *ahimsa* absolutely, without any reservations whatsoever. He felt that as *satyagrahas* were protracted struggles and as they could bring great suffering upon the *satyagrahi*, unless the *satyagrahi* was absolutely committed to *ahimsa*, he would falter at the crucial moment and lose himself in violence.

He was conscious that a large proportion of his followers did not believe in *ahimsa* as a creed He urged it to them as a political method, emphasizing at times that "a right act is right whether done for policy or for its own sake," and acknowledging on other occasions that "I have enrolled under the banner of justice all those who wish a secure it; and in doing so, as a practical reformer, I have not hesitated to take in those who I know are actuated by hatred." And he always stressed that violence was preferable to inaction, that he would recommend violence rather than countenance the emasculation of the country, that he would much rather that citizens were openly violent than that they were non-violent out of cowardice—out of a fear of being killed or injured in violent engagements.

He supplemented his fundamentalist position about *ahimsa* by additional strategic and tactical arguments. Among strategic reasons two seemed to him to be especially important. The experience of many countries, he said, shows that violent revolutions have not delivered power to the people; even when they have been progressive in the sense that they have overthrown a privileged class, they have ended up delivering power to a new, tightly knit oligarchy. Moreover, given the relative power of the State apparatus, violent movements must necessarily be secretive, limited to small groups and, therefore, elitist. They will not afford masses the opportunity to participate in them, to discover the power they have *vis-a-vis* the regime. For this reason, even if such violent movements are successful in dislocating a regime, their cleansing effects, he said, would be short lived.

One can infer many tactical arguments from his writings and the records of his conversations. Three can be noted in passing.

First, he felt that the regime forfeits its moral authority when it deploys physical force against the people. Popular movements will scarcely be able to acquire the moral authority that the regime forfeits if they adopt the same sanguinary means. Even when these means are deployed on behalf of the people's interests they will pull the moral standing of the movement many notches closer down to that of the regime.

Second, the relative police powers of the regime are so great and so mobile that they can snuff out violent uprisings rapidly and decisively. Our subsequent experience of Naxalbari and Telangana shows that because of the far superior physical power of the State apparatus and because of its far greater mobility, violent movements lose their focus very rapidly and degenerate into haphazard terrorism—alienating the populace and achieving little. In these circumstances to urge people to take up arms is to ask them to sacrifice themselves in useless heroism.

Third, his view would have been that as the large scale manufacture of arms within the country cannot be hidden for any length of time, as arms cannot be stolen from elitist defence forces, those who urge violent movements must be proceeding on the assumption—and Subhash Bose's INA was an instance in point—that other countries will supply arms. It is traitorous as well as foolish to advocate a course that starts by wanting to set things right at home and ends up mortgaging the country to foreigners.

For these obvious reasons and, of course, for more basic ones, he felt that popular movements must remain perfectly non-violent. By remaining non-violent, by conducting every act in the open they will neutralize the initial advantage that the regime has because of its control over the State apparatus. By remaining non-violent they will afford an opportunity for the broad masses to participate in the movements and experience the power they have *vis-a-vis* their rulers.

But doesn't it all depend on a leader? After all, so much incendiary material is always lying around in a poor country and yet nothing ever comes of it. What can anyone do until the Messiah appears?

Gandhiji's view was that just as we must look beyond individuals who occupy office, so also must we look beyond individuals who happen to be leading popular movements at any time. Deliverance will not come by the strength of one leader but by the effort of the people themselves. It follows by implication that, if conditions remain unchanged, they would have remained that way not because the leader who called them to battle has failed to do his job but because the people at large have not made the requisite effort. A leader can only point the way; the people, if they are to reach the goal, must trudge the road themselves.

Gandhiji used to say that his object was not to transform the people into parasites by making them dependent on a leader; his object was to make them self-reliant. It was neither his mission, he said, and it was beyond his capacity to be a "knight errant wandering everywhere to deliver people from every difficult situation." His "humble occupation," he said, had been to show people how they could overcome their own difficulties.

The *sine qua non* for popular movements is not the single individual who will lead them but the band of individuals who will follow him and form the vanguard: individuals who will stand up to the powers that be, men of conscience whose aims transcend their personal interests, who think of the country and the people rather than themselves.

Gandhiji's entire life was a search for the methods by which such individuals could fortify themselves against the pressures that regimes and their agents would undoubtedly bring to bear upon them. Much of his teaching was devoted to specifying these ways and to dispelling the various hesitations that keep all of us from joining the great struggles of our times. The *Gita*, Gandhiji was to affirm after his experiments and introspection, spelled out the conditions that would make the individual invulnerable: that he give up all attachment to his possessions, including among these the attachment to his ultimate possession, his body, that he rid himself of all false attachments to his friends and relatives, that he free himself from conventional ambitions.

We do not have to think long to see the relevance of these teachings to our concerns. If I am attached to my possessions, then I am vulnerable to anyone who can deprive me of them and I am beholden to anyone who can help me enlarge them. As governments can do all this better than anyone else, I am both vulnerable and beholden to these governments. If my attachment to my brother takes the false form of an obsession to help him get along by acquiring jobs and licenses, I am naturally mortgaged to the authorities who can give or deny jobs and licenses. If I am a prisoner of conventional ambitions—if, for instance, I am a careerist, if rising to the top of the civil service, the pyramid of my firm or university, is an obsession with me—then naturally I will remain beholden to those who influence institutional success of this kind. Similarly, if I have not overcome my dread of physical pain or even death, I shall always flinch from confronting those who can commandeer superior physical might.

Gandhiji used to say that the test of a man's devotion to the ideals he espouses is his willingness to die for them and that we would attain true *swaraj* only when we had learned to die with

## The Role of Popular Movements

fearlessness and love in our hearts. Then, he would say, we would indeed have grasped the teaching of the Hindu seers that the body was *maya*, that the only real entity was the soul and that it was an entity that no tyrant could touch, much less hurt. Then, at last, we would be invulnerable.

The individual who has imbibed these teachings is always prepared and, indeed, he is happy, to face the consequences of his acts. It was this spirit of willingly accepting the consequences of following their conscience, that distinguished the *satyagrahis* during the independence struggle. One has only to recall the remarkable statements that Gandhiji, Jawaharlal Nehru, Sardar Patel, Jaya Prakash Narayan and others made at the trials at which they knew they faced long periods of incarceration and, yet, at which they refused to enter even a formal defence on their behalf. It was this spirit which made them look upon prisons as "His Majesty's Hotels," to look upon each fresh persecution by the government as just evidence of the fact that they were indeed beginning to get their message across, to look upon the destruction of their conventional careers as the end of a bondage that left them free to thenceforth devote all their time and energy to serving the country, to view each fresh tyranny as yet another occasion to test their devotion to the cause.

Gandhiji—even as Krishna in the *Gita*—was just as concerned to dispel the hesitations that keep individuals from consecrating themselves to the country's cause and that of the people.

Among these was the fear of failure. The fruits of political action do not ripen for decades and decades. The individual hesitates to enter the fray fearing that it may all turn out to be a failure, that he may devote all his life to a cause and yet in the end the cause may elude him, that he may put in decades of effort only to discover in the end that he has not made the slightest difference to the existing state of affairs. Out of this fear of failure most of us stand back till we are more or less certain that the cause has a good chance of succeeding. And so, recalling once again the teaching of the *Gita*, Gandhiji emphasized that the *satyagrahi* must take up a cause because he believes it to be right and not because some calculus has shown him that he is likely to succeed in the conventional sense of the term. Indeed, Gandhiji taught, failure is impossible in a righteous struggle for the vital thing in such a struggle is not to reach a conventionally defined goal—even though one's struggle to reach the goal must be unsparing—but to make the effort.

Hence, the individual should cast away the fear of failure. Nor should he wait for others to join him. For him the struggle against an unjust system must first of all be a struggle for self-purification, an effort to set his own conduct right. The best preparation for a struggle against an unjust system, Gandhiji would say, was to set one's own house in order and this part of the struggle was entirely within the individual's control. As it was within the individual's control and as it was, in any case, a precondition for the success of the overall struggle against the system, there was no reason for the individual to postpone his efforts until others joined him. Even a single individual acting morally, Gandhiji used to emphasize, is bound to improve the state of affairs: even a single lamp, he would say, dispels the deepest darkness. The evil that the "great" do is done through the hands of ordinary individuals and, thus, to the extent that the individual's misconduct is contributing to the sorry state of affairs, the individual's efforts to rectify his conduct would directly improve this state. Moreover, Gandhiji said, it is highly probable that the individual's sacrifice and example would inspire others to join him and this, in turn, may produce big results. But, even though this was the probable sequence of events, the *satyagrahi* must scrupulously avoid falling prey to the temptation of these probable results. Were he to do so, he would be back to weighing the prospects of "success" conventionally defined and would, thus, be kept from taking the first steps. Rectifying one's conduct is an essential preparation for the struggle in a mundane sense too. Once the issue is joined, the rulers will use every device to discredit, expose, browbeat the individual. If his social conduct has not been spotless then nothing will be easier for the rulers than to discredit him and, in case his conduct is still hidden away, to send him scurrying around to cover up his past. How would such an individual have the stamina, the stature and even the time for the struggle?

Just as the individual should not wait for others, so should he not postpone the first step for the day when he has perfected himself in every way. Instead, Gandhiji stressed, he should take the first step forthwith and then concentrate on each subsequent step, acquiring in this way perfection through praxis rather than sitting back helplessly until full perfection descends upon him. Nor should he postpone the first step until some great battles are joined; instead he should make right conduct the hallmark of everything he does, acquiring strength for the great battles through his daily conduct. Nor, indeed is the first step shrouded in any great mystery: as a first step the individual must dissociate himself from the regime that is harming the country and the people. A single act of defiance, an uncompromising declaration about the true nature of the regime—anything, in fact, that ruptures the individual's links with the system that he has concluded is pernicious for the country—is as good a first step as any.

Only the individual who is preforming *tapas* in this form— who is striving ceaselessly to improve his conduct, whose efforts to serve the people are unremitting—only he can claim that he is taking his stand on his conscience. We have noted above that Gandhiji reaffirmed the individual's right to defy all authority when his conscience convinced him that obedience would be a compromise with untruth and evil. This affirmation of the right was not, he said, a license for everyone to do as he pleases, for everyone to insist that he had a right to go his own way irrespective of its consequences for the society as a whole. The right enjoined a heavy duty: that the individual consecrate himself to truth and justice and to the service of the people. A conscience was not something that everyone could conjure up in a day dream.

"But isn't all this just idle idealism? Shouldn't we posit something that is much more practical, something that is closer to people's present conduct, something that accepts people for what they are and then builds on that?" It is precisely this attitude— the attitude of so-called practical men—that brings entire peoples to a sorry pass. Gandhiji always stressed that an individual should not dilute his demands upon himself, that leaders should not dilute their demands upon the people, that an ideal should not be debased because of some presumptions about an individual's capacity or the people's capacity, that were such a thing to be done, all would be lost.

The ideal must be posited in its purest form. The people would then strain their capacity to live up to it. But if the ideal were diluted to gain adherents, all would be lost from the beginning itself. The Ganga, he would say, does not leave its course in search of its tributaries. Euclid's point and line, he was fond of reminding his readers and listeners, could never exist in practice and yet an entire discipline had been built upon their idealized conception.

Moreover, the difference, he always pointed out, between those like him who affirmed an ideal and strove towards it and those who dismissed the ideal as being "just idealism" did not lie in the fact that one set was idealistic and the other set was practical. The numerous decades that he had spent in public life and the success that had attended his efforts, he would say, did, after all, entitle him to claim that he was practical. Rather, the difference lay in the differing assessments the two sets had as to what was realizable in practice.

His experience, he said, had taught him that even if the ideal was not attained by all, the very fact that a few strove towards it—and that they strove ceaselessly towards its undiluted form—would make a material difference to the state of affairs, that the striving itself would bring the ideal closer to realization even as single drops of water would ultimately make their way through the hardest rock. Moreover, he said, history showed it to have often been the case that what was dismissed as being utopian at one stage had become commonplace at the next. All would concede that this had often been the case in technical matters. Why then, he would ask, was it impossible in the affairs of one's self, in the affairs of the people at large, in matters relating to the individual's conduct?

Popular movements that aim at reconstructing a country and a society do not need supermen. Throughout his life, and especially in his autobiography, Gandhiji took pains to show that he had hewn himself out of ordinary material, that anyone who made the requisite effort could do the same. The movements he led and the ones that are associated with his name show that not just individuals but entire masses are capable of taking their stand on principles and acting in a disciplined manner until their stand has been vindicated.

He used to point to the fact, for example, that thousands had been involved in the *satyagrahas* in South Africa, that all of them had been ordinary men and women, that the *satyagrahas* had lasted eight long years and had entailed great hardship for each of them and yet not one of them had deserted his post, not one of them had compromised his principles.

The greatest message that Gandhiji holds out for us is precisely to dispel the myths that a country owes its prostrate state to some mysterious factors, that the ways to set things right are equally mysterious, that we must await supermen to uncover these ways and to lead us to them. Gandhiji's teachings and his example show us that the important thing—and the difficult one—is not of discovering what is right, of discovering what needs to be done or of convincing people that such and thus is the correct standpoint but to make them do what they already know to be right.

Even more important, the truly important thing—and the even more difficult one—is not to make others pursue the right path but to bring oneself to doing so.

And, finally, that the most important thing—and the most difficult one—is not of resolving to do so at some future occasion, of resolving to take up the cudgels in some great engagements but of taking the first step and taking it now.

Thus, the *sine qua non* for popular movements is not the single superman who will lead them but the band of ordinary individuals who will consecrate themselves to the cause of the country. And the *sine qua non* for each of them is not that they build up stamina for the ultimate engagement but that they take the first step.

# Mrs Gandhi

## 5  Creeping Paranoia*

> **insecure**, *in-si kur'*, *adj.*, apprehensive of danger or loss: exposed to danger or loss: unsafe: uncertain: not fixed or firm—*adv.* insecurely—*n.* insecurity
> **melancholy**, *mel'en-kol-i*...indulgence in thoughts of pleasing sadness...
> **paranoia**, *par-a-noi'a*, *n.*, a form of insanity characterised by fixed delusions, esp. of grandeur, pride, persecution...

Mrs Gandhi is back at her old game—spreading canards, hurling vague, unsubstantiated accusations, conjuring conspiracies against herself and letting forth the Goebbelsian lie—a lie so big, so unashamed that people will say to themselves, "may be she exaggerates, but at least a bit of it must be true."

Her latest is that today far graver excesses are being committed than during the Emergency.

Even thoughtful observers are liable to regard such assertions as yet another manoeuvre and debate their worth or otherwise as a manoeuvre—whether or not they are "shrewd," whether or not they are "well-timed," whether or not they are "calculated."

*September, 1977.

This is the wrong way of looking at such assertions. For by viewing them as just parts of a manoeuvre we attribute an ephemeral, transient quality to them which is not warranted. The statements do not reflect a mere manoeuvre. They reflect her character—a commodity, unlike the manoeuvre of the moment, that will be around as long as she is.

To argue this out in detail would require an extended analysis of Mrs Gandhi's psychology—an enterprise that is not worth the while. I will draw your attention to just two features of her character.

## Insecurity

Mrs Gandhi's central characteristic is an insecurity so deep that it can only be characterized as congenital, an insecurity that has its roots in grave doubts about her own adequacy.

Recall the facts about Mrs Gandhi's growing up—facts and not the fiction of hagiographers: a household dominated by an imperious grandfather; anxieties and quarrels—not always subterranean—among the women, quarrels common to so many extended families; severe—suppressed but nonetheless severe—tensions between the father and the grandfather, who would not brook, as Nirad Chaudhuri has noted, a rival modernism in his household; the impression of the child and the adolescent that her mother was being neglected by the father and persecuted by the aunts; a less than successful academic career, the effects of which on the insecure adolescent must have been accentuated by the father's love—a love he was fond of displaying—for books, for intellectual pursuits; a lacklustre marriage; and, finally, a derivative existence in the father's household.

Moreover, contrary to what a superficial view might suggest, the way Mrs Gandhi acquired power and retained it could only have driven the insecurity deeper. Having held scarcely a single elective office of any consequence, she was catapulted into the Prime Ministership by the manipulations of a few bosses. Only those who have been acclimatized by long struggle can take such a sudden change in altitude without driving their insecurities and anxieties deeper.

Similarly, Mrs Gandhi retained her power by manipulations

within the parlour and by fooling the masses. Observers were heady at her success. But "success" of this kind works enigmatically on the subject's mind.

It develops in the mind of the one who succeeds a contempt for the rivals one is so easily able to outmanoeuvre as well as a contempt for the masses whom one is able so easily to fool. But most of all the successful subject develops self-contempt: while the rivals, the distant colleagues and the people at large may or may not know the distance between the slogans and the reality, between the professions and the practice of the leader, the fraudulent leader and his close henchmen know it for certain. And with this knowledge comes the fear of being found out, of being exposed by an event that suddenly gets out of hand, by a mistake. This insecurity breeds secretiveness and obsessive calculation. These, in turn, increase the distance of the leader from the masses. And the distance cannot but enhance the insecurity: floating in the air, the leader comes to see his increasing dependence on an ever shrinking handful. Now *they* become phantoms in the leader's mind, *they* too can never be trusted, *they* too seem to be scheming and plotting for their own advantage: do they know too much? are they hobnobbing with my rivals?

Thus, the very processes by which Mrs Gandhi acquired and retained power—processes which observers took as proof of her decisiveness, her sure touch, her self-assurance—in fact, these very processes heightened her innate insecurity.

The manifestations of this insecurity have never been far to seek. I shall recount only one or two.

Recall her obsessive concern with self-protection, the frequent forays against colleagues, comrades and even minions being the most publicly known example of this concern. In her political career at least it seems that she has never been able to bring herself to trusting anyone for long. By the end, anyone outside the reach of her informers and enforcers was in her eyes a threat to her.

'...Wary and secretive, (Hitler) entertained a universal distrust. He admitted no one to his counsels. He never let down his guard or gave himself away. "He never," Schacht wrote, "let slip an unconsidered word. He never said what he did not intend to say and he never blurted out a secret. Everything was the result of cold calculation".'[1]

'In order that he should triumph (Hitler) was ready to knock down those who helped raise him up. It was a characteristic he was to retain until the very end of his life, as can be seen from his dismissal of Goering in 1945.'[2]

Or think for a moment about her confidantes—they reflect the familiar obsession of the insecure leader, the obsession of surrounding oneself with manifestly mediocre men. Hitler and his banal entourage pictured so graphically by Speer, Nixon and his low level crooks, Mrs Gandhi and her Yash Pal Kapurs and R.K. Dhawans.

'Few of the party leaders were more than mediocre men, and few were even efficient. Most of them were unintelligent, grasping, jealous, and incompetent, and jockeyed for place by telling tales against their rivals, or else boosted each other's morale by organising "spontaneous" crowd demonstrations for one another. With the possible exception of D'Annunzio, there seems to have been no living Italian for whom Mussolini felt any admiration. When he later claimed that party leaders had let him down, the answer must be that he had subordinates which he deserved and whom he had himself advanced. No doubt he deliberately promoted their rivalries and conflicting policies. Frequently he replaced nearly all the ministers and party leaders in a sweeping "change of the guard," and he publicly boasted in 1929 that he used to announce these wholesale changes without even consulting first with the people he intended to appoint or dismiss. This was a revealing manifestation of *ducismo*.'[3]

Similarly, it is only the deeply insecure individual who seeks and accepts reassurance from sychophants. This alone explains how Mrs Gandhi could bring herself to accept and approve the vulgar and third rate paeans that sychophants

---

[1]Allen Bullock, *Hitler, A Study in Tyranny*, Penguin, London, 1962.
[2]Paul Hayes, *Fascism*, Free Press, New York, 1973.
[3]Denis Mack Smith, *Italy, A Modern History*, University of Michigan Press, Ann Arbor, 1959.

churned out during the Emergency. How insecure must the individual be who seeks solace and reassurance in such offerings of sychophants as the following—this one being a poem composed by Mir Mushtaq Ahmed, Chairman of the Delhi Metropolitan Council, and presented by him personally to Mrs Gandhi in November 1976:

> 'The truth,' the Mir mourns, 'they
> would not let her know who on untruth
> thrive, fatten, grow.
> But she stands for people's glory
> And knows fully well the real story
> She dares to live and swear by truth
> Untarnished, unblemished, uncouth
> Its time the sychophants beware
> Or else their deeds would lay them bare.'

And don't blame the sychophants. They would never have peddled such stuff unless they were sure that the lady relished it. Anyone who doubts this knows nothing about the workings of a sychophant—he knows nothing of the meticulous homework that goes into first ascertaining what the object of his flattery wants.

Or consider next the obsessive anxiety to snatch all credit for every success and the equally obsessive anxiety to dust off blame for every failure.

Recall Gandhiji's accepting full responsibility for Chauri Chaura—a solitary incident in a distant settlement, an incident with which he could not have been even remotely connected. Here is a man secure in his knowledge of his own worth. He knows that he will not be diminished by failure and mistakes. He openly acknowledges them and even characterizes them grandiloquently—he calls them "Himalyan blunders." Contrast this with Mrs Gandhi's feverish efforts to dust off all blame for the excesses of the Emergency—to overzealous officials, to opposition infiltrators in the administration, to intelligence officers, to State governments. But when it comes to snatching credit for a success, it is another story entirely. Who was the architect of the Bangladesh victory? None but her, of course.

'Mussolini was careful to take upon himself all the credit for any success, because this not only fed his vanity, but it also prevented his lieutenants from gathering any popular support and becoming anything but abjectly subservient to his person. For the same reason he discouraged them from taking any bold initiative. In return they were allowed to strut in fine uniforms and amass private fortunes, the chief losers being the Italian people who consequently were exploited and misgoverned by the dregs of the nation. Yet though Mussolini tried to monopolise the credit for success, he always found someone else to blame for failure, and perhaps he reached that last fatal pitch of delusion where he genuinely thought that he could do no wrong. . . .'[4]

## Pretensions to Aristocracy

The second feature to which I want to draw attention concerns the aristocratic pretensions which Mrs Gandhi has internalized in her psyche.

It has become customary to think of the Nehrus as aristocrats. Such a characterization is an over-simplification. It keeps us from getting to the complexities of their make-up. The Nehrus were not aristocrats—they were, as Nirad Chaudhuri has noted, pretenders to aristocracy, climbers in short. Like other Kashmiri pandit families they were minor officials in Kashmir. Having migrated to the plains, they set themselves up as aristocrats of a distant land. Motilal was the most conspicuous representative of these ambitions, of these pretensions. Pandit Jawaharlal came closest in the family to transcending them.

Mrs Gandhi grew up at a time when the efforts of the family to convince itself and others of its aristocratic mien were at their apogee. She internalized the pretension.

Now, this pretension to aristocracy has had two consequences. First, it heightened the insecurity born of other reasons—to the other anxieties was added the pretender's apprehension of being found out. The second consequence flows from the successful internalization of the pretension: having successfully convinced herself that she was truly of

[4]Smith, *op. cit.*

# Creeping Paranoia

aristocratic stock, she also internalized the corollary notion common to aristocrats, that they alone are fit to rule.

Once one has convinced oneself that one alone is fit to rule, one has no difficulty in convincing oneself that one's personal interest is the interest of the group, of the country. After all, if I alone am fit to run the country, anything or anyone that weakens me, weakens the country. It is thus that she got around to believing that opposition to her was actually treason, that it was indiscipline which would harm the country itself.

The point is that she does not just mouth the slogans, she *believes* them. It is for this reason that she has no pangs at all when she sacrifices someone who has stood by her, someone who has helped her, or when she does down a colleague. To her these moves do not appear as moves to further herself; they appear as unpleasant things that have nevertheless to be done in the interests of the cause, of the country. (The innate insecurity helps, for it predisposes her to believing that these colleagues and minions have begun conspiring against her in any case.)

The reader must remember that the notion that has been internalized is not "the interests of the country are my interests," but that "my interests are the interests of the country." So that when, as we clearly saw in 1975-77, the interests of the country diverge from the personal interests of the leader, the former are what are jettisoned.

> Megalomania and not internalized pretensions to aristocracy were what led to this identification in the case of Hitler, but the effect was the same: 'Throughout his career Hitler showed himself prepared to seize any advantage that was to be gained by lying, cunning, treachery and unscrupulousness. He demanded the sacrifice of millions of German lives for the sacred cause of Germany but in the last year of the war was ready to destroy Germany rather than surrender his power or admit defeat . . . . For a long time Hitler succeeded in identifying his own power with the recovery of Germany's old position in the world, and there were many in the 1930s who spoke of him as a fanatical patriot. But as soon as the interests of Germany began to diverge from his own from the beginning of 1943 onwards, his patriotism was seen at its true

value—Germany, like everything else in the world, was only a means, a vehicle for his own power, which he would sacrifice with the same indifference as the lives of those he sent to the Western Front . . . .'[5]

In aristocratic households—as in households that are on the way to aristocracy—children are liable to be pampered and neglected at the same time, pampered by servants and poor relatives who fawn over them and cater to their whims in the hope of thereby endearing themselves to the household, and neglected by preoccupied parents. The children thus imbibe the insecurity characteristic of neglected children as well as the extreme self-centeredness of pampered children.

Today in Mrs Gandhi's eyes every move, for instance, to restore the rule of law is just another device to get at her: if someone tries to ferret out the corrupt in the Congress, she sees in it a plot to do her in; if someone were to kill the half-carried Constitutional amendment by which, for instance, a Prime Minister is immune from prosecution for any criminal or civil act, she would only see in it another effort of her opponents to put her behind bars. The point is that she will not just be saying these things for propoganda. She will be saying only what she actually believes.

There is also the aristocrat's exaggerated view of one's hardships, of one's "sacrifices." Has anyone made as much political capital out of giving anti-British speeches to dolls or from spending a few months in prison, as she has? Do you recall her statements during the emergency that no head of government had borne as much criticism and abuse as she had? She *believed* what she said: the statements reflected both the aristocrat's fury at being criticized at all and the aristocrat's exaggerated notions of the hardships one has borne. Do you recall her statements during the Lok Sabha campaign of how no family had sacrificed as much for the country as her family? She would cite the gift of a family house to prove this. The aristocrat is so preoccupied with the enormity of the sacrifice entailed in giving up one of two or several family houses that he never stops to think that the

[5]Bullock, *op. cit.*

sacrifices of those who did not have houses to donate may also have been considerable.

## Predictable, Defensive but Dangerous

It is because her strategems and her statements reflect not just expedients of the moment but deep traits of her character, that they should not be dismissed lightly. Given the chance she will act predictably: she will act her nature.

No strategem will be out of bounds—for she truly believes that she and her kin alone are fit to rule us. She will not hesitate for a moment before fomenting strikes or worse, for she will have no difficulty in convincing herself that, even if these inconvenience the country for the moment, they will be in the country's interest for they will help bring back to power the only one who is fit to govern.

Similarly, she will be, as she has been, the merchant of fear—thrusting her anxieties on to the country itself. Thus, she will fan the fears of the Harijans, of the minorities, of industrial labour. Having incited these groups she will then play upon the dread of the ruling class—the dread of insecurity, of disruption. She will talk of growing lawlessness, of mounting crime. She will remind the industrialists of how her emergency had given them the security they crave, of how no one but her can protect them from the hordes. From her point of view all is fair for she—in her mind even more than in the mind of that clown—is India.

So, it is a predictable game. And it is a defensive one.

Mrs Gandhi is acting the way she is today not because she spies an easy kill. She is doing so to protect herself. She fears that unless she can keep reminding her rivals in the Congress that she is still a leader of substance, they might move to throw her out of the party. Moreover, through her contacts in the bureaucracy and the police, she knows that the evidence is piling up. She is desperate that, before the first instalment of this is released, she should be able to establish herself as one who is fighting for a cause—some cause, *any* cause; of course, the more altruistic, the better—so that when she is ultimately brought to book for some misdeed, she can proclaim herself a martyr, so that she may be in a position then to scream that the government is prosecuting her only because she is trying to help the Muslims, the Harijans, the poor.

Thus, it is a predictable game, a defensive game. But it is not a game that is bound to fail. Not by any means.

Mrs Gandhi embodies the fears and anxieties of the ruling class. Members of her class may will turn to her as the only one who can keep the people—who are for them just locusts—from devouring them. Moreover, the collaborators of the emergency period are her natural constituency, a potential springboard. The civil servants, the politicos, the journalists and others who helped her, who made hay, who lauded the dictatorship—they are under a psychological compulsion today to run down every thing, for that alone can justify their collaborationist conduct during the Emergency: "we knew all along that this *Kichri* won't work." Only thus can they dress their fearful collaboration as precognition. They are ready fuel for her touch.

And, most of all, whether she will come back or not depends on whether or not the new government does its work well. Her opponents may once again accomplish for her what she is not able to do for herself.

Therefore, do not dismiss her statements and actions as mere ploys. Remember Cicero's verdict that the character of Ceasar was well enough established in his youth for citizens to have been able to predict the harm he would do to the Republic and that, therefore, he should have been dealt with appropriately before and not after he wrought the evil.

# 6  Liar: An Appropriate, if Unparliamentary, Word*

In recounting the harrowing tale of demolitions the Shah Commission has taken up the people's case. In one mad spree after another one hundred and fifty thousand structures were demolished in Delhi.

And there was no formal, official decision at any level of the Delhi Administration or the Central Government that this was to be done. A hundred and fifty thousand structures affecting at least 700,000 human beings and no formal decision at all. There is extra-constitutionality for you.

Listen to Mrs Gandhi: as recently as four weeks ago she was asked by a journalist about individuals who had no official or constitutional *locus standi* exercising power during the Emergency. Her reply was, "... The question you are hinting at is that these people took part in Government decisions.... But it is the truth that no political decision was discussed with any of the people who were supposed to be in the caucus." The questioner persisted: "But a number of people had first hand experiences of interference in the administration by these unconstitutional authorities." And her answer? "I am sorry to say that I do not

*December, 1977.

believe it. But I know what I have done. I have not discussed politics with any member of my family."

Well, today the Shah Commission was told by official after official that files were being taken to Sanjay Gandhi *on a daily basis*, that he was ordering the suspension and promotion of officers, that he routinely asked a social worker—a man known for his honesty, his self-effacing services to the poor of Delhi— to deposit Rs 1.8 crores with him if he wanted him to alter his imperious decision, that he was present with his mother at meetings convened to discuss the question of demolitions, that he was personally present at the demolition sites and pronounced that documents presented by the victims were not adequate grounds to stay the demolitions, that his mother gave S.C. Chabra a half hour dressing down one midnight because this officer—known for his uprightness, integrity and efficiency—had incurred the wrath of Sanjay Gandhi. All this is not just coming to light now. The script of a documentary prepared by his crony—Navin Chawla—at that time had clearly referred to the fact that it was "under the guidance of the Youth Congress Leader Sanjay Gandhi" that 7 lakhs people were being shifted by the Delhi Administration. Just to make sure that the listener had not missed the point within three sentences the documentary referred again to the "guidance and push of Shri Sanjay Gandhi."

What would you call a person who in the face of all this swore that Sanjay never saw files, never took decisions affecting government, that he never attended meetings, that, in fact, "I have not discussed politics with any member of my family?"

The case—the harrowing details of which will unravel only when the common men and women take the stand at the Shah Commission in the coming days—also gives the lie to Mrs Gandhi's much touted concern for the poor.

When in his interview, the journalist reminded her that MPs like Subhadra Joshi had brought the hardships and injustices to her notice and she had done nothing to stop the excesses, she answered "I did, I did speak to them to look into the matter. I did speak to the concerned authorities."

Well, one "concerned authority" after another has deposed in affidavit after affidavit that the facts are the other way around: *they* spoke to her about the excesses, *they* sent her written memoranda, and *she* kept silent, *she* passed on their letters to the Congress President (presumably to have them pulled up), *she* stopped acknowledging their letters, *she* rejected one recommendation after another which might have stemmed this madness. A stage was reached when an MP (who was, incidentally, one of her drummer boys, a proponent of limited dictatorship and a lefty to boot) "was told that his letters in this connection were being torn and thrown in the waste paper basket by R.K. Dhawan, Additional Private Secretary to the Prime Minister."

Indeed, she fanned the fires, she egged the officers on to be even more ruthless, she pronounced the programme "an excellent one," she gave the impression, to use Jagmohan's apt expression, "to liquidate the problem as expeditiously as feasible. . . ."

"Liquidate the problem," "vanquish the opposition"—words of the compassionate *sevika*.

The details as they will unfold will also give the lie to her much touted secularism. The President was gravely distressed—two former Ministers have testified—about what had happened to the Muslims in the course of these demolitions. The coming days will reveal how much her heart bled for these victims. (Surely, at least as much as it bleeds today for the victims of the Andhra cyclone?)

And with all the protests, representations, with all the wailing that was reaching her, with the fact—as Raghuramaiah has testified—that she was personally holding meetings, taking decisions about these demolitions, with all this she cannot now plead that she did not know what was going on.

But what were the motives for the programme, for the ruthless manner in which it was carried out? There were three motives.

The first—as Sri Chand Chabra suggested—was the most important: to announce, to let everyone—the bureaucrats, the politicians, the people—know that Sanjay was boss. Anyone, anything that stood in his way would be bulldozed.

The second was the motive common to all dictatorial cliques —to spread terror, to tell the people that the regime is *un*reasonable, that it has a heavy hand.

The third motive is one which the rich share with Mrs Gandhi and her son—to get the poor out of sight, to throw them across the river, so that they do not spoil our morning walks, so that they do not offend our eyes, so that their filthy presence does not enhance our guilt, so that we can show our visitors—specially our foreign guests—what a beautiful city we have. The familiar gesture of the rich: to hastily stuff dirty clothes in the closet, to dump them in the bedroom, the "store," before the visitors arrive in the drawing room for the cocktail.

This motive lingers among the rich today. The poor must not forget this: the rich are bent upon creating a dual society in India and given another emergency they will again welcome the barbarities needed to do so.

In "liquidating" this problem Indira Gandhi and Sanjay worked on their behalf.

In the coming days the hearings will reveal the inhuman sufferings of the poor, of the common men and women of our city. They will also reveal the cold callousness of Indira Gandhi and her clique, of the same Indira Gandhi who even today exploits the deaths of Harijans, of cyclone victims to her own advantage.

Every reader must remember this in the weeks after January when the time comes for Indira Gandhi to appear before the Shah Commission.

What if she appears in sackcloth and ashes and says "I do not want to go into details about what has been said and what will be said; as the head of the then government I accept full responsibility for whatever excesses took place during the Emergency?"

Of what consequence would such a blanket statement be?

Is this country so supine, so petty, that all it is hankering for is that one individual should utter one sentence?

Before being satiated with any sentence of this kind, the country should look minutely at Mrs Gandhi's record of speaking the truth. A simple tally of statements during the Emergency and after it with what is being revealed now—from the records, affidavits and oral testimony—will do. Mrs Gandhi has never had any difficulty in saying one thing today and its opposite tomorrow.

Given this record, the people must remember that Mrs Gandhi's confessionals, her I-accept-the-responsibility statements, will indicate repentance only if they pass two touchstones.

First, they must be detailed. Whatever their content, general blanket statements will indicate that she stands by what she did, that she has now concluded that the enquiry is hurting her politically and that her best course is to help bring it to an end quickly. Her sincerity will be evident only if she helps the Commission re-construct the record in a *detailed* manner—of how she and her clique usurped power, how they misused it.

Readers who exclaim "but that she will never do" are in fact saying that she will never be sorry for what happened.

The second touchstones requires a longer time: we should ascertain the extent to which Mrs Gandhi abjures office and position and instead devotes herself to working among and with the people; to use her own expression, to what extent does she become a *sevika*?

Mrs Gandhi has never worked with or among the common people of our country. The people should not believe her confessionals till she has spent at least as much time working among and with them as an ordinary constructive worker as she spent riding their backs.

Constructive work is the one and only *pashchatap* for a politician. Disbarment from office is the one and only punishment.


## LIES, LIES, ALL THE WAY*

In boycotting the Shah Commission Mrs Gandhi has acted true to form. Having suppressed the truth for years she has refused to assist a commission that is ascertaining the facts.

The boycott and the submissions on her behalf go beyond legal niceties and fine points of procedure. The operative aspects of the long-winded procedural submissions were three: that Mrs Gandhi should not be called to testify as a witness; that, if called, she should not be asked questions regarding matter such as the circumstances leading to the proclamation of the emergency, the institution of false cases etc., and, third, that if called she should not be asked to make a statement on oath.

The petty legalisms aside, is this a stand that someone who

*January, 1978.

has nothing to hide would take? Even as the lawyers quibble, even as writs are filed and warrants issued, this is what the people will be asking themselves. They will not miss the real purpose of the boycott even as they saw through the procedural objections for what they were—a pretext to walk out with the fig leaf of legalisms. The people know better.

For what is being exposed in the Shah Commission is not just the enormity of the crimes but also Mrs Gandhi's record of speaking the truth.

The big lies that formed the foundation of the Emergency—allegations about conspiracies to plunge the country into anarchy and violence, about calls to the armed forces to rebel etc.,—have already been exposed. But the lies were not limited to these. They were innumerable and they touched every aspect of governance in those 19 months.

*Arrests*

Again and again (e.g., on 12 July 1975) we find Mrs Gandhi saying that the number of arrests are "a very meagre" proportion of the population. On the same day in an interview to the *Sunday Times* and *Observer* she asserts that only one-fourth of the arrests made since 25 June are of a political nature. By 24 August the untruth has become more elaborate and specific: "Although some people are under detention, the whole opposition is not under detention. In fact, most of them are out and most of those who are in prison are not political people. They are what are called 'bad elements' who the police have on their lists and others belong to those parties which we have banned." By 4 March 1976 she is asserting that "the overwhelming number" of those detained belong to the banned organizations.

Even as the round-up is being intensified all over the country, Mrs Gandhi asserts (in an interview published on 24 August 1975) that "people are being released almost every day." She repeats this or similar statements again and again (e.g., on 23 and 27 September 1975, 20 February, 12 and 31 March, 14 April 1976) to give currency to the untruth that everything is being relaxed.

Her minions take up the cue. On 1 January 1976, Bansi Lal

asserts that the Government has released most of the people detained under the emergency. "Now," he says magnanimously, "it is for them to behave properly." In an interview, the text of which is released on 30 April 1976, the major-domo Om Mehta tells *Excelsior*, a Mexican daily, that "most of those detained after 25, June 1975 have been released and that only those believing in terrorist methods are still under detention." Morarji Desai will be happy to know that he believed in terrorism.

Nor do the untruths stop at the numbers detained or the type of persons in detention. She does not spare the conditions of detention. On 27 June 1975, when there is panic in the jails, she says that the arrested leaders are being well looked after and are being provided with "comforts and facilities." She repeats the assurance in her Red Fort address on 15 August 1975. By 12 October 1975, she is telling the *Sunday Telegraph* that "I don't think there is any deliberate solitary confinement except that there are a couple of people who are kept in houses." As a year goes by she is able to claim she has certificates to prove her assertions. The allegations of harassment in custody, she tells the assembled Home Secretaries and I.Gs on 20 October 1976, are unfounded: "Most of the leaders who have been released from detention have themselves conceded that they have been exceedingly well treated." The dead Snehlata Reddy would have certainly corroborated that. What a pity she died as a result of the "comforts and facilities" she was provided.

*Pre-censorship*

And guess when pre-censorship was lifted? On 4 October 1975 Mrs Gaddhi says in an interview on German TV: "Censorship has already been liberalized a great deal. There is no pre-censorship now." She repeats this to the Australian Broadcasting Corporation on 25 October 1975: "Censorship is no longer the same. There is no sort of pre-censorship now." And she repeats it again to American agricultural leaders who visit her at her home on 20 February 1976.

But, of course, it is difficult to lie consistently. Having maintained for months that "there is no sort of pre-censorship," in a message to the AINEC she hesitates to make as unqualified a statement; after all, at least a few of the members of the association will have some personal experience of what is going on; so she says instead that "restrictions on papers have already been greatly relaxed. Pre-censorship is applied in only very few cases." On 12 March 1976, speaking on the Swedish TV, having maintained for five months that "there is no sort of pre-censorship now," Mrs Gandhi says that "by and large there is no pre-censorship now."

## Use of Police Force

Throughout the Emergency Mrs Gandhi maintains that she has imposed her draconian rule only to put democracy "back on the rails," that she has put an end to "an unconstitutional agitation by constitutional means."

By 9 July 1975, she is saying in an interview that she cannot think of anyone who has done as much to strengthen democracy in India as she has. (People would have had less reason to be surprised at her claim in the recent midnight ovation that India had never been freer than it was when she was Prime Minister—"Never, Never"—if they had believed her more during the emergency!) By 15 August 1975, *she* is quoting Jawaharlal Nehru's call: "freedom is in peril, defend it with all your might."

On 21 August 1975 this claim became much more elaborate. She tells an enthusiastic interviewer from Bombay, "So far as I know force has not been used at all even in a small way anywhere," and, "there is no use of force whatsoever anywhere in the country. The truth is," and this is news to us even today, "that the police have had less work since the Emergency than ever before."

By 19 April 1976 she is telling the San Francisco Examiner: "You can go anywhere and see that there is no police state atmosphere. In fact, throughout the Emergency we have not had to use the police at all and the people are relaxed."

On September 1976, she goes on British TV to say that "there is no forcing or compulsion" in the sterilization drive and that, in fact, "we do not believe in forcing anything on any people or on any state."

## Big as well as Small

The lies are indiscriminate. They cover matters big as well as small. On 17 June 1975, soon after the Allahabad judgement, she asserts that "barring a few, the reaction of the press to the verdict has been quite sober; the world press particularly has been very understanding. Newspapers outside the country were, by and large, sympathetic to me." In the coming weeks this solicitousness for foreign papers is to do an about-face. The moment they start attacking the Emergency, she screams out that they have never wanted to see a strong India, that they are the same ones who in the past opposed the Mahatma and her father, that they are specially opposed to her as they know that she will not give in to foreign pressure. A complete about-face in just two weeks.

And she begins asserting that the Emergency has nothing to do with the Allahabad judgment, that any suggestion to the contrary is a canard. "Another canard," she tells the *Daily Telegraph* on 12 October 1975, "that was spread and is still being spread is that the whole decision was taken by my son and one of my personal assistants who have absolutely nothing to do with it. My family has been very much maligned and, of course, my son is not in politics *at all*." Not even a little bit, Mrs Gandhi?

## Kamaraj

Even the dead are not spared. The moment poor Kamaraj dies—sad at what is happening, making public statements in village after village, town aften town in Tamil Nadu against what is happening—she is quick to appropriate him. On 5 October 1975, she tells a memorial meeting in Delhi that her personal bonds with Kamaraj always held strong "for he was very close to the ideals and principles I believe in" and that "during the last two months he was anxious that his people should work with us during these difficult days. I hope," she has the audacity to say, "everyone, particularly the people of Tamil Nadu, will give their attention to this ambition of his. Our comrades and his comrades should work together. This was his desire . . . ."

Barooah, never to be outdone in a lie or in hyperbole, is in his usual form at the same meeting. To those of Kamaraj's followers who feel helpless today he says: "The spirit of Mr Kamaraj lives and his spirit is embodied in the person of our beloved Prime Minister, Mrs Indira Gandhi. I, therefore, suggest that all those who believe in Mr Kamaraj's ideals of political and economic freedom of India must rally round the banner of Mrs Gandhi."

This myth is to be sedulously cultivated over the coming months. By the time Mrs Gandhi reaches Madras and a correspondent exclaims that in joining her party the Congress (O) people in Tamil Nadu have "responded to her call," she retorts that "they have really responded to the call of Mr Kamaraj." And, as she is now thinking beyond Tamil Nadu, she uses the dead Kamaraj for one final throw: "He had taken the initiative (for the merger) and was hoping some other States would also follow. That is why there was delay."

*Violence*

Even though she is the one who has unleashed the coercive apparatus of the State on a hapless citizenry, she repeats endlessly that the Opposition is the one that had planned violence, murders, kidnappings.

She has been saying since 5 January 1975, that the murder of L.N. Mishra is but "a rehearsal" of which she is "the real target," that it was "a well thought-out political murder." In her address on 26 June 1975, she links this assassination and the attempt on the Chief Justice's life to the activities of the Opposition. Throughout the Emergency—in almost every single public speech of which a record survives—she refers to these incidents, attributes them to the Opposition and insists that there are threats to her life.

She extends this canard. On 17 July 1975 she tells the biennial conference of anti-corruption and CBI officers that the Opposition was bent upon violence, that "the authorities are still finding weapons and bombs not only at RSS headquarters but all over the place." Speaking to Mexican journalists in an interview published on 25 July 1975, she again says that "although the programme given at the meeting itself was non-violent, we had full information that there was another parallel programme. And in fact arms and other things have been recovered."

Even though this is the refrain of her speeches throughout the coming months, the evidence about the weapons and bombs that have been recovered is never disclosed. Indeed, nor is anything disclosed about the alleged political connections of those who have been accused of either the L.N. Mishra murder or the attempt on A.N. Ray's life.

## Evidence

Indeed, Mrs Gandhi's standards of evidence to support her own assertions are very nebulous indeed. Throughout the Emergency, she insists that the opposition to her is receiving "financial, moral and other help" from outside the country. She repeatedly portrays herself as the beseiged heroine who is being encircled by opponents in the pay of foreigners.

But when the question of adducing evidence arises she says that she has no evidence, that such evidence as she has is "circumstantial" consisting of what the US and others did, to take an example nearby, in Chile, that she does not have the counter-intelligence machinery that would enable her to collect the evidence to substantiate her charge. By 1 January 1976, these claims reach their apogee: it is not for her she says to prove foreigners' involvement but for *them* to prove that they have not been providing financial and other support to the Opposition! Nothing surprising in that. After all, under MISA the government does not have to prove that you are a smuggler; you have to prove that you are not. (Have you ever thought how you would prove that you are *not* a smuggler?)

But there is nothing new in these loose standards of evidence. In the late sixties Mrs Gandhi used to publicly claim that she had "faced bullets" in her life. Evidence? You were to dig that up on your own. She used to claim that the Jan Sangh had conspired to kill her. As Rajinder Puri has recorded in *A Crisis of Conscience*, when the Jan Sangh MPs forced the government to produce evidence to substantiate the charge at a Parliamentary Consultative Committee meeting all she could do was to withdraw the allegation.

### An Old Habit

Nor is this a recent habit. In her new book, *Mrs Gandhi's Emergence and Style,* Nayantara Sahgal records that Mrs Gandhi's reports about her entire childhood are coloured by this unfortunate habit. At one point she quotes a remark of Mrs Gandhi about her imprisonment to an interviewer in 1969: "I was regarded so dangerous," Mrs Gandhi tells him, "that I was not even given normal prison facilities." Nayantara Sehgal quotes entry after entry from the diary of one of Mrs Gandhi's fellow prisoners—Mrs Vijayalakshmi Pandit—published in 1946 which shows that "far from being treated as dangerous and deprived of normal facilities, Nehru's daughter received specially courteous treatment."

### Under Oath

Nor should the reader think that Mrs Gandhi is any more particular about facts when she is under oath than she is ordinarily. The long judgment of Justice Sinha establishes again and again that she is as unreliable a witness under oath as otherwise.

She tells Justice Sinha in her written deposition that "rostrums were constructed at some places" where she addressed the meetings. She, however added, Justice Sinha records, "that the rostrums were constructed by private contractors under the direction issued by the State Government and that none of the gazetted officers... were in any manner connected with the construction thereof." Justice Sinha then records "overwhelming evidence" in page after page that establishes that her statement is not true.

Then there are the evasions and somersaults on the question of her tour programme which—unfortunately for her—had been sent to all and sundry and could not, therefore, be hidden.

The evasions and mis-statements reach a climax on the question of the date by which she had in effect become a candidate from Rae Bareily. When her oral testimony about the AICC decision conflicted with her additional written statement, she demurred: "There appears to be some mistake in the averment contained in this paragraph of the additional written statement." She went on to deny that the parliamentary Secretary of the AICC

## An Appropriate, if Unparliamentary, Word

had announced her candidature on 29 January 1971. She was then shown the additional written statement in which she had stated that the announcement had in fact been made. After going through the statement she replied that "even though it was so stated therein, she did not recollect about it." "She was then asked," records Justice Sinha, "whether she could say with certainty that no announcement was made by the All India Congress Committee on 29 January 1971 about her constituency and she only replied that she did not know whether any such announcement was or was not made. Pressed further, she said that she had read the additional written statement before signing it and that, to the best of her ability, she took care that whatever was contained in the additional written statement was true. She, however, added that the language contained in the additional written statement was legal language which she found difficult to clearly understand. All that I would say," concludes Justice Sinha, "is that the statement made by respondent No. I fails to satisfactorily explain the inconsistency."

Proceeding further, Justice Sinha cites a passage from her answers to the interrogatories in which she clearly acknowledges that the decision had been taken by the AICC about her candidature. "All that she said," notes Justice Sinha, "was that the decision was tentative and could be changed by her." When she, however, entered the witness box she took a different stand and said that so far as she knew no decision about her candidature was taken by the All India Congress Committee." When the attention of Mrs Gandhi was invited to the aforesaid reply given on her behalf she again said that she had no knowledge if the All India Congress Committee took even a tentative decision about her constituency. Now, says Justice Sinha, "if she had no knowledge about any such decision, how and under what circumstances it was admitted in reply to the interrogatories served on her, remains unexplained."

A little later a tape of Mrs Gandhi's press conference on 29 December 1970, is played back to her. In it she has been asked whether she was changing her constituency to Gurgaon in view of the fact that "a short while ago there was a meeting of the Opposition leaders and there they said that the Prime Minister is changing her constituency from Rae Bareli to Gurgaon." She answered "No, I am not." When questioned in cross-examination this is what she said about this question and answer: "It is wrong to assume that while giving the reply . . . I conveyed that I was not changing my constituency from Rae Bareli at all and emphatically held out that I would contest election again from Rae Bareli. In my opinion, there is no basis for this assumption." Justice Sinha's laconic conclusion is: "I have given my very careful and dispassionate consideration to the aforesaid reply given by respondent No. I during her cross-examination and I regret my inability to accept it."

And so on and on. No wonder then that Mrs Gandhi's counsel spent so much energy on trying to keep her from having to testify as a witness, from being asked questions and from having to say things under oath.

*New Beginnings*

It is entirely in the fitness of things that the very first sentence of the very first resolution passed by Mrs Gandhi's new party should contain the lie "this convention . . . in which a majority of members of the AICC are also present . . . ."

Like the Emergency this new party associated with Mrs Gandhi's name is born of a lie.

# 7  On Dealing with a Politician*

By her refusal to testify under oath Mrs Gandhi has done more to announce her guilt to the country than anything anyone else could have done.

She has also offended popular sentiment. Our long suffering people are not blood-thirsty. Even those who suffered directly during the Emergency are not thirsting for revenge. But they are a decent people, conscious of right and wrong, of what is honourable and what is not. They expect at the least an honest admission of what went wrong, an open acknowledgement of the sufferings that were heaped upon them.

By walking out on Justice Shah, by her contemptuous attitude, Mrs Gandhi has spat at the people's face.

The spitting *per se* is no surprise. With her pretensions to aristocracy, Mrs Gandhi has always held the people in contempt.

But why has she chosen the boycott as the occasion for reminding the people of her contempt for them? Primarily because, in the face of overwhelming evidence, she could not have sustained the lies she thrust on us during those 19 months. "It is best," she reasons, "that on one excuse or another, I should stay away. Proceeding on overwhelming evidence, Justice Shah

*January, 1978.

will lay bare the facts that I cannot controvert in any case. But by staying away, I will always be able to claim that the verdict is *ex parte*, that I was not given a chance to state my version of the facts." What is one more lie where there has been a torrent already?

"Moreover, the boycott has the incidental advantage of starting a side-show. Instead of having them focus on the main issues that are being bared in the Shah Commission, I will divert the people's attention to peripheral issues. I will drag the Shah Commission to my level—it will then appear to the public as a mere complainant in a local court, rather than as a tribunal searching out the truth. And, then, *I* will be the centre of this drama, not the issues."

So, boycott it is.

This is a pathetic stance. Mrs Gandhi's uncontrite bluster will not fool anyone. Today Mrs Gandhi is the leader of a rump. She tried desperately to capture the Congress, so that she could keep screaming that the only reason her conduct is being bared is to wipe out the Congress. This manoeuvre failed. Now she will be shouting that every Congressman who gives evidence is doing so only to discredit her new party. Her current state is well reflected by the people she was able to muster for shouting slogans on her behalf outside the Shah Commission premises—a miserable fifty or sixty.

Today her followers consist of only two types. First, there are those who are so hopelessly mixed up with her misdeeds that they have nowhere else to go. Caught with her in the interlocking webs of mutual complicity, they will have to stand by her, and she by them. They will be, as they are, the hard-core of any group she now forms.

Second, there are those who have been pushed into her camp by local factional considerations. Thus, if Patil goes to Brahmanand Reddy's group, Urs cannot but walk to her, if Swaran Singh goes one way, Dhillon and Zail Singh cannot but go the other, if Brahmanand Reddy is on one side and Chenna Reddy on the other, Vengal Rao must necessarily be vacilating in between.

What a contrast to 1969. Then Mrs Gandhi was "an issues candidate"—not in fact, but in the minds of many. Many joined her, many boosted her because they thought that she was the great white hope of the Indian revolution. Today not one of her followers is with her for any comparable reason.

"But isn't the crucial difference that she was in power then and is not in power now?" No. The crucial difference is that the people know her better today. Then they had only three years of her record to go by; today, they have eleven.

This record establishes two things beyond doubt. First, she doesn't care two hoots for any issues: she has not fought for office so as to implement some policies; she has espoused policies so that she may capture office. Second, her record establishes—even in the eyes of our professional politicians, accustomed as they are to double dealing and chicanery—that she is not a person anyone can trust.

All this puts her at a low ebb today. But none of it spells her political demise.

The principal determinant of that will be performance of the Janata governments. If things go on sliding the way they have been in Bihar, UP and Madhya Pradesh, people will soon feel—and they will soon start acting on the premise—that their trust has been betrayed. The objective situation will worsen and the more articulate, better organized sections—students, unionized labour—will be ready fuel.

As these are inflamed, the insecurities of the rich, the owners of industry, will be heightened and what they will begin to recall about the Emergency will be its "peace and security." And such are Mrs Gandhi's skills at dissimulation, of functioning at many levels simultaneously—that even as she inflames students and labour, she will project herself as the "law and order" candidate.

Similarly, even as she deploys those sacks of money raked from the rich, she will be projecting herself as the candidate of the poor. This is apparent in the very first moves: that standard invocation of "socialism," a word she has mutilated all these years, the conscious effort to give decorative positions in her party to persons with a lower-class, lower-caste, appeal-to-minorities halo: Buta Singh as General Secretary, Tirpude in Maharashtra, Urs in Karnataka, Narasimha Rao in Andhra. They will count for no more after the elections than have their numerous predecessors, but they are good advertisements till then and so she will make much of them.

The only way for the Janata to counter all this is to do its duties as a government better. The Janata governments should work harder because the people have reposed trust in them and not because Mrs Gandhi is to be neutralized. But the latter will be an incidental and certain consequence. For if the Janata governments work there is nothing Mrs Gandhi can do which will get her back. Conversely, if they fail to work there is nothing that anyone says which will keep her from getting back. The people harassed, betrayed will forget her record, the indictments.

The second danger—and for her the second opportunity—comes from the continuing factionalism within the Janata party. While the speculation is always about whether or not the Central leaders are getting on, the crumbling—if it commences—will start in the States. Joshi in MP has to go for "natural reasons." Trials of strength are on for Devi Lal in Haryana and Shanta Kumar in HP. If these three dominoes fell, will others not sense opportunities in Bihar and UP.? Will the 1967 situation not be recreated? And will she not then be back in the buying and selling trade? And the reason that things in MP, Haryana and Himachal have gone so far without being rectified is that the Janata party secretariats—even the Central office in Delhi, with that considerable reservoir of talent—have not been doing their work: they could have intervened earlier to check the high-handedness of a Devi Lal or the factional sniping at Shanta Kumar. Just as they can now do much more than they are in ensuring that the Yadav and Karpuri Thakur ministries work better.

In fact, one is appalled to see that the party is not moving to take advantage of even obvious opportunities. It too is waiting for others to do its work, it too is waiting for its opponents to commit suicide. Consider, for instance, the case summaries released by the Shah Commission. Any party interested in reforming our public life—or even in the narrow objective of exposing the misdeeds of the Congress governments during the Emergency—would have ensured that each of the case summaries is translated into each of our languages, that they are mailed *gratis* to every primary school teacher, every postman in every village, that is to the communication nodes in our society. If the party is not well enough organized to do even such things—things involving minimal effort and expense—then indeed a great deal of time has been wasted. By now it should have been possible not just to post literature to large numbers but in fact by now *mandals* should have been in place in *mohallas* and villages which could have been actively discussing issues in weekly meetings.

But the basic requirement is not of propaganda and posting literature. It is of work. If the party is to be any different from the Congress, if it is to be any more than a mere electoral machine, it must be organized around work. The party talks of priority to agriculture. Why does it not make it a rule that only those who distinguish themselves in translating this priority into an operational reality will advance within the party? Or take even prohibition. Where is the public education that should be the foundation of such a move? The government and the party are relying exclusively on administrative circulars and legislative resolutions. Hardly the Gandhian way of attaining this Gandhian objective.

So, the party should be built around work. And the party must be build for work. For the transformations the Janata governments have promised our people cannot be achieved by secretariats and legislatures. A party built on work and able to work in every hamlet alone can ensure land reforms, area planning, what have you.

Similarly, the way to convince the Harijans in Andhra and Maharashtra that Narasimha Rao and Tirpude are just decorations that will be discarded soon is not counter propaganda but to field candidates who have actually worked with and for the dispossessed. If the Janata in Andhra consists of even bigger landlords than the Vengal Rao Congress then how will the landless repose trust in it? It is useless complaining about Mrs Gandhi's fraud if one's deeds are no different. To carry conviction with the masses, you must be a party of the masses.

Thus, doing one's work well, deeds that are obviously different from the conduct of the other, the painstaking, patient political education of the people, these are the only ways to deal with a political adversary. To expect that Mrs Gandhi will commit suicide is to pray for manna. To hope that some magistrate will indict her and that will be end of the matter is to play the fool. A politician has to be dealt with politically.

# The Sequel

# 8 Yesterday's Bullies

## WATCH THEM SQUIRM

Yesterday's bullies are scurrying like rats today.

The very persons who were telling us that the facilities in Indian jails are just unbelievably good, that the prisoners are gaining weight, those very persons are securing one anticipatory bail after another, mortified of spending a few nights in the *havalat*.

The very persons who were telling us that there was no reason to feel agitated about the hundreds of thousands they had hurled into jail ("they are just a small proportion of our population"), those very persons are running around destroying records ("just personal files," mind you), those very persons are manufacturing excuses so that they do not have to appear personally in the courts.

The very men who spat insults at generals and admirals, the men of great calm and resourcefulness who, we were told, would weather all storms, in whose hands the country's defence was safe as they were unflappable, those very men now run for cover under their hypertensions and their heart conditions.

And you should hear the stories about their complete collapse inside the lock-ups; of how, even before the interrogators had so much as shouted at them, they fell upon the policemen's feet, of how they howled or mercy, of how they promised to squeal about the Memsahib herself. And how, from the moment he got his bail, each has been trying frantically to find out what the others in the lock-ups have squealed about him.

Strutting around like the cat's whiskers today and grovelling and cringing tomorrow—this is the character of bullies.

We should look at their behaviour closely, not because they deserve attention, but because what is being revealed about them tells us a great deal about our political system.

The important point is not that they are contemptible but that these hollow, contemptible men acquired such authority, such legitimacy in our polity, that they received such acclaim, such deference.

After all, these are the very men before whom Ministers, MPs, civil servants, policemen, academics, editors were prostrating themselves till just a few months ago. These are the men whose fatuous inanities about the Constitution, about defence and development strategies, about the education system, were being imbibed as wisdom.

Why did they appear so tall then? Circumstances and the illiterate people have given the answer: not because they were tall, but because we were on our knees.

Will we commit this lesson to heart so that the next time around equally hollow men reach the top or these very men "stage a comeback," we will see them for what they are? Or, will Ministers and MPs take to paying homage again? Will civil servants again do their bidding—hiding their careerism behind the plea that their service rules bind them to obeying orders? Will our editors again bring out pictorial features about them, about their "dynamism," about their "ability to get things done?"

So, we should observe their behaviour closely and ask what it is in our political system which brought this *kaai* to the top. Is all well with a society which grovels before such men but does not spare so much as a thought for the idealism of young men who, upon being tied to trees, upon a pistol being held to their heads, have the courage to say that if they were freed they would still struggle for the poor?

We should also observe closely the working of the legal system. Observe how many of these fellows get the *Hydrabadi goli*. Observe how they get their anticipatory bails for the asking. Observe, once the cases start, the innumerable clauses and sub-clauses these follows are able to invoke in their favour. And contrast all this with the helplessness of the simple tribal who is dispossessed of his land by the *shahukar* from the plains, who retreats into the forest and clears some land to keep himself from starving, and who is then arrested for violating the Forest Act.

Contrast the clauses that come to their aid with the helplessness of those who have been languishing in jails for seven years as undertrial prisoners.

Contrast the way the law works for them with the way it works for those who, having been acquitted on the charge of having committed a crime, are now facing trial for conspiring to commit the crime for which they have been acquitted.

And while you are at it, count the number of landlords in our vast country who have been sentenced for not paying minimum wages or for exacting a higher-than-legal share of the crop from their tenants.

What does all this tell us about the judiciary, about the legal system? Is he not right then who tells us that "Law is but the convenience of the powerful?" (And incidentally the one who said that was not Mao nor some raving Naxalite. But Gandhi.)

Think too of those ageing buffaloes in the Congress Working Committee. They still do not have the courage to disown these men. In fact, some of them bleat out (yes, these buffaloes bleat) that the Government has no business investigating the embezzlement of six crores as the Congress has not filed any complaint! Not just that: they rush to provide succour circumstantially. They pass a resolution charging "torture" and "third degree methods." Old Bansi the lily-livered, getting oxygen for his asthama, and Snehlata dying inch by inch denied even elementary medical care, dying in harrowing torment from attacks after attacks of the same asthama: who are the torturers?

But what can one expect from these fellows? They are creatures of the men whose character is now unfolding before us. Thus, they are not just hollow men. They are so hollow that even the hollow bullies found them hollower than themselves. The bullies placed them where they are because they were confident that these buffaloes would dance to every tune. Such is the Congress that would be a national alternative! Such is the Congress in whom many had detected a "progressive force"!

The great harm these bullies and these buffaloes have done to our country once again proves the ancient adage: a country need not fear strong men, but it must dread weak men strutting around as strong.

Finally, the pusillanimity of these bullies has a lesson for would-be usurpers too. The Memsahib, on all accounts, was a parlour politician par excellence. In order to survive, such a politician must cut down every man of substance. Soon enough he has weakened all around him. Soon enough he is surrounded only by weak men and henchmen. None of them is now strong enough to challenge him. But, for the same reason, no one is strong enough to help him deliver the goods. Strength in the parlour is weakness in the country.

The dialectic is the nemesis.

## SPINELESS STALWARTS*

The Shah Commission has begun hearings on what is liable to be one of the most important cases before it. The case summary on "Events between 23rd and 25th June, 1975" documents astonishing facts:

- The proclamation of the Emergency had nothing to do with the law and order situation. Fortnightly reports of the Governors to the Presidents and of Chief Secretaries to the Union Home Secretary spoke of the law and order situation being well under control. Thus in telling the President that 'information has reached us which indicates that there is imminent danger to the security of India...' Mrs Gandhi lied.
- Indeed the officers whose job it was, among other things, to keep track of the law and order situation—the Cabinet Secretary, the Home Secretary, Secretary to the P.M., the Director, Intelligence—have all testified that they were not even informed, to say nothing of being consulted. Nor was the Law Minister or his Ministry consulted about the procla-

*December, 1977.

mation. The decision and the proclamation were entirely the work of hacks who had no official or constitutional *locus standi*.

- Preparations for the arrests were begun well before the rally on the afternoon of the 25 June. The close allies of Indira Gandhi—Urs, Vengal Rao, P.C. Sethi, Hardeo Joshi, Bansi Lal, Zail Singh, Kishan Chand and many others—were informed about the decision over a period of at least three days before the proclamation. And yet Indira Gandhi told the President she could not consult the Cabinet because there was no time to do so.
- The President was hustled into signing the proclamation even as he and his Secretary were in the midst of consultations about the constitutionality of the proclamation.
- In the letter she sent to the President, Indira Gandhi tried to insinuate that it was the President who was alarmed at the deteriorating law and order situation and had, therefore, decided to impose the Emergency. Even Fakhruddin demurred at this and so a revised letter was sent subsequently for the records. (But, the reader will recall, Indira Gandhi did not give up this insinuation: the first sentence of her broadcast on 26 June was: 'The President has...,' laying the responsibility on the old man.) Chief Ministers were used as messengers and Air Force planes were misused for what was a political ploy solely to keep an individual in power. The records were fabricated to show the flights as 'training flights.'
- The Cabinet was not consulted even in the most perfunctory manner. Only one Cabinet Minister—the latter day hero, Brahmanand Reddy—was told about the decision. He meekly suggested that as one emergency was already in force, all the arrests etc., could be decreed under it. But when Indira Gandhi stuck to her decision, all he could do was bleat that 'as she knew best what was good for the country...she could take a decision.'

There is a host of other disclosures and it is to be hoped that every citizen will acquaint himself with this crucial case summary.

It is in the context of these startling disclosures—all documented by official records and affidavits—that two recent developments are to be seen: the stand Mrs Gandhi is taking and the stand that Congressmen are taking in the wake of their working Committee's "advice" to boycott the Shah Commission.

Mrs Gandhi has suddenly developed a touching faith in proper procedures, in the dignity of the Parliament, in fundamental rights guaranteed by the Constitution. What a farce.

Her substantive points are two: that the procedure followed by the Shah Commission is not legally justifiable and that, as the Parliament ratified the Emergency proclamation, he cannot look into it.

There is nothing to either of the points.

Under the Commissions of Enquiry Act, the Commission can adopt such procedure as it deems fit. The Act is absolutely unambiguous on this point. Mrs Gandhi complains that no opportunity is being given to cross-examine the witnesses. In fact, by sending written statements—full of half truths and political inuendo—that are widely reported in the press, *she* is the one who is able to have her say and at the same time escape cross-examination.

As for the Parliament ratifying the Emergency, so was the Enabling Act under which Hitler assumed dictatorial powers approved by an overwhelming majority of the Reichstag. And indeed, the record clearly indicates that he followed all the prescribed procedures much more meticulously than Mrs Gandhi and her bunch. Were these facts to preclude any subsequent Commission from examining the genesis of his Emergency, the *mala fide* intentions which underlay it and the use that was subsequently made of it?

Mrs Gandhi has one simple objective and that is to stay away from the Commission as long as she can. She knows that the evidence against her and her clique is irrefutible and that if she comes and lies she will surely be hauled up for perjury.

And the Congress "leaders" are once again being the spineless stalwarts that they are. They are desperate that some one should do their job for them: that some one should put Mrs Gandhi in the locker so that she is off their backs. But they are still too frightened to do anything themselves.

She cracks the whip, the Working Committee passes a resolution and now, pleading helplessness, they refuse to appear.

They have given affidavits. They have been passing tid-bits to the Commission's staff in private. They are praying that the Commission will finish her politically. They know that she, her son, her coterie will abuse and humiliate them as they did in the past. Yet, they refuse to stand up.

Their stand is as indefensible as it is unpardonable. The question today is not whether one individual should or should not appear before the Commission. The hearings are an occassion to educate the country about the manner in which it was hijacked. When these Congressmen are not willing even to help reconstruct the record how can one believe their protestations that they would never let such a tragedy occur again?

The country will rue the day when resolutions of political parties come to determine who should and who should not appear before Commissions of Enquiry. Today these Congressmen are "obeying" a Working Committee resolution "advising" them not to appear before the Shah Commission because, they say, of the dictates of "party discipline." What if the same Working Committee passes a resolution tomorrow that, while they may obey the Commission's summons, they should not say anything prejudicial to Indira Gandhi or to the record of any previous Congress Government?

People often wonder what Mrs Gandhi will do if she ever gets back to power. There can be little doubt that she will act as she did. Whatever the truth about that, there can be no doubt at all that these Congress "leaders" will behave exactly as they did during the Emergency and as they are behaving now: they will be doormats for ever. Rats can't help being rats.

Our only consolation is that Mrs Gandhi will take this whole bunch down with herself. They will drown with her as they do not even have the courage to cry out for help.

"WISDOM OF THE HIND"*

Another day of startling disclosures at the Shah Commission. Indira Gandhi and her coterie decide one fine day that all who oppose her should be put in the locker and kept there. Everyone executes this order without any thought whatsoever. Without any

*December, 1977.

thought, that is, except that unless he executes the decision, he might be inconvenienced. So, it is the other man's freedom, his life, versus my inconvenience, my likely transfer to an inferior posting. The law of the jungle. . . .

The case summary and the evidence establish the unambiguous intention of Indira Gandhi and her clique: get my opponents out of the way and keep them out.

- Therefore, blank, cyclostyled arrest orders are issued with a standard ground for detention that too has been cyclostyled.
- Warrants for arrest, the then ADM (South Delhi) has testified, are filled in by police officials *after* information is received that the person concerned has been arrested.
- In faraway Bangalore, the Commissioner of Police, states in a secret letter that he has passed detention orders against Vajpayee, Advani etc., 'after scrutinizing the material placed before me and satisfying myself regarding the need for their detention.' The records give the lie to this; full two days after this letter, the Home Secretary of the State is still informing Delhi that he is sending 'our special police officer' to Delhi to collect the grounds for detention.
- There is once again the effort of Indira Gandhi and her clique to pass responsibility to others: as Sushil Kumar testified, the Centre is itself empowered under MISA to sign the satisfaction forms, but the usurper's instinct is unfailing—your evil must be done by the hands of others.
- The concerns of officials—officials to whose supposed residual idealism even at that hour JP is appealing—their concerns are evident. Bhiwani Mal, the then IGP (remember his swagger?) tells us: 'What really worried me at that moment was whether we would be able to organize an operation of this magnitude at such short notice.' The Secretary (Law & Judicial, 'Law' and 'Judicial' of all things) is asked his opinion about the use of cyclostyled forms for MISA warrants. His response is not about the morality or propriety of the fascist step. Instead it is that 'there is no specific provision prohibiting use of cyclostyled forms for MISA warrants but the courts generally do not like such practice.' The fastidious courts! Later he is summoned and asked to hang around Raj Niwas in case he is needed. He waits dutifully till 5 A.M. and is not asked for. Next

day he learns what has transpired. And his lament? 'I then felt that I might have been the Law Secretary of the Administration but indeed I was not amongst its confidants.'

But the most important disclosure is that on that fateful night in Delhi *only* 67 persons were taken in under MISA, in Haryana *only* 70 persons, in Andhra *only* 11 persons. And yet the city, the states went dead.

How easy it must have seemed. This lesson will not be lost on the next usurper. And unless our people are fortified by new values, by new organizations so that millions and millions will not play dead just because 67 or 70 or 11 are whisked away, freedom will not be safe.

The disclosures teach many other lessons too.

Laws cannot be framed on the presumption that only good men will administer them. The reader must glance at the solemn assurances that K.C. Pant gave to Parliament in 1971 that MISA would not be misused. There is also that letter which Indira Gandhi wrote to Morarji swearing that she would not use MISA against her political opponents. And yet the apprehensions of each of the Opposition speakers in the parliamentary debates were borne out to the letter. (And K.C. Pant and his ilk who had been doling out the assurances never protested. Her Majesty's loyal *Karamcharies*.)

This lesson should not be forgotten. The debate is once again on about whether MISA should or should not be repealed. Once again some individuals (perhaps no less honourable than K.C. Pant) are doling out assurances that they will not misuse the Act. When you hear the new assurances, recall the old ones.

It is also clear that procedures cannot protect a country from the dictator's bulldozer. There is a revealing sequence in the case summary. Someone, raising a procedural point, says that JP, Morarji etc. should be arrested under Cr. P.C. and not under MISA. He is overruled because arrests under Cr. P.C. would mean that the detenus would have to be produced before courts in a few days. So, it is MISA. But the MISA forms can't be typed soon enough. Use the cyclostyling machine. Even filling in information on the cyclostyled forms is taking time. Well, sign blank orders. The ADM has to be satisfied about the grounds. Order him to take the policeman's word for it. . . .

The sequence vindicates JP's point to the letter: you won't be able to help by raising procedural objections, you will be able to help only when you refuse to obey illegal, immoral orders and are prepared to take the consequences.

The case summary includes a document that Indira Gandhi will use much in the coming months. In this top secret letter she advises Chief Ministers to use the new draconian powers "very sparingly and with the greatest care" and she reminds them of their responsibility to have the detentions reviewed periodically. "Let it not be said that this amending Ordinance is in any way being misused or misapplied." (In the event it is misused wholesale. Of the total arrests under MISA, 80 per cent are under the amended Ordinance. And Bahuguna, virtuous of late, presides over the largest misuse.)

On the basis of this document she will again lament that her only misfortune has been that her lieutenants have never listened to her advice that they be gentle, civil, just. No one will be taken in by this self-serving prattle. If she acknowledges that she knew what was going on, she comes out as unbelievably callous. If she insists that she did not know what was being done, she comes out as unbelievably negligent and incompetent.

But there is an important point to her secret letter and the country should not be so obsessed with establishing her guilt as to miss it. Her guilt and responsibility are, of course, there. But they are not her's alone.

Hundreds and thousands share them. They too must be brought to book. To heap all the blame on her will be gross escapism. And it will be dangerous for our future. For unless the generality of civil servants, of policemen and, indeed, unless the average citizen is made conscious of *his* responsibility in what happened, nothing would have been learnt. The next usurper would find things no more difficult.

The low point of the hearings came early in the day. Indeed, with the very first witness, Inder Gujral, our current Ambassador to Moscow. He typifies the cringing politician who has floated to the top in our country. Deposing ("with the wisdom of the hind," as he said three times) he did all he could to say things in such a manner that he would neither offend his past employer, Mrs Gandhi, nor his current employer, the Janata Government.

The situation in June 1975 was not normal, he said. (To say it was normal would have offended his last employer). But it was not abnormal either. (To say that it was abnormal would have offended his present employer). Was the law and order situation alarming? "Not to my knowledge (that to satisfy his present employers) but (lest this cause offence to his last employer) I was not in charge of law and order, so I would not know." And so on and on. All the way from Moscow, merely to mumble. (One almost begins admiring Kishan Chand for at least now telling it like it was.)

Gujral could not resist a parting mumble. Lest his hedging appear too obvious and offend his current employers, he let it be known while getting up: "But by that it should not be understood that I think the Emergency was justified." I bet that when some sympathizer of Mrs Gandhi confronts him with this sentence, he will exclaim: "But I did not say that I thought the Emergency was unjustified."

Thus is our country represented abroad. By the wise hind.

## ON CONTEMPT AND RESPONSIBILITY*

The Shah Commission hearings are the most important adult education classes in the country today. Even a single day at the hearings is of the greatest value. Each case summary, each question of Justice Shah points to some general issue.

The parade of witnesses is itself instructive. The simple, transparently sincere victims—as on 18 November when the Commission considered the arrests of Bhimsen Sachar and others—and the peacocks of yesterday: the Kishan Chands, the Sushil Kumars, the Bhinders.... We can see these peacocks without their plumage now: men who are nothing without their *gaddies*, their uniforms, the ranks behind their names—LG, DM, DIG (R), SP (CID). The honest, unadorned idealism of the victims contrasts so greatly with the petty evasions of these "officers of the State," with their interminable recourse to "vide DO letter number x, oblique y, stroke z...."

This contrast raises the general question: whom and what

*November, 1977.

should a polity honour; whom and what should it hold in contempt?

We are often told that whatever our differences with individuals who occupy an office, we must not do anything to pull down "the dignity of the office itself." Remember all that shrill chanting about "the dignity of the office of the Prime Minister," about "the supremacy of the Parliament?"

This practice of attaching a halo to the office which is larger than the worth of the individual who occupies it is pernicious. It is a fascist cloak. The only effect of invoking "the dignity of the office" for discrediting or stifling dissent is to protect the person occupying the office.

People will not be free if they are mesmerized by the mystique of an office.

A polity which invokes "the dignity of office" to silence dissent or disagreement is acknowledging the fact that the individuals who occupy the offices of State are no longer able to command the regard of the citizenry by their conduct and now need to be propped up by incantations about "the dignity of their office."

An office, an institution is no more than the persons who man it.

After all, if a bunch of frightened ADMs sign arrest warrants —as each of the ADMs questioned in the Bhimsen Sachar case did—just because some policeman told them to do so, then should the people not hold them in contempt? And how is the "court" which they embody any more than them? Should the "courts" manned by such "magistrates" (what a perversion of the word) not be held in contempt?

If some senile old man (and an opportunist to boot) ratifies a fraudulent emergency, if he puts his seal on to one fascist ordinance after another, one dictatorial "law" after another, should the people not hold him in contempt? (I am thinking of the senile and aged Hindenburg, of course!) And what is his office beside him? Does it make any sense to say that while we may disapprove of what he has done "as an individual," we must respect what he has done "as the President?"

Similarly, when 191 collaborators in the Rajya Sabha raise their hands for the 42nd amendment when they are asked to raise them (the vote was 191 to zero), is their conduct not contemptible? Are *they* any different from *their conduct*? And is the *"institution"*—in this case the Rajya Sabha—any different from *them*?

When the overwhelming majority of judges acted to deprive us of *Habeas Corpus* did they deserve our regard? Did the institution they filled deserve our regard?

To the extent that the institution—the Rajya Sabha or the Supreme Court—was other than the acts of these collaborators, it was so because of the acts of other individuals: those members of the Rajya Sabha whose deeds had led the usurpers to throw them in jail, the single dissenting judge. That is, the institutions were different, they were not wholly tarred only because of the specific acts of other individuals—*not* because of any mystique inherent in the institutions *per se*.

And who is responsible for bringing the institutions into contempt? Not the casual observer who, upon observing the conduct of the MPs, the judges, the President, concludes that they have been reduced to a contemptible level. But the legislators, the magistrates, judges, Presidents whose conduct has actually tarred their offices.

Moreover, does a deed become honourable just because the prescribed procedures have been followed?

At the hearing about the arrests of Bhimsen Sachar and associates, two ADMs admitted that they signed the warrants before the sheet stating the grounds for arrest reached them. But one ADM tried to distinguish his conduct by pleading that he had done so only after the sheet had reached him. (Of course, he, alongwith the other two, admitted that he had done nothing to satisfy himself about the veracity of the alleged "grounds." Each of them said that even if they had wanted to do so, they could not have done so as they had no independent investigating agency at their disposal; they had to rely on what the police told them; so much for the Act which makes a fine point of insisting that a civilian officer and not just a policeman must satisfy himself about the veracity and adequacy of the "grounds for arrests.")

The question is: does the conduct of this ADM become more justifiable, more honourable because he ensured that the sheet of paper stating the "grounds" was with him before he signed the warrant—because he followed the prescribed procedure a bit more than the others?

The more general question is: does the conduct of an officer of State—in this case the ADMs—become honourable just because he is following orders—in this case, of the DM?

The point is best seen by viewing an extreme case: not just of imprisonment—as in the Bhimsen Sachar case—but of extermination—as in the case of the Jews in Nazi Europe.

Now, two facts are noteworthy.

First, three decades of meticulous search have failed to turn up a single written order of Hitler specifically directing anyone to exterminate the Jews. Not a single written document bearing his signatures or in his hand.

Does this fact absolve Hitler of the responsibility for what happened? In settling this question are we to go by the absence of a written document or by the general ideological framework that Hitler had created for the regime, by the brutal state that he had fashioned, by the oral exhortations he hurled at his subordinates about the "final solution" (and about which written evidence exists in the diaries and minutes of discussions kept by Himmler, Goering, Speer, Heydrich etc., and to which many— e.g., Eichman, Speer etc.,—later testified), by the well-documented and well-publicized attention he gave to details in the case of other matters which were much less central to his vision of the new world (for instance, by the attention he paid to the details of Speer's architectural plans)? So much for the relevance of written documents for establishing the culpability of the head of the government—whether it is a Hitler or an Indira Gandhi.

The second point is that just as no written document exists recording Hitler's orders, a number of written orders, decrees "laws," inter-ministerial "agreements" exist prescribing not just the general policy of extermination but the details of how this was to be done. These orders, decrees etc., are signed by the highest officers of the Reich—Himmler, Heydrich, Thierack (the latter being the State Minister for, of all things, Justice) and others.

Thus, for instance, there is the decree dated 16 February, 1942, by Himmler "concerning (individuals) of German stock in Poland." It authorizes that their children should be taken from them and sent to families "that are willing (to accept them) without reservations, out of love for the good blood in them." There is the inter-ministerial agreement of 1942 between Himmler and Thierack, the Minister of Justice, that certain categories of prisoners could be "worked to death." There was another "agreement" between Himmler and the President of the Reichsbank that all valuables recovered from the dying Jews—the melted gold fillings from their teeth, rings, watches etc.,—were to be deposited into an account of the SS bearing a cover name. Similarly, there were formal orders permitting the use of Jews for medical experiments. There was a formal, detailed, written plan, called the Plan for the Extraordinary Pacification Action, which spelled out the details for exterminating the Polish intelligentsia. There were formal orders decreeing the murder of "mentally ill" Germans. And so on and on. There was literally a plethora of written orders.

Now the point is: is the action of officials of the Reich who kidnapped forty to fifty thousand Polish children under the decree of 16 February 1942 to be condoned just because they were carrying out written orders? Or is the action of the SS personnel who exterminated almost 6 million to be condoned because they were merely implementing Himmler's orders or inter-ministerial agreements between Himmler and the Reich's Minister of Justice? Or is the action of the various "doctors" who, invariably without any anaesthetics, subjected their hapless victims to increasing air pressure or increasing cold till their lungs burst, till they froze to death, or who used them for bone grafting experiments, who inflicted gas gangerene wounds on them—are these to be condoned just because all this was done on a written authorization? Is the murder of 70,000 "mentally ill" persons humane just because there was a written order that this be done?

The lesson of history is clear: no head of government can evade responsibility on the plea that no written document bearing his or her signature can be found ordering the heinous acts; and no officer lower down the line can evade responsibility for a heinous act merely because he can produce a written order from a higher up.

"But will ordered administration not become impossible if everyone starts deciding things for himself?"

No. The presumption underlying the question is either that

ordered administration requires people to do unreasonable things and that, being reasonable, decent people, they will refuse to do them if they are encouraged to think for themselves or the presumption is that most people are so unreasonable, so perverse that while administration requires only reasonable things to be done, being perverse, officers of State will not do them and, therefore, they should be conditioned to obeying orders thoughtlessly. Neither presumption is defensible. Over the years not thinking for oneself has become an alibi for passing the buck, for evading responsibility, for not being innovative, for sheer laziness, for covering one's tracks.

A more fundamental point is involved too: a society that can keep going only by conditioning its officers of State to stop thinking for themselves has rotted at the core; it is many steps towards authoritarianism already; at each crisis it will be plunged into atrocities and inhuman conduct; in modern times—what with the sophisticated technology, with the armed apparatus at the command of the officers of State—it will be literally defenceless against barbaric conduct.

The lessons, thus, are clear: for a polity to be free, no officer of State must abdicate his duty to think for himself; second, its citizenry must know that each act of every officer of the State must be judged in itself—the fact that a good man has performed it does not make it good necessarily, the fact that someone has ordered it does not make it honourable by itself, the fact that in performing it the prescribed procedures have been followed does not add to its intrinsic worth; third, the citizenry must know an individual—a leader, an officer of the State—by his deeds alone, not by the office he holds, not by his lineage; and, finally, the citizenry must know that an institution, an office, is no more than the individuals who man it, it deserves no more deference than it acquires by their conduct.

# 9 Kidnapped, Not Arrested*

The case summaries about detentions in Delhi establish that citizens were not arrested during the Emergency, they were kidnapped.

Consider the facts these case-summaries reveal:

- Magistrates sign partially filled and even blank warrants.
- They sign warrants when they know that the grounds are vague and insufficient; they sign the warrants even when they know that there are no grounds at all for arresting the victim. Indeed, they tell us that they took it to be a part of their jobs, of their duties, to fabricate these grounds. "We were also told...," says one of them on oath, "that in case the grounds in any particular case were considered inadequate by us, we should fabricate such grounds as might be felt by us to be sufficient...."
- Persons are picked up on warrants signed by magistrates who have no jurisdiction over the areas in which the victims reside.
- Material on which the grounds for arrest are to be based is furnished many days *after* the person has been locked up and it is then ante-dated.

*February, 1978.

- Lists of persons who are to be picked up are unsigned, they are often conveyed orally, even over telephones.
- The Act says that the detention of a person must be reviewed by the State Government within 15 days of a person's detention; it becomes the "policy" to dispense with this formality among others and to routinely ante-date the grounds as having been put up within the stipulated period.
- A "policy" is laid down that magistrates should consider whatever grounds are furnished by the police as "adequate" when, as the police and intelligence men now tell us, the police itself knew that the grounds were flismy, invented and often entirely non-existent.
- People are hurled into prisons because they offend some courtier—an Arjun Das, an Ambika Soni—or just, as in four representative arrests the Intelligence Bureau reported even at that time, "to oblige a cloth merchant."
- The statutory four monthly review of detentions is reduced to being an empty face and decisions about the fate of citizens are taken when a courtier—the punk, Navin Chawla—lunches with a lady of the court—"Ambi" as he calls her—at the Maidens Hotel.
- The advice of courts, their strictures, their decisions are routinely disregarded: a court asks for a report in three weeks, the report is never furnished; it says someone should be released, he continues in detention; it issues summons asking that a prisoner should be produced before it, mere jailers disregard the summons; it pronounces some detentions 'illegal' and adds for good measure that they exemplify nothing but 'plain, simple, high-handedness,' '*Nadarshahi* of the government'; the strictures have no effect on the government; a High Court directs that parole be given and is put in its place by two lines from a two-bit officer: 'in view of the decision of the LG very recently...rejecting the request for parole, there is no question of recommending the request only on the direction of the High Court'; when the High Court presses for a parole the LG thunders on the file that his government should have the Supreme Court expunge the remarks of the High Court and have it 'give a categoric ruling that the High Court should not impinge on the jurisdiction of Parliament which is implemented through the Adminis-

stration; by the next sentence his thunder becomes ominous: 'the persistence in its attitude by the High Court will unfortunately lead to an unseemly confrontation....'

● An ADM avers that he orders the detention of a journalist because the DM tells him that 'this person has incurred the displeasure of Smt. Ambika Soni'; the records show that the person is not an activist, the Intelligence Bureau reports that 'he does not belong to any political party'; in spite of all this the ADM has no difficulty in putting his signatures to a long and elaborate lie. 'Shri Virendra Kapoor is an active worker of RSS/BJS. The RSS organization has been banned by Government for having indulged in subversive activities. He is reported to be indulging in undesirable and subversive activities. He has been holding secret meetings against the Government. His activities are prejudicial to the internal security of India. He is an active supporter of the movement launched by Shri Jai Prakash Narain against the Government. He is a potential danger to the security of the State. He is a trouble maker and expert in exploiting the situation. He devotes his time and resources in making propagananda against the Government....'

● Once in the clutches of the 'law,' the victim passes from hardship to hardship, from humiliation to humiliation: he is shunted off from Tihar jail to the jail in Bareilly; there the jailers insist that he must have some connection with the criminals who broke out of Delhi jail and so put him in solitary confinement in a tiny cell, they subject him to various humiliations and put him on to 'C-class food'; he narrowly misses being put into leg irons....

● In another case, the alibi of the ADM for the manifest untenability of the grounds now is that he signed the detention order "without reading the document."

● An innocent student is kidnapped because he is thought to be someone else; all concerned soon realize the mistake; but again and again they confirm the continued detention of the poor fellow as being necessary for the security of the country.

● Unknown to hundreds of thousands of citizens 'records' about them are built up over the years; these records—untrue from beginning to the end—form to this day the basis of 'police verifications' that may determine whether you get a job that you otherwise deserve or not; these records are the handy raw material from which ingenuous accounts of your subversive activities are fabricated at a moment's notice.

Even with all this homework, the grounds are comic, though their consequences are cruel: an 83 year old author who, as an SDM put the matter at that time, 'could hardly see when he appeared in court,' is shunted off to prison on the grounds that three and a half years earlier 'he alongwith others expressed concern over the continued decrease in Hindu population due to the family planning scheme,' because three years earlier he went in a procession to the PM's house 'whereat along with others he criticized the government in the usual strain,' because three years earlier 'he resigned from the Jan Sangh and joined Lok Tantrik Sangh formed by Balraj Madhok,' because three years earlier in a public meeting 'he alongwith others paid tributes to the freedom fighters who sacrificed their lives for the country's independence...'; and a magistrate signs these grounds thus fulfilling the requirement of the Act that the detention order is based on 'the subjective satisfaction' of the detaining authority about the adequacy of the grounds.

Are these detentions "arrests" or they "kidnappings"? In what sense are our policemen guardians of "law" and "order"? What "law" and what "order"? Guardians or habitual violaters? Are our magistrates dispensing justice or are they busy "legalizing" crimes of the State-apparatus? Which is the party of violence in our country: the ghost of the CP-ML or the police? Who is the recruiter of "extremists" in our country: the RSS *pracharak*, the CP-ML cell-leader or the State apparatus itself?

## THE GUARDIANS OF LAW*

We cannot even begin to determine what needs to be done about the criminal habits of the State apparatus until we get two false notions out of our heads: the notions that these criminalities occurred because some administrative arrangements were inade-

*February, 1978.

quate or because some provisions of the law were deficient.

One ADM after another, for instance, has said that he could not but take the grounds for detention furnished by the police at face value because he had no independent investigative agency to verify the grounds.

What if these ADMs had their "independent investigative agencies"? Would that have made any difference whatever? After all, there is no reason to presume that their particular investigative agencies would have resisted being misused when no other investigative agency showed any such resistance. Moreover, is it really the fact that these ADMs certified the grounds of detention just because they did not know that the grounds were fabricated? Have they not themselves testified, one after the other, that they were fully aware that the grounds were "vague," "insufficient," "inadequate," "fabricated," "invented," "non-existent," suffering from "fatal illegalities"—to recall just a few of the expressions they have themselves used?

Therefore, we should not feel reassured tomorrow if the new Government were to say that "it has taken adequate steps" to prevent this particular lapse because, for instance, it has furnished these ADMs with an "independent investigative agency" each.

Second, the crimes did not occur because MISA or some other statute was deficient.

After all, MISA does insist that the magistrate satisfy himself about the adequacy and veracity of the grounds for detention. It is the magistrates who chose to obey the Bhinders and the Bajwas. The statute does provide for a four monthly review of the detention of a person. The individuals in the review committee chose to be dumb ciphers.

No police manual authorizes third degree methods. No jail manual authorizes torture. No law required the outgoing Chief Justice to certify that the prisoners were being looked after "with maternal care." Nor did any statute require the new Chief Justice to hold that to insist that prisoners had a right to approach the courts when the executive did not want them to do so would be wrong as it would amount to doubting the intentions of the executive.

No statute required any of this. Moreover, the usurper never has any difficulty altering the statutes according to his convenience. The detention cases provide yet another instance of this truth.

A law Secretary is asked to review the arrests and help prepare the grounds of detention. He finds that "in a majority of cases there were no grounds at all and in others the grounds were flimsy and inadequate. I told the administration," he states, "that the detention orders could not be sustained....Some attempt was made to make up the deficiencies with the help of the CID and other police agencies but no tangible results could be achieved...." Did any of this embarass the usurpers? Not at all. They just decreed a new "law" that dispensed with the requirement of having to show the victim or the courts the grounds for detention.

To add falsehood to arbitrariness, they insisted in court after court that they were keeping the grounds secret—not to hide their patent untenability, not at all, my lord—but only because disclosing them would jeopardize the security of the State.

The failure then was not of administrative arrangements or of statutory lacunae. The failure was of individuals. They did not lack information. They did not lack statutory authority. They lacked guts.

The usurpers—the Bhinders, the Bajwas, the Navin Chawlas—were, of course, responsible for the crimes. But so were all those who abdicated all the formal authority that went with their offices.

No one exemplified these abdicators better than the pitiable Kishan Chand the then Lieutenant Governor of Delhi. The detention cases establish him as a callous toady.

Do you think that is too harsh an expression?

Consider first the evidence of his callousness.

A prisoner's brother dies. He applies for parole to help his brother's family and attend to other formalities. Kishan Chand rejects the application saying that "since...the last rites would have been performed by this time, no usual purpose would be served in giving parole to the detenu."

A prisoner's condition deteriorates at an alarming rate in prison. He does not respond to treatment. A doctor to whom the case is referred certifies that he is suffering from "acute liver disease" and is seriously ill. Kishan Chand rejects the application for parole on the grounds that "the detenu is not in any imminent danger of life."

In the case of an aged patient, who applies for parole on medical grounds, the jail doctor certifies that "the patient will need surgical treatment as soon as possible." The file journeys for 45 days. Later, after another application for parole is submitted, the case is referred to a physician. She records:

> 'His main disability is frequent attacks of dizziness which are very incapacitating. This has been attributed to insufficiency of blood supply to the brain from narrowing of blood vessels. He has other evidence of cerebro-vascular disease in the way of considerable loss of memory and endigenous depression. In addition, he has severe disease of the bones of the cervical region with pain and enlargement of the prostate gland with urinary symptoms. In view of his age and the multiple disabilities he has, he may be considered for release on parole.'

But Kishan Chand is unmoved: "Since these diseases are not of recent origin, release of the detenu on parole is not necessary for providing medical treatment to him."

Someone's close relative is stricken with cancer. He is refused parole for even three days to see the relative.

In case after case Kishan Chand turns down the advice of courts, of the central Ministry of Home Affairs, advice which would have resulted in a little more compassionate treatment of the hapless victims.

But while he—like all the functionaries he typifies—is strong to the weak, he—also like his tribe—is weak to the strong. He is a toady to them.

Someone is arrested for smuggling antiques. He has several CBI cases against him. He has been arrested for smuggling a year earlier also. He manages to get out on parole for a week because he says his wife is unwell. Kishan Chand rejects his request for extending the parole, noting:

> 'The detenu, Shri B.R. Sharma is a notorious smuggler in antiques. Simply because his wife had developed suicidal disposition is not a sufficient ground for extending his parole. The proper course would be that his wife gets appropriate

medical treatment. The request for the extension of the detenu's parole is accordingly rejected.'

Five days later he is asked, without being furnished any new material, to reconsider his decision. He now extends the parole "on compassionate grounds."

The smuggler continues to obtain one extension of his parole after another. Restrictions on his movements too are removed in due course.

At last the Review Committee says that the latest request for extension of the parole should be rejected. Kishan Chand rejects it. The next day, the very next day, the same officer sends him a note saying that he should approve the extension. He approves it.

Just a little later, he is not just approving extensions he, in a literal parody of his earlier note, is recommending that the detention order itself should be revoked:

'In view of the fact that the wife of the detenu, Shri Bali Ram Sharma, has developed suicidal tendencies and her condition continues to be precarious, I would again submit that the detention order of Shri Bali Ram Sharma under COFEPOSA may be revoked. As I had submitted in my earlier note of 16.11.77 it will suffice if Shri Sharma is proceeded against under the case registered against him under Sections 379/411 for having concealed a number of antiques for smuggling purposes in his farm at Chhatarpur which was raided by the local police on 26th September 1975 and for which there appears to be ample evidence.'

Needless to say, the smuggler continues on parole throughout the Emergency and is finally released two days before the election results. So much for the much trumpeted use of MISA against smugglers.

Another person, detained for his involvement in cases of cheating and forgery, gets parole even without applying for it.

Yet another lucky fellow is arrested because of his involvement in several cases under the Gambling Act, the Opium Act, the Excise Act and several other acts. Kishan Chand insists that the fellow be detained under MISA even though his officers tell him repeatedly that ordinary criminals cannot be detained under MISA. He confirms the detention and reconfirms the continued detention four months later.

But now arrives a short epistle from the redoubtable Bhinder: "We find that this criminal is quite old and has also written a letter of apology. It is, therefore, recommended that he may please be released so that he is given a chance to lead a normal life."

The Chief Secretary—not one to take up cudgels with Bhinder—sends the file to Kishan Chand with the non-commital note: "If approved this case may first be placed before the Screening Committee."

But Kishan Chand will have none of this pussy-footing. He orders the release forthwith: "We should be guided by what DIG(R) says and agree to his release."

We thus have usurpers on the one hand and callous toadies on the other with timid careerists in between.

And the new government tries to put us to sleep with the lullaby that it is ensuring that henceforth the Preventive Detention Act will not be misused; the new clauses, it tells us, will see to that.

But it wasn't the absence of these clauses which landed one hundred thousand in prison the last time.

## THREE MODEST PROPOSALS*

Proposals for making the police and bureaucracy safe for our people must reckon with one cardinal fact.

This fact is that the arbitrariness, callousness and toadyism which have been revealed in the detention cases are not exceptional aberrations. They are the stock-in-trade of our police and administration.

We do not get to hear as often about them in part because these features, even though they are inflicted on the poor day in and day out, do not affect persons of our class often in normal times; and in part because commissions as thorough, as expeditous

*February, 1978.

and as conscientous as the Shah Commission are themselves exceptional in our country.

Anyone having the slightest acquaintance with the police, for instance, knows that, even though much good work is done, arbitrariness, callousness, being on the right side of the rich and well-connected, toadying to one's bosses, are the staples of a police career.

The new recruit is weaned on illegality, he matures in a culture of illegality and by the time he reaches a position of responsibility he knows down to his very bones that the pliant magistracy will always legalize his illegalities.

Bribes, it seems, are necessary for recruitment. In 1975-76 a scandal broke out about the recruitment of sub-inspectors to the Delhi police: it seems that aspirants for the posts had paid sums as high as Rs 12,000 to Rs 14,000; and the only reason we got a glimpse into this state of affairs was that some who had paid the asking price were not included in the list of successful candidates. Will a person who has paid such an entrance fee be honest in his dealings with the public?

Posts are auctioned and policemen at all levels testify that the "cuts" travel all the way to very high-ups.

Policemen regularly receive fixed *haftas* and monthly charges from shopkeepers, touts, gamblers and others. These, they say, are shared, once again, with officers at very senior levels. Indeed, these are the one set of "taxes" which the shopkeepers etc., just have to pay on time. Penalties for delay or foot-dragging are certain and swift.

Policemen and young officers grow up in the service seeing their seniors accept bribes, indeed they grow up collecting money and other perquisites for their bosses, they grow up seeing the latter misuse governmental facilities—the office car, the office phone, the retinue of official attendants—for personal ends. As they grow in the service they come to know that their promotions, their postings to lucrative assignments, all depend on how well they serve—not the people—but their bosses.

How can they be expected to respect abstract notions of "law," properiety, civility, service?

The senior officers do not mind, they even encourage illegal and arbitrary conduct of their subordinates just as the politicians do not mind and even encourage the illegal and arbitrary behaviour of senior officers. Firstly, the well-being, the "cuts" of the superiors directly depend on the malfeasance of the subordinates and, secondly, they know that only the compromised subordinate—the man who has much to hide—is a reliable instrument.

Given this culture, we must realize that we are dealing with mercenaries: they will desist from evil behaviour, from conduct that harms the citizenry, only if the penalties for doing so are terrible.

This is the first clue about what needs to be done once the commissions have completed their work.

The only way to prevent such arbitrariness, callousness and illegalities in the future is to mete out exemplary punishment to those who have been responsible for them in the past. There is only one way to keep the Andhra policeman from killing young boys and girls in cold blood and lying that the deaths occurred in "encounters" and that is to ensure that a dozen of the guilty are actually indicted and punished for murder.

What is true of the police is true of every other service also.

The second thing we need to do is to ensure fuller public disclosure about the conduct of the state apparatus *vis-a-vis* human rights.

The principle here should be of *automatic* disclosure of the relevant information.

Thus, for instance, each jail must be asked to publish every month a complete list of prisoners, their current status (whether they are being held as under-trial prisoners, whether they have been convicted etc.), the crimes for which they are being held, the period each has already served, the special conditions which have been imposed on the person (e.g., is he in solitary confinement, has he been put into iron legs etc.), whether he is in need of and is receiving medical attention and so on. The statement must also contain details about the jail as a whole: the number of persons it can accommodate, the number of taps, latrines etc., the average quantities and types of food that have been served to the prisoners and so on. These lists must be published and they must be made available to the prisoners.

Do not let anyone bamboozle you into thinking that the publication of these data will cost a great deal. The data are already available with every jail warden. Publishing them will cost almost nothing, specially when the cost is compared to what we spend on, for instance, the police apparatus. And this is the one part of our expenditure under the head "Law and Order" which will be well spent. When expenditure under this head increases, it usually means that the police establishment or the jail establishment have been enlarged. The insignificant increase proposed here will help inform the citizens as to what is happening to their brothers and sisters rotting in the jails.

As first steps in this matter of full disclosure I propose we start with the following.

First, all governments should hold a census of all prisoners in jails on a given day—for instance, May 1 this year. The census should cover the sort of items that have been listed above. The census will reveal vital and surprising information and in addition, it will provide a bench-mark on which the periodic releases of data proposed earlier can be based.

Second, police records that have been accumulated against all political activists over the past, say, ten years should be mailed to each of the subjects. Recent revelations have clearly established their tendentious intent, their fraudulent contents as well as the misuse to which they can be put.

There is no danger to the security of our country in following this course. It is perfectly possible to separate the police records of smugglers, spies and the like from those of political activists and to release only the latter. Indeed, the police and intelligence agencies already keep these records in separate categories. No complicated exercise will be required.

The extent to which the new governments resist such a demand, to that extent we should know that they are no different from the old governments: to that extent we should know that they too are continuing to compile identical records about individual citizens, to that extent we can be certain that they too will use them for the same purposes as their predecessors.

The proposal is a litmus paper. Its consequences are greater for the governments—for their accepting or resisting such proposals will tell us a good bit about them—than for us as citizens. Indeed, one thing about these police records that the current disclosures prove is that no honest political activist need fear them in the least. When a regime decides to pick him up it will not go by the facts of what he has been doing. It will just pick him up and concoct stories—from fabricated records if these are available, without them if they are not.

My third proposal is related to the second. Groups of responsible citizens—members of Parliament, some judges, civil rights activists—must be allowed full access to jails so that they may inspect the conditions for themselves and also check the veracity of what is being put out by the jail administrations.

"But how will any of this prevent the usurper? He will just suspend the publication of such data. He will just stop allowing your 'responsible citizens' from visiting the jails."

He will indeed But that is not a fatal argument against the proposal.

First, his stopping all such releases will itself constitute a visible and important signal to the populace, a signal that things are not normal any longer.

But the second reason is the more important one: the sorts of things we have come to know during the Emergency are the daily life of thousands and thousands in our prisons today. So, the information flow, the access to jails will perform a very useful function in the years before the usurper takes over. We should not be so obsessed with the emergencies as to stop attempting to alleviate suffering in the periods between the emergencies.

The usefulness of the data cannot be denied. They will force us to look at the horrors that Mary Tyler and others have described. They will at once inform us that many are even today rotting in Andhra's jails as under-trial prisoners, that they have been held as under-trial prisoners for periods as long as seven years. They would focus our attention at once on heinous practices—such as the one of rounding up young boys whenever the jailers want extra labour—that are now being revealed.

There are many other proposals that one can list, of course: setting up of committees to oversee the work of our police and intelligence agencies, for one. But I have much less faith in them than in punishment of those in the state apparatus who are proven guilty in this round, in requiring automatic disclosure of information and in ensuring access to jails and police lock-ups.

We can be certain that no government will legislate any of these proposals till it is compelled to do so. After all, there has been a purpose in reducing the police and the bureaucracy to the present immoral state over the years: the ruling groups, the successive governments have not been solving our basic problems and have needed unthinking instruments which will help them put the lid on the problems. Therefore, the present governments too would want things to continue as they have done in the past.

Even modest proposals, therefore, will have to be fought for every inch of the way. This is the challenge for civil rights groups, for Bar Councils and the like. They must mobilize public opinion and compel reluctant governments to enact these and similar proposals.

For these are matters of life and death. And there isn't much time.

# 10 The Shah Commission and Our Future*

With the conclusion of the demolition cases the first round of the Shah Commission's hearings has come to an end.

By their equanimity and patience, their diligence, their sense of fair play, Justice Shah and his excellent team have proven that they can deal with all direct challenges to the Commission —whether these be in the form of Indira Gandhi's cheap theatre or Charan Singh's presumptuous pronouncements.

The real danger for the Commission, therefore, does not come from these sources but from the fact that the people's interest in the proceedings may sag over the coming months, that for various reasons they may fail to see the terrible significance that these proceedings have for their day-to-day lives. This is specially so because as the long cross-examinations start, as the swarms of lawyers (those master obfuscators) get into the act, the hearings will become less and less spectacular, less and less "newsworthy."

There are many who pray for the *denoument:* not just Indira Gandhi and her shrinking clique but all those who are today being undressed in public—the politicians, policemen, civil servants. And I do not mean just the officers etc., whose direct

*December, 1977.

involvement in the crimes is being bared. I mean the walking dead in the Congress, I mean the police and civil administration as a whole. A very numerous and well-connected lot.

For thirty years they have strutted around by overawing the people, by making themselves out to be larger-than-life, by making themselves out to be little Ceasars and little Solomons. They are now being exposed for what they have in fact been: often cringing toadies and careerists, scoundrels and criminals sometimes.

They cannot bear their camouflage being ripped off. They desperately want the hearings to stop or the public to stop paying attention to them.

We must consider the reasons on account of which their desperate prayers may well come true. And we must find ways of dealing with them. For were the public attention to waver, were it to fail to see the relevance of these proceedings to its day-to-day life, the outcome would not just be a tragedy, it would be fatal.

"But this government is doing nothing except holding inquiries after inquiries. Shouldn't it stop squandering its energies on these and start dealing with rising prices, strikes, production and the like?"

Whether the government is doing something about prices, production and the like or not is a debatable matter. But one thing is not debatable: if the government is not doing anything about these matters it is not because it is pre-occupied with the commissions. By implying the contrary, its critics are in fact being too generous to the government; they are providing it the alibi of the commissions. If the economic ministries fail to formulate or implement coherent policies, or if the governments in Bihar and U.P. fail to govern, it is surely not because the ministers or officials concerned are busy assisting the Shah commission.

"But how long must we go on raking up the past? We spent years and years wailing about the British. Are we now to spend years wailing about Indira Gandhi?"

The work of the Shah Commission is important—and it deserves the unwavering attention of every citizen—precisely because it is *not* about our past. But about our future. Events of the recent past are but an occasion for us to construct a text, a

## The Shah Commission and Our Future

guide that may help us avoid similar catastrophes tomorrow.

"But it is clear as daylight that Indira Gandhi and a handful committed terrible crimes against the country and the people. Why not just throw them into the slammer and get it over with? Why go on and on with this interminable legal business?"

Such impatience—often most vocally expressed by those who kept silent during the Emergency—is entirely misplaced. What we have been through is a comprehensive collapse of the system and the foundations of a liberal polity are by no means secure. If a few individuals come to be punished, they are to be dealt with merely as visible symbols of what was and is wrong.

The hearings are important because they go beyond the question of establishing the guilt of individuals—they are educating us about the system: can the Constitution be fortified; must our officials obey all orders; indeed, must they obey orders even if they are—as the Police Act would have it—"legally given"; can they escape the consequences of their acts merely by producing a file that contains a written order from a higher-up; can a higher-up escape responsibility merely because no written order in his or her hand can be found; what does the "supremacy of the Parliament" mean when that round building is full of supine collaborators; what is the role of the judiciary—is it to go by the letter of each law with the small "l" (no *habeas corpus* if there is a "law" saying "no *habeas corpus*") or is it to upheld the rule of Law with the capital "L"; is freedom safe when the seniormost police officers take to behaving like armed criminals rather than as upholders of the law, when they start fudging records, lying, conspiring to hide the truth, as if all this was just a routine day's work? And so on. The hearings are the occasion for us to consider and debate such fundamental questions.

Indeed, their significance in this respect goes far beyond these specific questions. Their most important contribution today is to expose our rulers, to de-mythologize them. A people cannot be free if they hold their rulers in awe as demi-gods. They will be free only so long as they are a bit contemptuous of their rulers.

The hearings are helping cut the rulers to size. This is the very first step in a people's political education.

"But you keep talking about the system. The poor don't even have enough to eat. What are the Janata governments doing about food, about jobs, about prices?"

We must pay attention to the commissions not because of the Janata governments but—if it comes to that—in spite of them.

Indeed, one of the greatest dangers is that either the failure of some governments to deal with economic and other problems or the fact that some of them may start conducting themselves in a manner that is no different from the Congress governments, that one of these will lead the people to dismiss the work of the commissions with the shrug: "Why go on about the commissions, the governments are not going to do anything in any case? What is so strange about the disclosures in the Shah Commission? If you enjoy disclosures of that kind all you have to do is to visit Haryana today."

We must remember that the outcome of the commissions is much more important for our future as citizens than for the future of the Janata governments. Indeed, I am certain that at least some of the reforms that the commissions will recommend will have to be fought for by the citizens—governments in general, whether Janata or not, will find them inconvenient, they will want to shelve or dilute them; the people will have to insist that they are put into effect.

When will we learn this lession, that our fate does not depend on what governments do or not but on what we do? Remember all those lectures of the election campaign about how one of the first things the new governments do would be to improve our jails? "We have seen the appalling conditions at first hand, we have suffered from the lack of medical care, from the filth and overcrowding. We vow we will make our jails reformatories." And in that flush of emotion, all this was sincerely meant. But have you heard any reports lately of which government has done what to improve our jails?

When J.P. says that *Lok Shakti* must be organized, that it must be harnessed, he is not just mouthing a slogan. He is spelling out the difference between life and death.

Nor should we be misled for a moment by the fascist talk of the middle classes and the rich who try to pooh-pooh the commissions by exclaiming, "what is the use of all this when the poor are starving?"

When power is so concentrated in the hands of the rich and the middle classes as it is in our country today, it is the poor who

## The Shah Commission and Our Future

need an open society most. Ever heard of a rich man being forcibly sterilized? Of the seven lakhs who were uprooted by the demolition squads, how many were rich, how many were Secretaries and Joint Secretaries?

Finally, we should not let the theatre Mrs Gandhi may stage distract us. What if she now files a writ? What if she refuses the summons? (The fact that she would be doing so after having earlier told Justice Shah that she will come when summoned will only mean that she is being true to form). Warrants will then be issued. What if she again insists on being arrested and on being trucked to the Commission? And then refuses to answer any questions?

There will be much drama. What will be her purpose in staging it? Merely to make the people focus on her rather than on the issues that are coming up, on the questions she has to answer, on the answers (evasive?, untruthful?, circumlocutory?) she is giving or not giving.

The citizens must refuse to be parties to the drama, even as onlookers. Indeed, it would be best if all except those who have some actual function to perform at the hearings stay away on the days on which she is to come and on which she may stage the theatre. Oblivion—nothing would be better than oblivion, an actress left with no one to watch her performance.

# New Beginnings

## 11  Intellectuals and the Interregnum*

The Emergency forced us to look at ourselves, as if in a mirror. I would presume that most of us fell a few notches in our self-esteem.

If one goes by what our friends and colleagues are now telling us about their "true feelings" about the Emergency, about how intolerable it all was, about how they always knew that all that propaganda was balderdash, about how they knew from the very beginning that the dictatorship was "not viable"—if one goes by all this and more, one would have to conclude that almost everyone was outraged and incensed all along. And yet, anyone who tried getting a few elementary, riskless things done—to sign a statement or two, to write an article, howsoever oblique, to write for a cyclostyled news-sheet, to carry messages or material—knows how few were prepared to do anything. All those "true feelings," all that outrage, all that inside information, all that precognition, and no deed? *"Yahan to Bhai,"* as the Acharya would say, *"baat hi ka kaam hai, kaam ki baat nahin."*

We are fair-weather revolutionaries. How radical our conversation, how strident our voices, how vivid our accounts of Giap and Ho, when the sky is clear. And how quickly we become

*July, 1977.

"just academics" when the clouds gather, how quickly we remember that we are just "men of letters," how demanding our teaching load suddenly becomes, how practical our concerns then, how hoarse and low our whispers.

'And did it take all that much to crush us? Fifty or so of the most audacious people were deprived of work in their professions. A few were expelled from the party, a few from the unions, and eighty or so protest signers were *summoned for discussions* with their party committee. And they came away from those "discussions" pale and crestfallen.'[1]

And were we lacking in the customary excuses?

'A multitude of excuses has been primed, pondered and prepared. Tripping up a colleague or publishing lies in a newspaper statement is resourcefully justified by the perpetrator and unanimously accepted by his associates: If I (he) hadn't done it, they would have sacked me (him) from my (his) job and appointed somebody worse! So in order to maintain the principle of what is good and for the benefit of all, it is natural that every day you will find yourself obliged to harm the few ("honourable men play dirty tricks on their neighbours only when they have to"). But the few are themselves guilty: why did they flaunt themselves so indiscreetly in front of the bosses, without a thought for the collective? Or why did they hide their questionnaires from the personnel department and thus lay the entire collective open to attack? Chelnov... wittily describes the intelligentsia's position as standing crookedly—from which position the vertical seems a ridiculous posture.

But the chief justifying argument is: *children*! In the face of this argument everyone falls silent: for who has the right to sacrifice the material welfare of his children for the sake of an abstract principle of truth? That the moral health of their children is more precious than their careers does not even enter the parent's heads, so impoverished have they themselves become. And it is reasonable that their children should

---

[1] A. Solzhenitsyn, "The Smatterers" in A. Solzhenitsyn (ed.), *From Under the Rubble*, Fontana Collins, London, 1976, p. 252.

grow up the same: pragmatists right from their school days, first-year students already resigned to the lie of the political education class, already shrewdly weighing their most profitable way into the competitive world of science. Theirs is a generation that has experienced no real persecution, but how cautious it is! And those few youths—the hope of Russia—who turn and look truth in the face are usually cursed and even persecuted by their infuriated, affluent parents.'[2]

'... One of the contributors to the present anthology was to have been an exceptionally distinguished person with a string of ranks and titles to his name. In private conversations his heart bleeds for the irrevocable ruin that has befallen the Russian people. He knows our history and our culture through and through. But—he declined. *What's the use? Nothing will come of it*—the usual good excuse of the smatterers.[3]

'... Albeit in a somewhat unexpected form, the intelligentsia in fact got exactly what it had spent many decades trying to achieve—and submitted without a struggle. And the one solace it has been able to suck on surreptitiously since has been that "the ideas of the revolution were good, but were perverted." And at each turn in history it has comforted itself with the hope that the regime was beginning to mend, that a change for the better was just around the corner and that then, at last, collaboration with the authorities would be fully vindicated.'[4]

So, the first thing the Emergency taught us about ourselves was that we lack even the most elementary courage. And we must remember that we collapsed without struggle in the face of the *mildest possible dictatorship*. I am fully aware of the excesses, of the tortures and deaths. It is not out of an ignorance of facts relating to these but because of knowledge about their extent that I am characterizing the dictatorship as the "mildest possible" one. When we compare the 19 months to what a Djilas or a Solzhenitsyn has had to stand up to, when we compare

---

[2]*Ibid.*, p. 249.
[3]*Ibid.*, p. 252.
[4]*Ibid.*, p. 244.

them to what may well be in store for us, no other characterization is defensible.

And yet we subsided like froth.

The few who picked courage found out how isolated they were —from one another and especially from organizations that reached the masses. Decorative switches on the wall, with no wires at the back. A simple affirmation of the truth is of supreme importance and those who affirmed it did a signal service. But it is not enough. The fact that we had no links with mass organizations left us painfully ineffective.

But one thing did not change: our "conceited cliquishness," our voluble contempt for each other.

I am always surprised at how ill we speak of each other. During those 19 months I was astonished how our intellectuals would just refuse to acknowledge the courage, the simple honesty, of the few among them who were refusing to bend: "he is bent upon making a martyr of himself"; "how cut up he is that he isn't being arrested; he is convinced that she is denying him the halo that will get him a ministership when he comes out"; "oh, you don't know, he is printing all that stuff *at her behest*; by getting fools like you to write, he makes her task of locating you rats easier and in the meantime she touts his magazine as proof of free speech; for heaven's sake, *wake up*, *he is her agent*"; "it's all very well for him to do it, he has all those lakhs stashed away"; "what's the damned point of writing all that from England, for God's sake; why doesn't he come back and really *do* something?"; "he—the Marwari that he is—is incensed only because he isn't getting those ads; give him those ads and then you'll see how committed he is to a free Press."

Nirad Chaudhuri once concluded that we had taken to envy *per se*, to *nishkama irshya*. For long this seemed an apt description. But after these 19 months, it seems quite inadequate. Our voluble contempt for others is not a reflection of envy; it is a reflection of self-contempt. Lofty in words, mercenaries and careerists in deed, we know ourselves; we hurl this self-contempt at others, refusing to believe that, unlike us, the other fellow believes in a principle, that he is courageous, that he is just plain honest.

To understand the intellectuals and their activities, writes

Gramsci in his *Prison Notebooks*, we must not focus on "intrinsic intellectual activities"; rather, we should look at "the ensemble or the system of relations in which these activities (and the intellectuals themselves) have their place in the general complex of social relations."[5]

This is a large subject. Here I can do no more than draw attention to two relevant facts.

Most intellectuals are middle-class intellectuals. The hallmark of the middle class is its economic dependence on other classes. The obvious consequences of this dependence have been heightened in India by two factors. First, there is the age-old practice of co-opting the organic intellectuals and leaders of the exploited groups;[6] this practice has been developed into a fine art; it has been one of the principal devices by which our society has contained rebellion, protest, pressures for reform. The device is in full use today: the intellectual, wherever he is, is quickly co-opted, given the privileges or at least a smattering of the privileges of the ruling class and thus converted into an official ideologue. Second, in recent times, the complete centralization of patronage has made the manipulation of the dependent middle-class intellectual much easier.

Thus, because of their class dependence which makes possible the traditional device of co-opting potential trouble-makers, and because of centralized patronage our intellectuals today are, what Marx and Engels in *The German Ideology* call, official ideologues: ideologues whose function, as that of the Brahmins of old, is to perfect for the ruling classes their illusions about themselves, their situation, and their era.

The second feature that we may note briefly is the basic division of labour—between manual and mental work—which appeared and was ossified very early in our history, and which capitalism is today driving deeper. Intellectual activity cannot but reflect the general process that results in division of labour (increasingly

---

[5] A. Gramsci, *Prison Notebooks*, Lawrence and Wishart, London, 1971, p. 8.

[6] Gramsci uses the term "organic intellectual" to describe those individuals who organically belong to a class and who, because of various factors—their own intense experience, their native ability, etc., —come to articulate, almost to embody, the aspirations, interests and anxieties of their class.

complex and narrowly specialized), and production for exchange rather than for use (reification). Among intellectuals, the high status of "pure theory" and the disdain for popularization of the results, are but a reflection of this extreme division of labour and the resulting compartmentalization of society.

Mao and Gandhi are one in perceiving the consequences of this state of affairs. Mao's views on the relative importance of being "red" over being "expert," on the crucial importance of everyone (academics, theoreticians, etc., included) working with and amidst the masses, are well known. His programmes aim, among other things, at doing away with the basic division of labour between manual and mental division, a division to which Marx had attributed so much of what was wrong. Some of Gandhi's harshest passages are similarly reserved for the expert without any ideological moorings, without any values that transcend his narrow personal interests. As early as in 1908 in *Hind Swaraj* he rails against professionals, like doctors and lawyers, who care nothing for veracity, for their fellow man, for the community, for the country, and are interested only in enriching themselves. His constructive work programmes were designed to alleviate the pernicious effects of this at least among his immediate colleagues. And he held among the principal results of his individual *satyagrahas* the fact that they, as in the case of the Kheda *satyagraha*, "compelled the educated public workers to establish contact with the actual life of the peasants. They (the educated public workers) learnt to identify themselves with the latter. They found their proper sphere of work, their capacity for sacrifice increased. . . ."[7]

In the foregoing I have proceeded as if it is correct to describe Indian intellectuals at least as "experts." Their work, even academic work, in many fields is so poor that this assumption may well be questioned. That they can get away with such shoddy work is to be attributed in part to the transitional stage in which our society is: feudalism has not completely gone, capitalism has not yet come to prevail, competition has not as yet replaced privilege. A degree, a job, confers a privilege that is not disturbed merely because another is more "productive," even in the narrow,

---

[7] M.K. Gandhi, *My Experiments With Truth*, Navjivan, 1959, Ahmedabad, p. 324.

capitalist, sense. And yet our intellectuals strut around asserting that against all odds, they are engaged in a mighty battle to maintain "oases of excellence" amidst the invading desert of mediocrity and torpor. Even if this were true, it would not suffice: "... To back quality against quantity means simply this: to maintain intact specific conditions of social life in which some people are pure quantity and others quality. And how pleasant it is to think of oneself as one of the licensed representatives of quality, beauty, thought, and the like. There is hardly a lady in the fashionable world who doesn't imagine she is performing this function of preserving quality and beauty upon earth...."[8]

Our situation, today, is no different from the situation of the Indian intelligentsia Gandhi described in 1908: "those in whose name we speak we do not know, nor do they know us."[9] It may well be worse: our specializations are narrower, the tug of economic aspirations is greater, our eyes are more firmly fixed on foreign lands. Not knowing the people, we are apt to tumble into one of two adjacent pits: either we will tend to deify them and expect them to work miracles or, out of contempt for them, we will convince ourselves that "they will never do anything," and, hence, will never do anything ourselves. In one case, we will go around urging adventurist positions; in the other, we will fail to extract what can be obtained from a given situation. Adventurist bravado will be swiftly followed by despair, by mutual recrimination and abuse for the inevitable failure, and, thus, by cliques and fragmentation. The second, defeatist standpoint is, even to begin with, one of gloom and cynicism, and of passing the blame in anticipation.

## An Interregnum

We are now living through a brief and unexpected interregnum.

The co-existence of different modes of production during the last three decades afforded a degree of autonomy to the intermediate class—in this period, those who manned the State apparatus, intellectuals and other members of this class were able to

[8] Gramsci, *op. cit.*, pp. 363-364.
[9] M.K. Gandhi, *Hind Swaraj*, Navjivan, Ahmedabad, 1962, p. 62.

manoeuvre and manipulate within a fairly wide terrain.[10] The contradictions within this system have prevented adequate change for over a decade. The Emergency gave us a glimpse of the manner in which this stalemate is likely to be broken. The unexpected restoration of freedom should not blind us to the underlying shift in the balance among different classes. The landed interests who, since independence, had been acquiring control of the organizations of the Congress and a few other parties and, by the late 1960s, had captured these upto the state level, have now made a spectacular thrust upto the national level. Along with the owners of industry, they are now poised to use the State apparatus openly and audaciously for their own purposes. Industrial and agricultural labour cannot but be sat upon in this process. And that must inevitably entail curbs on the freedoms of speech, organization, etc.[11]

Thus the vise is closing in. We have already passed through the stage when, in response to the increasing restlessness of the working class, the rulers attempt to buy them by populist rhetoric. In the next phase, as development is more openly and audaciously capitalist, intellectuals and other members of the intermediate class will have less and less room for manoeuvre. They will be under growing pressure to explicitly function as agents of the ruling class—of the owners of the means of production.

Possibilities for influencing the course of events will, of course, always seem to be around the corner. But chiefly they will be hallucinations:

'It is this transitional society that Tolstoy's heroes personify —subjectively honest representatives of the then ruling class who see the problem and the contradictions in the objective situation, but who cannot bring themselves to break with their class. Hence ... extreme possibilities crop up and are earnestly considered; serious steps are taken towards their translation into reality; but before the decisive step is taken, cont-

---

[10]Cf: K. Marx, F. Engels, *Collected Works*, Volume 5, Moscow, 1976, pp. 193-205; Hamza Alavi, "The State in Post-Colonial Societies" in H.P. Sharma and K. Gough, (eds.), *Imperialism and Revolution in South Asia*, Monthly Review Press, New York, 1973, pp. 145-173.

[11]Cf. Chapter 2.

rary tendencies appear, which are in part nothing but the same contradictions on a higher level, in part leanings that drag the heroes down to a compromise with reality. This produces a ceaseless movement in which all the important determinants of this life find expression in all their richness, but which very rarely leads to a really dramatic crisis, to a clean break of the previous phase. The lifelike quality, the inner richness of the characters rests on the fact that such extreme possibilities arise again and again, that the thorn of the conflict between social existence and consciousness never ceases to prick. But the movement is always almost a continuous circle or at best a spiral, never the rapid dramatic upheaval. . . .'[12]

Similarly, as the vise closes in, the scope for doing merely good deeds will become less and less.

'...the impossibility of an active life in this world of which we have just spoken is clearly expressed in *The Living Corpse* by Fedia into whose mouth Tolstoy, without mentioning his own favourite theory at all, even as a possibility, puts these word:
"A man born in the sphere in which I was born has only three possibilities to choose from. Either he can be an official, earn money and increase the filth in which we live—that disgusted me, or perhaps I didn't know how to do it, but above all it disgusted me. Or else he can fight this filth, but for that he must be a hero and I have never been that. Or finally and thirdly he tries to forget, goes to the dogs, takes to drink and song—that is what I have done and this is what it has brought me to."
'In Nekhlyudov's figure Tolstoy did of course attempt to present the individual good deed itself. But his inexorable truthfulness produces a quite different, bitterly ironical, result. Only because Nekhlyudov himself belongs to the very ruling class he hates and despises, only because in his own social sphere he is regarded as a good-natured fool, as a harmless eccentric bitten by the bug of philanthropy, only because he

---

[12] Lukacs in David Craig, (ed.), *Marxists on Literature, An Anthology*, Penguin, London, 1975, p. 326.

can make use of old family and other connections, can he accomplish his "good deeds" at all. And objectively, all these good deeds are mere insignificant trifles; they are as nothing in comparison with the horrible inexorability of the machine, and they fit easily into the amorous or ambitious intrigues of those who are part of the machine. Subjectively Nekhlyudov himself is forced—often unwillingly, often full of self-contempt, but sometimes also yielding to a temptation—to wear the mask of the courtier in order to be able to accomplish at least a few of his "individual good deeds." And where Nekhlyudov draws the Tolstoyan conclusions from the earlier critical vacillations of Konstantin Levin, he is faced with the hatred and distrust of the peasants who regard every "generous" proposal of their landlord as a new cunning attempt to deceive them and take advantage of them.'[13]

Finally, as the vise closes in flight will become less possible; in any case, it will offer no reprieve to the sensitive. And capitulation will entail ever greater humiliation, an ever increasing psychological price.

In such a situation, do intellectuals have any role to play at all? Or should they take the back-seat and wait till the politicians have sorted things out?

One reason for counsel of taking the back-seat arises from our habitual use of the word "intellectual" in such a way that while professosr of public finance and journalists, for instance, qualify to the category, men like Gandhi, Mao, Lenin, Ho Chih Minh, Giap, are all excluded. These men, who spent their lives in struggle, who expended at least as much mental effort in summarizing the experience of the masses for them, as physical effort in the struggles themselves, are the true intellectuals. And, as has been correctly said in the case of Lenin, they advanced *philosophy* by succeeding in *practice*. Once we put the matter thus, the question is not whether we should take the back-seat and let "politicians" sort things out or not (of course, we should not) but what our potential role can be and how we can equip ourselves for it.

Now, there can be little doubt that major transformations

---

[13]*Ibid.*, p. 314-315.

have had a major intellectual input and, conversely, failure at the intellectual level has often contributed to failure to extract what could have been obtained from a situation.

Only the pedants, who insist on reducing dialectical materialism to mechanical determinism, scoff at the importance of the subjective element at turning points. Those who have participated in real struggles—Lenin, Mao, Gandhi, and others—have never under-rated the importance of the subjective element. They have worked hard at understanding the subjective state of the forces of change and at transforming this state. Indeed, they did not spend their time working on transforming the objective base, they did not become technologists and engineers; rather they worked on the superstructure and within this most of all on transforming the subjective state of the masses. Mao was to note later on that revolutions had not proceeded strictly according to Marx's forecast: it had not been the case that the base advanced sufficiently, thus enabling the revolutionary forces to capture the superstructure; rather the sequence had been that, by a complex process, revolutionary forces had captured the state apparatus and had thus accelerated changes in the base.[14]

---

[14]Stuart Schram, (ed.), *Mao-Tse-tung Unrehearsed*, Penguin, London, 1974. Mao stresses this theme repeatedly. I shall have to confine myself to just one passage. Thus, in answering the question, "Is revolution in backward countries more difficult?" he says: "In western countries they have been having one great difficulty in carrying out revolution and construction. This is because the poisons of the bourgeoisie are very powerful and have permeated every nook and cranny. In our country there have been only three generations of the bourgeosie. However, in such countries as Great Britain and France the bourgeoise have a history of 250 or 260 years to more than 300 years. . . . Lenin said: 'The more backward the country, the more difficult its transition from capitalism to socialism.' Now it seems that this way of speaking is incorrect. As a matter of fact, the more backward the economy, the easier, not the more difficult, the transition from capitalism to socialism. The poorer they are the more people want revolution. In western capitalist countries both the employment rate and the wage standard are relatively high, and the bourgeios influence on the working people has been far-reaching. . . ." Cf. his "Reading Notes on the Soviet Union's Political Economics" in *Miscellany of Mao Tse-tung Thought*, Joint Publications Research Service, Arlington, February 1974, pp. 258-259. Mao's insistence on extending the concept of contradictions not just to within the proletariat but also to the

The ruling classes in all societies maintain their hold not just by direct domination but, as Gramsci would say, through establishing "hegemony" by internalizing notions and ideas in the minds of the oppressed which will keep the latter from acting to overthrow the system. The Indian philosophic and religious tradition constitutes one of the most highly articulated and effective examples of the hegemonic system. As societies progress, more and more subtle devices are developed to make those notions an "interiorized force" that will keep the oppressed in bondage. Ultimately, these notions are dissolved by practice. But, in helping the masses summarize the experience of their advancing practice and to bare for them the hegemonic ideology for what it is, the intellectuals have a concrete function. Moreover, many aspects of their training give them a natural advantage in fulfilling this function.

The importance of correct ideological orientation and interpretation is also seen in the fact that, for centuries, in China as well as India, for instance, peasant rebellions and the discontent of the masses was used by one part of the gentry to oust its rivals, to merely change dynasties or to replace native dynasties by imperial masters. A single, small but characteristic, example will suffice to remind us that this skilful manipulation continues to this day: recall the use that has been made by the rulers in the past decade of Naxalite adventurism to dull the conscience of the urban citizenry in India and to cover what the rulers have been doing to spread terror in the countryside.

Marx repeatedly pointed out that the development of the workers takes place in an extremely uneven and piecemeal manner. It is altogether impossible that they should develop the

---

psyche or mental make-up of an individual, is well known. For a brief recapitulation see, I.C. Hsiung, *Ideology and Practice, The Evolutions of Chinese Communism*, Praeger, New York, 1970.

Engels himself had dismissed as "fatuous" the notion that "because we deny an independent historical development to the various ideological spheres which play a part in history, we also deny them any effect upon history." He also stressed that his and Marx's insistent emphasis on the base had been caused partly by the fact that they were combating those who grossly neglected the influence of economic forces and structures. K. Marx, F. Engels, *Selected Correspondence*, Progress Publishers, Moscow, 1975, pp. 433-37.

correct ideological perspectives in a flash. Hence the important role of those who can help them summarize their experience and interpret their situation. In our own case, we have seen how erroneous, borrowed, paradigms have way-laid the organized workers in India. The Emergency exposed the pernicious unsuitability of these paradigms most dramatically. The working class was split and rendered impotent precisely by the "formula Marxists" who had adopted wholesale scriptures written abroad.[15] Moreover, unless a scientific explanation is presented to the masses, we turn them over to messiahs.

'To go,' Marx is reported to have shouted at the tailor-agitator, Weitling, 'to the workers in Germany without strictly scientific ideas and a concrete doctrine would mean an empty and unscrupulous playing with propaganda, which would inevitably involve, on the one hand, the setting up of an inspired apostle and, on the other hand, simply asses who would listen to him with open mouth.'[16]

Thus, it is not that there is nothing to be done. But to do any of it we will have, quite literally, to step out of our skin.

We must, first, shed a number of comfortable illusions.

The last three decades show that the system cannot be "reformed from within." Thus, it is futile to hope that something will come from peddling suggestions to the rulers or from "allying with progressive sections within the ruling party." The disillusionment of many an intellectual—from the sad figure of D.R. Gadgil on down—bears testimony to the former. And the

---

[15] For a narration of many of these rationalizations see Chapter 3. To see how a creative thinker adapts received doctrine and forges a new paradigm suited to the concrete situation, see accounts of specific struggles led by Gandhi and Mao. In Gandhi's case, for instance, see M.K. Gandhi, *Satyagraha in South Africa*, Navjivan, Ahmedabad, 1972; Mahadev Desai, *The Story of Bardoli*, Navjivan, Ahmedabad, 1957; Rajendra Prasad, *Champaran Me Mahatma Gandhi*, Bihar Rashtrabhasha Parishad, Patna, 1965. And in the case of Mao see, for instance, Mark Selden, *The Yenan Way in Revolutionary China*, Harvard, 1972; John E. Rue, *Mao Tse-tung in Opposition, 1927-1935*, Stanford, 1966; and W. Hinton, *Fanshen*, Monthly Review Press, 1966.

[16] Edmund Wilson, *To The Finland Station*, Farar, Straus and Giroux, New York, 1972, p. 197.

CPI's bankruptcy testifies to the latter: predictably its failure has been as total and as ignominious as that of those sections in the CCP who had thought that they would influence the policies of the Chiang regime by "strengthening progressive sections within the KMT."

Nor can anything be changed by mere cleverness. All the lefties who thought that they could change the regime's course by smuggling in a few progressive paras into the Plans, all of have been dealt with in time.

Nor can much be achieved by "reforming at least one part of the system." This is a common illusion: "I don't know about the entire system and so on; I feel that if I can only help in making excise duties more equitable, I would have done my job." The fate of the Gandhians since independence—dedicated as they have been "to keeping at least one or two lamps burning"—tells us, for the hundredth time, that the whole determines the parts and not the other way around; howsoever diligent and proficient I may be in embroidering my corner of the cloth, if the cloth is on fire, my work too will be consumed by it sooner or later.

Nor, finally, can we make a ruling class change direction merely by frightening it that, unless it does so, it will land itself in big trouble. As Baran once said, people do not generally commit suicide out of the fear of eventual death.

At each stage, the weak, the exploited, are the engine of change. And the "weak," the "exploited," the "workers," are not abstract categories. They are human beings who are prompted to act not by abstract doctrines but by practical necessity. Their principal teacher is their daily living experience, the struggles they participate in, "the stern but steeling school of labour." Finally, "it is not a question of what this or that proletarian, or even the whole proletariat, at the moment regards as its aim. It is a question of *what the proletariat is*, and what, in accordance with this *being*, it will historically be compelled to do...."[17]

Rid of illusions, with a correct appreciation of the prospects and engines of change, we must stop addressing the rulers. We must concern ourselves with the masses.

What does this mean? "I will offer you a talisman," says

---

[17] K. Marx and F. Engels, *The Holy Family*, Progress Publishers, Moscow, 1975, p. 44.

Gandhi. "Recall the face of the poorest and the most helpless man whom you may have seen and ask yourself whether the step you contemplate is going to be of any use to him. Will he be able to gain anything by it? Will it restore to him a control over his own life and destiny? In other words, will it lead to *Swaraj*, or self-rule, for the hungry and spiritually starved millions of our countrymen? Then you will find your doubts and yourself melting away."

For intellectuals this would imply, first of all, that we change our attitude even to purely intellectual work. Thus, for instance, when confronted by an erroneous philosophy, our object in combating in must not be mere academic disputation; rather, our object should be removing a hindrance to emancipation. Thus, to press the illustration, if we are studying some of the Indian schools of philosophy, our objective in commenting upon them should not be to win academic points purely within "the realm of ideas." Our objective should be to show how the doctrine of these schools enters or butresses the world view of our people and how it helps or hinders their further emancipation. Similarly, we must at all times guard against the danger that traps academics: of being carried away by the momentum of our specialized discipline, of losing ourselves in its fine, subtle, elaborate controversies, controversies that have no relevance outside the journals of that discipline. We must, at all times, refer what we are doing to the reality around us and test it against a talisman such as Gandhi's.

Secondly, it means that the subjects we work on must be those that will help the weak, the workers, understand their strengths and weaknesses, subjects which will enable them to interpret their situation correctly; in other words, those that will help them liberate themselves.

Third, we must view the weak, the workers, not as a passive receptacle for our views and pronouncements but as an active force. This implies an attitude that is sympathetic and critical at the same time. There is no place for hagiography. It is just as important to acquaint the exploited with their weaknesses as it is to acquaint them with, for instance, what Lu Hsun used to call the oppressor's "literature"—his web of "laws," his administrative circulars, his instructions to the police.

Fourth, our audience must be the masses and the active cadres who are working with them rather than fellow specialists in our discipline.

> 'Creating a new culture does not only mean one's own "original" discoveries. It also, and most particularly, means the diffusion in a critical form of truths already discovered, their "socialisation" as it were, and even making them the basis of vital action, an element of co-ordination of intellectual and moral order. For a mass of people to be led to think coherently and in the same coherent fashion about the real present world, is a "philosophical" event far more important and "original" thant he discovery by some philosophical "genius" of a truth which remains the property of small groups of intellectuals.'[18]

This entails that we learn the language—not just in the sense of the mother tongue etc., but in the sense of the mode of expression—that one can only acquire by "watching the mouth" of the people. It most certainly implies that we learn to put across our results in the media through which the workers and peasants absorb information and impressions.

Passion is an essential chemical in all this. Mere intellectual dissatisfaction with the existing state of affairs, unless it is accompanied by a warmth and passion for the alternative world, will always end in mere hopelessness: railing and wailing against what is, we will shrink back from the struggles—with all that they entail—which alone will produce the new; or, noticing that the new is not perfect (as it can never be) we will lose heart and take to railing and wailing again instead of prosecuting the new struggles that the new situation demands.

> 'The popular element "feels" but does not always know or understand: the intellectual element "knows" but does not always understand and in particular does not always feel. The two extremes are, therefore, pedantry and philistinism on the one hand and blind passion and sectarianism on the other. Not that the pedant cannot be impassioned; far from it. Impassioned pedantry is every bit as ridiculous and dangerous as the

[18]Gramsci, *op. cit.*, p 325.

wildest sectarianism and demagogy. The intellectual's error consists in believing that one can know without understanding and even more without feeling and being impassioned (not only for knowledge in itself but also for the object of knowledge); in other words that the intellectual can be an intellectual (and not a pure pedant) if distinct and separate from the people-nation, that is, without feeling the elementary passions of the people, understanding them and therefore explaining and justifying them in the particular historical situation and connecting them dialectically to the laws of history and to a superior conception of the world, scientifically and coherently elaborated—i.e., knowledge. One cannot make politics-history without the passion, without this sentimental connection between intellectuals and the people-nation. In the absence of such a nexus the relations between the intellectual and the people-nation are, or are reduced to, relationships of a purely bureaucratic and formal order; the intellectuals become a caste, or a priesthood (so-called organic centralism).

If the relationship between intellectuals and the people-nation, between the leaders and the led, the rulers and the ruled, is provided by an organic cohesion in which feeling-passion becomes understanding and thence knowledge (not mechanically but in a way that is alive), then and only then, is the relationship one of representation. Only then can there take place an exchange of individual elements between the rulers and ruled, leaders and led, and can the shared life be realised which alone is social force—with the creation of the "historical bloc."[19]

## From and To

Neither the requisite knowledge nor the language, to say nothing of the empathy and passion, will come about without our going to and learning from the masses. The exhortation "from the masses, to the masses" is common to Gandhi, Mao, Ho and others who have helped the masses change the state of things.

Working with, and among, the masses is the operational

[19] *Ibid.*, pp. 418-419.

meaning of "uniting theory and practice."

The prescription that we "unite theory and practice" certainly does not imply that we abandon theory, that we stop thinking. It is not an anti-intellect admoniton. We have already noted that there have been major intellectual inputs into each of the major transformations. Practitioners, *par excellence*, Lenin, Mao, Gandhi, Ho *et al.*, spent a major part of their lives in purely intellectual work. The balance in the case of Marx and Engels was even more on the side of intellectual work as against direct participation in political work.[20]

> For Marx and Engels, as Hoffman puts it in his uneven polemic, 'the question was not whether one was "active" or "merely theorized"; the question was whether one sought to build up a revolutionary movement in a correct and therefore scientific manner[21]...Can it not be said...that the greatest of Marx's endeavours, the volumes of "Capital," was nothing more than a "theoretical critique," and that when Marx drove himself to exhaustion and well nigh ruined his health in writing the work, he was simply "philosophising"...?[22] It is clear from the *German Ideology* that the Young Hegelians are practical in the sense that Marx and Engels call them "the staunchest conservatives" so that the real question can be more clearly posed: *not* are the writers practical or theoretical but *rather* is their practice conservative or revolutionary.'[23]

What relation, then, should theory have to practice?

> 'If the problem of the identification of theory and practice is to be raised, it can be done in this sense, that one can construct, on a specific practice, a theory which, by coinciding

---

[20] "... Since 1852, I was no longer connected with any association and was firmly convinced that my theoretical works were of greater benefit to the working class than participation in associations whose days on the continent were over," Marx, to Freilgrath (December 29, 1860), *Selected Correspondence, op. cit.*, 147.

[21] John Hoffman, *Marxism and the Theory of Praxis*, Lawrence and Wishart, 1975, p. 41.

[22] *Ibid.*, p. 43,

[23] *Ibid.*, p. 173.

and identifying itself with the decisive elements of the practice itself, can accelerate the historical process that is going on, rendering practice more homogeneous, more coherent, more efficient in all its elements, and thus, in other words, developing its potential to the maximum or alternatively, given a certain theoretical position, one can organise the practical element which is essential for the theory to be realised. The identification of theory and practice is a critical act, through which practice is demonstrated rational and necessary, and theory realistic and rational. This is why the problem of the identity of theory and practice is raised especially in the so-called transitional moments of history, that is those moments in which the movement of transformation is at its most rapid. For it is then that the practical forces unleashed really demand justification in order to become more efficient and expansive; and the theoretical programmes multiply in number, and demand their turn to be realistically justified, to the extent that they prove themselves assimilable into practical movements, thereby making the latter yet more practical and real.'[24]

Thus, what distinguishes run-of-the-mill academics from revolutionary thinkers is that, while the former are preoccupied with controversies within their profession, transforming the state of affairs is the conscious object of the latter's thought. While the technologist, the academic and the "practical man" take the overall situation as given and focus on their narrow technical task, the revolutionary thinker addresses himself to transforming the overall context. The conditions under which alone the theory of such revolutionary thinkers germinates, advances, and reaches maturity are obvious.

'The final word can rest with Lenin. His famous dictum that "without revolutionary theory, there can be no revolutionary movement," is often and rightly quoted. But he also wrote, with equal weight: "Correct revolutionary theory. . .assumes final shape only in close connection with the practical activity of a truly mass and truly revolutionary movement." Every

---

[24]Gramsci, *op. cit.*, p. 365.

clause here counts. Revolutionary theory can be undertaken in relative isolation—Marx in the British Museum, Lenin in war-bound Zurich: but it can only acquire a correct and final form when bound to the collective struggles of the working class itself. Mere formal membership of a party organisation, of a type familiar in recent history, does not suffice to provide such a bond: a close connection with the practical activity of the proletariat is necessary. Nor is militancy in a small revolutionary group enough; there must be a linkage with actual masses. Conversely, linkage with a mass movement is not enough either, for the latter may be reformist; it is only when the masses are themselves revolutionary, that theory can complete its eminent vocation.'[25]

*Intra-Movement Democracy*

The argument thus far has been that we must adopt the point of view of the masses, that to do so we have to learn from and then teach the masses, and that all this is possible only if we actually participate in mass struggles. After all, one cannot comprehend mass struggles, to say nothing of influencing them, by gesticulating from the sidelines.

But participation in mass struggles should not be taken to mean, as Stalinist parties would have us believe, blind obedience to party high-ups. Indeed, this notion, spread by party bureaucrats, must be resolutely combated. And the intellectuals are specially suited to combat it: their effectiveness is the first thing that suffers when democracy within the movement is stifled and their native proclivities *qua* intellectuals predispose them to independence, even to a bit of free-wheeling.

There is no reason, especially not in the current situation in India, to be defensive about this independence. Two considerations will show that fighting for intra-movement democracy now and in the foreseeable future, far from harming the cause, is essential to it.

The first concerns our immediate context. We have arrived at a juncture when the very fundamentals have to be re-examined.

---

[25]Perry Anderson, *Considerations on Western Marxism*, New Left Books, 1976, pp. 105-106.

The various lines—of "unity and struggle," of "critical support," of "annihilating the class enemy," of *"hridaya parivartan"*—have all been found wanting. How can the thorough examination that is required take place unless there is the fullest democracy within each branch of the mass movement?

The second is more fundamental. Experience shows that even when things get going, transformations take a very, very long time. Set-backs and errors along the way are inevitable. Moreover, nothing works forever. Sooner or later every revolution ossifies, every leadership becomes a bureaucracy. Thus, new struggles will always have to be launched. The intellectual—like everyone else who is committed to progressive emancipation—must, therefore, continually combat all tendencies which undermine the prospects for fresh struggles. The throttling of intra-movement democracy is certainly one such tendency.

In our own case, we have to fight not just the presumed omniscience of party bureaucrats and messiahs, but also naive shibboleths and dogmas. The more "committed" our intellectuals are—not in the sense that "the more immersed they are in mass movements," but in the sense that "the more volubly immersed they are in the affairs of parties and groups"—the more firmly imprisoned they are in these labels and dogmas. The lefty's cliches about Gandhi are no better reasoned than the Gandhian's unthinking prejudices against Marx and Mao.[26]

Such narrow dogmatism arises from a variety of sources: we are immersed more in academic disputations of the printed word than in action; our thinking is, abstract—even metaphysical—

---

[26] It is precisely for bringing home our proclivity to react unthinkingly to the lefty reader (of whatever hue) and the Gandhian reader that I have deliberately cited passages from authors as disparate as Solzhenitsyn, Lenin, Mao and Gandhi. I have often had "committed" intellectuals enthusiastically endorse a passage when I have told them that it is from a work of one from their camp, only to see them recoil when I have told them the name of the actual author, only to see them repudiate even the substance of the passage they had so recently endorsed just because of the name of the author. It is my experience that, perhaps because they spend more time with books, our lefties are more prone to these knee-jerk reactions than our Gandhians. Gandhi is particularly uncomfortable to them—as to all from our class—because he insists, first of all and above all, on the individual rectifying his own practice.

instead of being concrete and practical; we are lazy, labels settle the question and absolve us from the trouble of seeing how the thought of the *bete noire* can be developed creatively; we fear responsibility, the responsibility of taking a position on our own, without the prop of the scriptures, we fear running the risk of being proven wrong. We fear ridicule and ostracism from our associates who, we fear, will taunt us for forsaking the faith. But, most of all, the dogmatism has its roots in timidity: not having participated in mass struggles ourselves, we have no direct experience and, therefore, no self-confidence that we can think for ourselves, that we can judge passages, "lines," standpoints for ourselves without always referring them to the prescribed scriptures.

We must free ourselves from slavishness to labels and dogma. And the way to do so is action: that will dissolve these shackles.[27]

[27] A colleague suggests that to get the faithful to consider even the proposition that we should think for ourselves, I should cite the scriptures! Here then are a few sentences from a single speech of Mao at a single conference, the Eighth Party Congress of May, 1958:

'... Is there also the fear of being proletarian professors? I think there is. For instance, there is the fear of Marx. He lived in a very tall building, and one had to climb many flights of stairs to reach him, something unattainable in a lifetime. As I mentioned at the Chleng-tu Conference, do not be afraid, because Marx was also a human being, with two eyes, two hands, and one brain, not much different from us, except that he had a lot of Marxism in him. He wrote many books for us to read. We do not have to read all of them... I have not finished reading them; therefore, I am still downstairs. As we have not finished reading his books, we all belong downstairs, but do not be afraid. It is not necessary to read all of Marx's books. Reading some of the fundamental things will be sufficient, but what we have done has surpassed Marx. What Lenin said and did surpassed Marx in many aspects. Marx did not undertake the October Revolution, but Lenin did; therefore, Lenin surpassed Marx in the practical aspect. At that time, he had the conditions of the time. Marx never undertook China's great revolution; therefore, our practice also surpassed Marx. Principles are created in practice. Marx did not succeed in his revolution, but we did....

'We must not belittle ourselves or hold ourselves in contempt.

The first requirement for everything that has been narrated above is, as the Emergencey so forcefully brought home to us, elementary (and elemental) courage.

> As I have often said to some comrades, China was oppressed by imperialism for over 100 years and the people were intimidated by the propaganda of obedience to foreigners and foreign countries spread by imperialism; they were afraid of everything. Feudalism propagandised obedience to Confucius, making us feel inferior. We were inferior in the face of Confucius Since the opium war, we have been inferior in the face of foreigners, and we were afraid of them. Before that we were afraid of Confucius. . . . What was the reason? At that time, the saying was "rejecting the Sage is violating the law." Opposing the Sage was "violating the constitution. In regard to foreigners, I am inferior to them; in regard to Confucius, I am inferior to him. What kind of reasoning is this? I once asked some comrades around me whether we lived in heaven or on earth. They all shook their heads and said that they lived on earth. I said no, we live in heaven. When we look at the stars from earth, they are in heaven. But if there are people in the stars, when they look at us, wouldn't they think that we are in heaven? Therefore, I say we live in heaven while also on earth at the same time. The Chinese like the gods. I asked them whether we were gods. They answered no. I said wrong. The gods live in heaven. We live on earth, but also in heaven; so why shouldn't we be considered gods also? If there were people in the stars, wouldn't they also consider us as foreigners? . . . .
> 
> 'My purpose in citing so many examples is to show that the young people must surpass the old and the less educated can excel the more educated. Do not be intimidated by famous people and scholars. We must be courageous in thinking, speaking and doing. We must not be afraid to think, speak or do. We must liberate ourselves from the condition of having our hands and feet tied. . . .
> 
> 'Chia Kuei is a character in the play entitled *Fa-men Temple*. He served under Liu Chin. The latter was a court eunuch in the Ming Dynasty, but actually the "prime minister" possessed great powers. One time Liu Chin asked Chia Kuei to take a seat. Chia Kuei said: "I am used to standing; I do not dare to sit. It" was a slavish behaviour. The Chinese people served as slaves to imperialism for a long time. It is inevitable that a tail from this slavish behavior is carried over to the present. This tail must be chopped off; the work style of Chia Kuei must be knocked down. . . . There are two kinds of modesty: one is ordinary modesty and the other is modesty compatible with reality. The dogmatists copy from foreign countries. This is excessive modesty. Why do they not use their brains in whatever they do?. . . . When a proletariat copies from the

'Throughout the years of Soviet power, the intelligentsia has been well enough informed, has known what was going on in the world, and could have known what was going on in its own country, but it looked away and feebly surrendered in every organisation and every office, indifferent to the common cause. For decade after decade, of course, it has been held in an unprecedented strangle hold (people in the West will never be able to imagine it until their turn comes). People of dynamic initiative, responsive to all forms of public and private assistance, have been stifled by oppression and fear, and public assistance itself has been soiled by a hypocritical State-run imitation. Finally, they have been placed in a situation where there appears to be no third choice; if a colleague is being hounded no one dares to remain neutral—at the slightest evasion he himself will be hounded too. But there is still a way out for people, even in this situation, and that is to *let themselves be hounded*. Let my children grow up on a crust of bread, so long as they are honest! If the intelligentsia were like *this*, it would be invincible.'[28]

And this courage is not a matter of methodologies and viewpoints and "lines." Its roots are in the private being in his aloneness.

Is exhorting oneself and others, is listing all these desirables for oneself and others, useless? "What's the point, no one will ever step out of his skin." *Masjiden to rehtee nahin, tamir se kaya fayeda?*

It is, indeed, true that entire classes do not transcend their class interests. And so, it would be entirely unrealistic to expect

---

proletariat of another country, it is dogmatism, copying the bad as well as the good. This is not good. One must copy, but what one should copy is the spirit, the essence, not the superficial. . . . The universal truth must be combined with China's concrete reality. . . . We must be courageous in hoisting and uprooting. Improper self-confidence, mediocre self-confidence and false self-confidence are all not permissible. Modesty without a scientific foundation is not true modesty. True modesty must be compatible with reality.) *Miscellany of Mao Tse-Tung Thought*, Joint Publications Research Service, Arlington, 1974, Volumes I & II, pp. 91-97.)

[28] Solzhenitsyn, *op. cit.*, p. 250.

that our intellectuals—and the middle class to which they belong—will change wholesale. But history affords numerous examples of individuals transcending their group and class interests. Instead of lamenting that others will never change as a bloc, each should focus on his practice. *Hum sudhrenge, jag sudhrega.*

## SELECT BIBLIOGRAPHY

The following selection will acquaint the reader with a wide variety of views on the question.

Perry Anderson, *Considerations on Western Marxism*, New Left Books, 1976.
Paul Baran, "The Commitment of the Intellectual" in Paul Baran, *The Longer View*, Monthly Review Press, New York, 1969.
David Craig (ed.), *Marxists on Literature, An Anthology*, Penguin, London, 1975.
A. Gramsci, *Prison Notebooks*, Lawrence and Wishart, London, 1971.
Held and Nielsen, *Philosophy and Action*, Oxford, New York, 1972.
John Hoffman, *Marxism and the Theory of Praxis*, Lawrence and Wishart, 1975.
L. Hsun, *Selected Works of L. Hsun*, Foreign Languages Press, Peking, 1959, especially the talks on the "New Literature" and the "Shanghai Literature," in Volume III.
L. Kolawosky, *Marxism and Beyond*, Paladin, London, 1969.
George Lukacs, "On the Responsibility of Intellectuals" in G. Lukacs, *Marxism and Human Liberation*, Delta, New York, 1973.
George Orwell, "The Prevention of Literature," "Politics vs Literature: An Examination of Gulliver's Travels," and "Writers and Leviathan," in S. Orwell and I. Angus (eds.), *The Collected Essays, Journalism and Letters of George Orwell*, Volume 4, Harcourt, Brace and World, New York, 1968.
Mao Tse-tung, *Selected Works*, International Publishers, New York, 1954, in particular "Combat Liberalism," (Volume II) and "Talks at the Yenan Forum on Arts and Literature," (Volume IV).
*Miscellany of Mao Tse-tung Thought*, Volumes 1 and 2, Joint Publications Research Service, Arlington, 1974.
Hans Morgenthau, "Truth and Power" in his *Truth and Power*, Praeger, New York, 1970.
A. Shourie, "Economics, Economists and Policy Makers," *Economic and Political Weekly*, February 1975.
A. Solzhenitsyn, "The Smatterers," in A. Solzhenitsyn (ed.), *From Under the Rubble*, Fontana Collins, London, 1976.

## 12  Proposals for Bihar Students*

Constructive work is an essential part of revolutionary struggle.
From the point of view of revolution the objective of constructive work is not that of solving a particular problem. Rather, from this standpoint, constructive work has five objectives: (a) we should get to know ourselves, our weaknesses and strengths, a bit better, we should make ourselves purer and better instruments through the fire of work; (b) we should get to know each other better, we should be able to assess how far each of us will be prepared to go in the next round; (c) we should get closer to the masses; (d) through the school of work we should improve our understanding of the system in which all of us labour; finally, and most important of all, (e) the work we undertake and its results should enable the masses themselves to understand the nature of the system better.

When Gandhiji undertook the *satyagrahas* in Champaran, Bardoli and Khera his principal objectives were not that indigo cultivators should be able to get a slightly higher recompense from the millowners, that the land revenue assessment should be revised or that the collection of land revenue should be deferred in a particular year. Each of these was just the occasion for

*December, 1977.

## Proposals for Bihar Students

struggle. The principal objectives were precisely the five that I have listed above.

Today we are passing through a brief interval between two periods of struggle. Bihar students had a significant role in the 1973-75 movement. There can be little doubt that the coming convulsions will also demand much of them. That is why we should take up such tasks in this interval as will forge us into better instruments for struggle.

In our country—and specially in a backward province like Bihar—there are many, many institutions that need to be set right, many ways of doing and looking at things that need to be reformed. There is, therefore, no shortage of tasks that need to be taken up. And it would be presumptuous—and almost a bit foolish—for one to prescribe that tasks "a," "b" and "c" should be taken up and tasks "x," "y" and "z" should not be touched at all. In a situation where thousands of things are crying out to be done, it would be silly for us to set up a competition between rival lists of constructive work programmes, it would be silly for us to lose ourselves in acrimonious debates about the relative merits and demerits of these rival lists. Every programme will yield some good. I do not want to start a debate urging that we should only take up the tasks I shall list and not take up any other task. My objective is merely to put forth a point of view to friends and to translate it into a few representative concrete proposals.

Compared to other sections of society, students have one distinction: they are literate. Therefore, one of the things that society can expect of them is that they will take up tasks that only those who can read and write can accomplish, or at least, in accomplishing which the literate have a comparative advantage.

I believe that in the present context our students should identify such constructive tasks as have three specific features: they should bring us closer to our people, in particular to the depressed and dispossessed among them; in performing them we should come to understand our political system better and, third, the results of that work should enable the people, in particular the depressed and dispossessed among them, to understand the nature of the State better.

Of the various types of constructive work that can be taken

up, investigations, "studies" as our social scientists are apt to call them, are one kind. Undertaking investigations that reach beyond our normal curricula—curricula that all of us regard as completely unsatisfactory and inappropriate to our needs—undertaking such studies is the minimum that we can be expected to do. They will require time, of course, and some inconvenience also. But, if we are not prepared to set aside a little time and put up with a bit of inconvenience then we are not serious at all. All our sloganeering in the streets, all our defiant posturing is, in that case, just that much hot air.

Of the various subjects that suggest themselves, I believe that the following six will prove particularly instructive. I would suggest that students who want to play a part in JP's total revolution should undertake investigations on topics such as these and broadcast the results among the people.

The subjects are as follows.

First: *who owns the guns, who gets murdered and who is indicted for murder?*

We need three kinds of information to answer these questions: we need the gun-licences issued by the government, we need data about the social and economic background of persons who have been murdered and we need data about the social and economic background of persons who have been held guilty of murder by the courts.

It is easy to see that an examination of these data will reveal a good deal about the real state of affairs in the countryside. Consider, for instance, the fact that before sanctioning a gun-licence the government official is required to ascertain the "social status" of the applicant. The presumption of the official is that the applicant who is seeking a gun-licence should at least have something that is worth safeguarding and for safeguarding which a gun or a pistol is required. If a landless labourer were to request the official for a gun-licence, generally speaking the reaction of the official will be, "the fellow does not even have anything that is worth anything, what the hell does he need a gun for?" But if a landlord were to say that he should be sanctioned a gun-licence because he needs arms to protect his property then, whatever else he may think, the official is unlikely to tell himself that the landlord does not have anything worth safeguarding. Now, if in answer to the second question ("who gets murdered") we find that generally speaking the dispossessed and the downtrodden are the ones who get killed, then will it not show that, in the eyes of our State, while the life of a landless labourer is *not* worth protecting, the property of a landlord *is* worth safeguarding?

By ascertaining the facts listed above we will also be able to learn a good bit about other matters:

- Is it a fact that the proportion of downtrodden who get killed is higher than that of the landlords?
- Is it a fact that when a well-to-do person is killed, the culprit—or at least an alleged culprit—gets caught while the murders of the poor generally remain 'unsolved'?
- Is it a fact that even when the murders result from family feuds, from the personal hatreds or the factional fights of the landlords, the downtrodden are the ones who are held responsible?

The second topic worth studying is the following: *violent incidents and the State apparatus.*

We should take up some incidents from the past five or ten years of Bihar's history in which individuals from one class, say landlords, tried to pressurize or suppress individuals from another class, say landless labourers or tenants, by violent means. We should reconstruct the incidents dispassionately, almost clinically, and then try and answer the following question: when functionaries of the State—policemen or administrators—ultimately reached the scene, on whose side did they intervene? While the incident was still ablaze or in the aftermath, did they join the landlords in further crushing the downtrodden or did they intervene to protect the latter?

The third topic is: *a people's census of land rights.*

All of us know that in spite of all the noise and din about land reforms over the past thirty years, we have not had a satisfactory national census of land rights. Whenever such compilations have been made they have been put together on the basis of *patwari* records and the like. Now, it is well known that *patwari* records are not reliable—specially not in a state like Bihar which still has many vestiges of feudalism on its back. Therefore, we should take up some part of Bihar—backward districts like

Purnea and Champaran that are marked by poverty, extreme inequality and grave tensions would be ideal—and we should organize a people's census of land rights in that area. It should be a "people's census" in the sense that it should not be a census that has been put together by looking at official registers; rather it should be a census that has been built up by actually asking the tenants, the tillers themselves, as to who owns the land that they cultivate, how much rent they pay, what share of the crop from that plot they part with and so on.

A census of this kind will reveal a host of facts about our political and economic system. A comparison of the facts with the existing laws—for instance, of the crop shares that are extracted from the tenants with the maximum that is permissible—will itself be an eye opener.

The fourth study is to prepare a list of *Bihar's 500 largest landlords*.

While Bihar, like the rest of India, has passed reams of land reform laws, while it also has fixed ceilings on land ownership, it is well known that many in Bihar own and receive rent from thousands and thousands of acres. It would be really instructive to compile an authentic, irrefutible list of these landlords, their holdings, and the rents etc., that are exacted for these holdings by the landlords. Such a list, like the earlier census, will also have to be compiled by personal, on-the-spot inquiry and not from official records.

Once such a list is available we will be able to use it as a touchstone: we will be able to publicize it among the people and affirm that we will take the professions of successive Bihar governments about land reforms seriously after seeing what happens as a result of their actions to these five hundred, to their holdings, to the rent and other exactions they rake in.

The fifth topic worth studying is so obvious that it does not even need a summary justification: *the temples of Bihar, their keepers—the priests—and the priests' keeps*.

There is hardly an area in the country where the people are as heavily drugged by the opium of religion and superstition as they are in Bihar. This religion and these superstitions directly help the ruling classes keep the people under their heel: the religion and superstitions lead the people to internalize the empirical order, to look upon it as rational, as serving some higher purpose, to regard culture as nature, to regard the man-made social world as an immutable order decreed by some superhuman agency.

We should, therefore, examine the workings of the temples of Bihar. We should examine the properties and lands they control, the way they treat their tenants. We should examine the soporifics they peddle to the people. We should examine the living habits—the concubines and all—of the priests who strut around as the functionaries of God on earth.

Finally, we should put together a study that is of the first importance: *law from the point of view of the poor*.

Gandhiji used to say that law is but the convenience of the powerful. Today our liberal society boasts of equality before law as one of its great tenets, nay as one of its great achievements. Yet the equality is not even a formal equality, it is a sham. As a perspicacious thinker once put it—all that the Law in its majesty today affords is equal freedom and opportunity to the rich and the poor to die of starvation.

Palliatives are often touted about. Seminars urging the need to make the formal equality real never cease. Reports containing general exhortations follow reports containing general exhortations. Bills and resolutions are passed urging legal aid to the poor.

And yet things continue as they are.

We should document the state of affairs in minute and concrete detail. We are seeing before our eyes how the Indira Gandhis and the Yashpal Kapurs, the Birlas and the Jains are able to invoke clause after clause, sub-clause after sub-clause to prevent the cases from even getting off the ground, while the same clauses and sub-clauses come in handy for keeping the Girijans and Harijans and their sympathizers in prison for six-seven years as undertrial prisoners. The laws never suffice to prosecute a landlord for not paying the prescribed minimum wage or exacting more than the permissible crop-share. Yet they are never wanting in evicting a tenant or pauperizing a marginal farmer. A classic set of cases that need to be documented and exposed are the "conspiracy cases" launched against so-called Naxalites in Bihar's neighbouring state, Andhra Pradesh. I doubt if there is another set of cases that prove as well as these the fraud that is perpetrated on the poor in the name of law in our country. The inception of these cases, their preparation, the way they have been prosecuted, the time that has elapsed in their journies through various courts, the fate of the victims and their families during this period, the judgements that have been handed down, the apathy of the society to the proceedings—each one of these aspects speaks volumes about the nature and purposes of our much-flaunted Rule of Law.

I could go on listing additional subjects. The six I have listed should suffice as representative illustrations. We will not be able to study any one of them by pouring over official reports or by spending our time in libraries. This is one of their virtues.

To study them we will have to establish and strengthen our contacts with the people, specially with the poor and the downtrodden among them. And there can be no doubt that the effort to dig up the facts about these simple subjects will teach us a lot about the system in which we live today just as publicizing the results of our investigations will help deepen the people's understanding of the system.

# 13  The Janata Year

## TOUCHSTONES*

Through the elections the people have once again proven for themselves the lesson that Gandhiji held out for all of us—that the people are powerful, the potentates are not.

Whether something can be accomplished or not in the reprieve that we now have will depend on whether or not the people are vigilant, on whether or not they shed fear, on whether or not they get organized.

In the large, the outcome will be determined by the economic forces with which we have become all too familiar—growing unemployment, urbanization, poverty and the like. In many respects the Janata Party is but a linear projection of trends within the Congress itself over the past 30 years. Thus, to mention just one instance, the landed interests which had been gradually extending their hold over the Congress organization and by the mid-60s had come to completely dominate it at the provincial level, have in the Janata party now made a spectacular breakthrough up to the Centre also.

For this reason, many have no doubt about the economic and

*April 1977.

other policies that the new government will follow, just as they have no doubt about the eventual outcome.

In a sense (and thank the Janata-*Janardhan* for that) we are back in 1973. There are, of course, two crucial differences: the people are more self-confident and, second, the very process by which the new leaders have acquired power will keep them from doing a June 25 on us soon.

It is probable, therefore, that in this round the contradictions of the system will be exposed even more unambiguously than they were in the first half of the seventies. How far will things drift this time? Will the demand again grow in the ruling classes for another strong man? Will some new pretext be found for another *coup*?

My purpose here is not to speculate about these possibilities. It is merely to list a few ready-reckoners by which the reader may assess whether the new government is going to be at all different from the pre-June 1975 Congress government.

Many complicated indices can be listed—about the balance between different classes, about unemployment, about numbers below the poverty line, about rates and compositions of investment and what not. These are the important indices—they give us glimpses of factors that will determine the eventual outcome. My check-list deals with much more modest items. But they are tell-tale items and there are two advantages to them—the information about them will become available much sooner than that about the more esoteric indicators and, second, almost all of it will be within the grasp of the ordinary citizen himself.

My check-list covers four aspects: corruption, enquiries, restoration of a free society and a few aspects of the economic scene.

*Corruption*

Through his day-to-day dealings with the State apparatus, the citizen will know how far the government is fulfilling the pledge of a clean administration.

I offer but two bits of litmus paper. First, a declaration and two pledges. Every member of the new party who holds office (in the party or in government) must publicly declare his assets and income and those of each member of his immediate family (whether adult or minor, married or unmarried); he must also declare his past as well as present associations (financial, managerial, or of any other kind) and that of every member of his immediate family with any concern engaged in commerce, industry or agriculture. Furthermore, he must pledge to bring this declaration up-to-date every year and he must pledge that should a mis-statement be found at any stage in his declarations he will voluntarily retire from public life for at least ten years.

We have become so accustomed to corruption in politics that the instinctive reaction of the reader will probably be—"but you are asking for the impossible; no politician will agree to follow this prescription."

There is no reason for us to tailor our requirements according to what the standard politico will do or not do. If we begin doing so, the game will be lost even before it is begun. The point is that an honest man will have no difficulty in complying with the declaration and the pledges. Gandhiji, by whose name the new rulers swear, would have had no difficulty with them. JP, on whose shoulders they have reached their new offices, would have no difficulty with them. To the extent that the declarations, etc., of the new rulers fall short of the preceding formulation, to that extent we will know they have things to hide.

"But why not just the ministers? Why every holder of office of the party? Is it not enough that we make sure that the ministers are honest?" The Janata Party is not the mighty *Shiva:* it cannot confine poisons to parts of its body. Ministers at the top will not be honest unless *all* levels in the party are honest. Gandhiji, whom the new rulers like to quote, used to say that an organization which starts relying on rogues to do its work, will soon have rogues at its top. The recent history of the Congress is living proof of this maxim. So I am afraid, it is all or nothing.

"But then why not 'every office-holder of the party?' Why all members adult or minor, (married or unmarried) of his immediate family also?" Unfortunately, we live in the land of *benami*. There is hardly a politician in India who keeps assets in his name. Many of the assets (cash, jewellery, to say nothing of accounts abroad) are not in anyone's name. And our formulation, far from being too stringent, doesn't even touch these. But at least we should take account of the current practice of

Indian politicians and rope in all members of their families. Surely, we have not forgotten Sardar Pratap Singh and Bakshi? Those who talk so much of the assets that Sanjay is said to have accumulated will concede that they would have got nowhere by merely asking Indira Gandhi to declare the assets in *her* name. Will they now themselves be less forthcoming than they would have wanted Indira Gandhi to be?

"But is it not enough that these declarations be filed with the PM or with the party office? Why must they be made available to the public?" The reader will probably be surprised to know that it has been common practice for Ministers to file a declaration of their assets and those of their spouses with the PM for years. And a fat lot of difference that has made. Public scrutiny alone will ensure that no mis-statements are made. Public scrutiny alone will enable us to compare the assets and incomes of our rulers with their professions of socialism and Gandhism.

"But what is this about associations with firms of profit?" Firms invest in our politicians. They keep them. They maintain them and their families. And they are rewarded once the politician has access to office. This declaration of associations will help us spot the favours done to firms and the reasons thereof.

"But the pledge to retire for 10 years is just too much. Why not leave it to the government and the party to deal with the liar in the way they deem fit?" We have seen how governments and parties deal with those of their members who are caught with their hands in the till. If the fellow is an ally, his conduct is attributed to innocent forgetfulness; if he is to be whipped into line, the information is used to blackmail him. No, there is no substitute for a public pledge. And let the fellow forget the pledge when he is caught. The people will remember it.

And now for the second bit of litmus paper. There has been much talk of the subversive influence of multi-nationals and other foreign concerns. Boeing, Piper Aircraft and others are in the air. We are told that one of the ways in which these firms eat into our vitals is by bribing officials and politicians.

The sincerity of the new rulers in dealing with this problem will be guaged by whether or not they ask every foreign company in India to disclose names of all Indians who have received commissions and other payments from it during the past, say, 10 years. Every company should be told that, should the government's subsequent enquiries indicate that it has lied, it will be barred from doing business in India.

"But is this not too sweeping a requirement?" Far from it. It should ultimately be extended to requests to foreign governments for urging their banks to disclose the names of Indians who have accounts in them. It should ultimately be extended to cover Indian firms. And so on. But if the new rulers do not even take the first step that has been suggested above, we will know that their talk about the corrupt and subversive practices of foreign firms is just that much blather—the talk outsiders indulge in before they become insiders.

## Enquiries

You cannot come across a single person today who feels in the least responsible—to say nothing of feeling remorseful—for the heinous events of those 19 months. Politicians, who till yesterday were strutting around as the cat's whiskers, blame it all on over-zealous officials. And there isn't an official who admits to zeal, far from an excess of it. At best, all the blame is being put on the *Chandal Chowkdi* or our *swadeshi* gang of four (people still do not have the courage to include the fifth in the gang). And this gang is not repentant at all; on the contrary, it is convinced that the country will soon repent for having thrown it out.

Now, it should be obvious that a country of 650 million cannot be stunned by 4 or 5 individuals. The nineteen months represented a systemic failure. Nothing of what transpired could have happened without the enthusiastic cooperation of thousands of eager *apparatchi* and the tacit cooperation of thousands more. After all, none of the 4 or 5 arrested anyone; none of them tortured anyone; none—I would presume—grabbed the money with his own hands.

The nature of enquiries that it will launch will tell us whether the new government is interested in exposing the system that failed or in just trapping the five.

The heinous acts, the malfeasance, the crimes against the nation of the five must be thoroughly exposed and they must be brought to book for them. If they are not prosecuted with the greatest vigour, we will conclude—the sanctimonious drivel notwithstanding—that deals have been made.

But, if the enquiries are limited to the four or five individuals, we will conclude that the government is just interested in hunting down individuals rather than in exposing the system that collapsed, rather than in educating the country so that it may be better equipped for the next *coup*.

The government should also know that enquiries limited to just four or five may well end making martyrs of them. And a government that itself has a few against whom strictures and charges have been levelled in the past must know that the strictures and charges are soon forgotten, that the individuals soon enough find their way back to high office. Some of them even turn up as members of code of conduct committees.

Thus, the government's sincerity about its democratic professions, about its pledges to rebuild institutions, should be judged by whether or not it institutes four general enquiries: a commission to reconstruct the events of the 19 months, expose the instruments that were used, to affix responsibility all along the line; second, a commission to enquire into corruption during the Emergency; third, a commission to enquire into maltreatment and tortures in police custody and jails; and, finally, a commission to enquire into excesses of the executive during the Emergency.

The enquiries must spell out the instruments that were used—from the harassment arm of the government, the CBI, income tax raids, etc., to the police, the censor and all—and they must expose the individuals who wielded them. They must tell the country what happened to the decision-making process: was the lapse of having a pliable President sign the Emergency proclamation a day before the Cabinet met just a solitary oversight or had illegality become the norm; who gave and in what form were the orders given for the vasectomy drive; who ordered beatings and tortures in police custody and in jails; who withheld medical treatment from ailing detenus; and so on. They must also report how the government machinery was subverted by putting operators in key positions in the banks, in financial institutions, etc.

Only in this way will the country learn, only in this way will our opportunist civil service and our immoral police learn. Otherwise—whether the four or five are sequestered or not—the

## The Janata Year

country will be as ill-prepared for the next assault as it was on 25 June 1975.

Three additional points about these enquiries must be borne in mind.

First, the enquiries must afix responsibility unambiguously. Officials, ministers, others must be named. Consider the vasectomy drive. What was the minister doing? He—and others like him—now blame everything on unnamed officials. Was the fascist Maharashtra law the work of a lone doctor or was there official and ministerial encouragement? When the Centre added a few more turns to this fascist screw, did officials do so in the dead of night? Was the minister so negligent that he did not even know what laws his officials were pushing, that he did not know—when everyone even in the bazaars knew—what was happening in the vasectomy camps? If he knew, what did he do about the law, about what was being done in the name of planning families? What about ministerial responsibility?

Indeed what about the collective responsibility of the Cabinet? What about all those who sat silent at Cabinet meetings and are belching in self-satisfaction today? We must not forget that they—and the despicable Congress MPs who lauded every turn of the screw—are trying their hardest to divert the country's attention from themselves by hurling all the blame on to four or five individuals.

Second, the punishment must match the enormity of the crimes. We should not, as the venerable Acharya has said, be squeamish and mealy-mouthed: punishment is the right word. It must be exemplary so that it registers on the collaborationist and opportunist ethos of the civil service and the police. This is not a call for *badla*. Anyone who tries to dismiss it as such will be doing so dishonestly. It is a plea for teaching those who man the State apparatus a lesson.

The danger is that the new ministers—so new to office, so flushed with the first experience of "power"—will be satisfied with symbolic gestures, with sending a fellow to Lakshadweep, another to the Andamans: *aji use uchal kar kale pani patak dala*. And the recent recruits to the cause of freedom—those who sat silent through the 19 months—would be only too eager to encourage leniency all around. Now that the campaign is over, they are desperate to have everyone return to business—as usual. Every disclosure, every reprimand, every punishment raises the question: what were *they* doing when all this was going on? (Waiting, of course. Waiting for the right moment. While thousands were rotting in jails, they were waiting. While some of them were being tortured, while some of them were being denied medical treatment, while some of them were dying, while their families were suffering, our friends here were waiting. Waiting, my foot. They were shivering in their *dhoties*.)

If the officials are guilty, if these pups really deport themselves as little Ceasars, why is the government unleashing them on the hapless tribals? And just look at the signal that is being transmitted to the collaborationist civil service and police: with the memory of these symbolic reprimands, when the next *coup* comes, the officials will still be telling each other, "I say, do as the new *chandal chowkdi* tells you; at worst when the *raj* changes, you'll be transferred. But if you refuse to do their whim today, God knows what may happen to you...."

The third point is that the enquiries must be people's enquiries and not just bureaucratic enquiries. People at all levels must be involved in determining the norms for fixing responsibility, in collecting evidence, in determining the appropriate scale of punishment.

"But will this not deteriorate into a witch-hunt? What do the people know about fixing responsibility, about evidence, about what punishment is appropriate and what is not?"

How quickly the scales are turned! Suddenly now the people do not know how to assign responsibility! Till yesterday they were the *Janardhan*. Now they don't know how to collect evidence and afix punishment. *They* are the ones who have delivered us from the dictators. Not those who today presume exclusive knowledge about enquiries and evidence and accountability. Will our "democrats" once again and that, too, so quickly, show their customary contempt for the people?

Thus, the new government should be judged by the thoroughness and comprehensiveness of the enquiries it sets in motion.

## Restoring Freedom

Repealing every single black law, every black amendment pushed through by the previous government is but the first step—though obviously an essential step—in restoring freedom.

Freedom was not snuffed out in our country because of these "laws." These "laws" could be enacted—and that too with such ease and amidst such apparent acclaim—because freedom had been snuffed out.

Therefore, the new government will be judged by how far it moves in helping recreate the preconditions of freedom.

This is a large subject. I will offer but three simple tests.

First, we should see what the government does to expose and reduce the intelligence and police apparatus of the State.

The Indian people are unarmed. Recent events have conclusively demonstrated that the enormous police and intelligence apparatus that has been built up is incompatible with a free society. It is certainly incompatible with the Gandhian society that the government says it wants to help create.

It is also clear that the apparatus is not necessary if a regime is genuinely working for the interests of the people. The extent to which it maintains it, to that extent we will know that the regime has not been able to win the people over and that will be so only because it will not be working for them.

Exposure as well as actual reduction is necessary. The country must be told the ways in which intelligence agencies have come to be misused. It must be told about the torture methods that have been introduced into Gandhi's India. It must be told about the centres and "chambers" where specialized cadre and equipment have been assembled for these. The country must be given a full account of the numerous young men and women who are said to have died in "encounters" with the police. The government must regularly publish information about detenus. It must permit observers to regularly visit the jails and talk to the prisoners. There are absolutely no technical difficulties in publishing data of this kind and in allowing access. If the data are not published, if access is not allowed, we must conclude that things are not different from what they have been, that Gandhiji's name is once again being appropriated by a bunch that has no intention of moving towards a Gandhian society.

Secondly, we must watch—and each of us will soon know by his personal experience—what the government does to reorient the harassment machinery of the government (from the income tax raider, the sales tax inspector to the *patwaris* and policemen in the villages) and what machinery is set up to ensure redress to the citizen.

Tyranny and terror—a glimpse of which the upper classes had during the 19 months—are features of the daily lives of the poor. In the villages the State apparatus nakedly functions as the arm of the landed interests. We should, therefore, watch out for reports about encounters between the landless and the land owners, between employees, and employers, and ascertain on whose side the State apparatus intervenes in each encounter. We should see whether the past record of the apparatus always intervening on the side of the landlords, the employers, is at all different from now on.

The third test is about electoral reforms. We should watch and see what happens to the role of big money in the elections. A party that is actually working with the masses does not need the enormous amounts of money that the Congress used to rake in. As its haul increased, so we knew that it was doing less and less work with and for the people; so we knew that it was ceasing to be a political party, that it was becoming a mere electoral machine. Now that the Janata Party is the ruling party, will it be any different? Will it also start making distinctions between those who are corrupt "for themselves" and those who are corrupt "only for the party?" The coming assembly elections will provide an early indication: *honhaar birvaan ke hot cheekne paat.*

## The Economic Scene

The new government has pledged itself to many things during the campaign: the abolition of destitution, guaranteed employment, reduction of income disparities to 1:10 and so on.

All of us will be watching the usual indices for gauging its progress towards fulfilling these pledges. Its candour on these matters will itself be a good indication. As the situation worsened over the years, Congress governments became more and more taciturn on all these questions. A glimpse into what is happening on the ground will be given by how forthcoming the government is with data about numbers on the employment registers, the numbers who have acquired jobs through its special schemes, the kinds of works that have been taken up, the number of workers who have been laid off and retrenched and so on.

My check list—of five items—is just illustrative.

First, we should see what is happening to investment. The stagnation of investment rates for the past 10 years has reflected the underlying stalemate in a synoptic way. So we should see what happens to these rates: whether they limp along as they have done for a decade or whether they rise; and if the stalemate is indeed broken, we should see how it is that it has been broken. The betting is that if it is broken at all, it will be by giving full rein to private firms and to foreign firms including the multi-nationals. If this indeed turns out to be the case, it will be really interesting to see how these firms are brought around to doing the Gandhian things—in the goods they produce, in the way they treat labour, in their relations with government and the society, in the technology they adopt.

Second, we should see what is done to reorient the productive system for producing the goods that the poor need (but for purchasing which they do not have the means) rather than the goods that the well-to-do want. Many small things will tell the tale: the fate of controlled cloth, the number of ration shops in the villages, the quantum of goods supplied through them and so on.

Third, decentralization. Progress towards this objective will by itself tell us whether a single item can be plucked out of Gandhiji's teaching and transplanted in a society that is otherwise rushing towards "modernization" and capitalism. In Gandhiji's thought, decentralization is but an element in a comprehensive scheme—a scheme that is no less than a plan for an alternative civilization. For him a good index would be the extent to which units at each level—the individual, the family, the locality, the village, the block, the country—are self-sufficient. The government—given its class background etc.,—can hardly be expected to bring about such a large re-structuring. To gauge whether it is doing anything at all in this matter, we should watch three of the crudest indices: (*a*) is it able to reorient the R&D effort in the country so that its starting point is the poor man's life, the things he needs, and its objective is to ascertain what can be done to help him acquire these; (*b*) is it able to get our skilled personnel—our architects, our engineers, our doctors, our academics etc.,—to work for the poor, specially for the poor in the villages; (c) is it at least able to shift a substantial part—say, one-third—of its own bureaucracy, specially its senior bureaucracy, from Delhi and the State capitals to the district and the block headquarters?

Fourth, we should see what stance in adopts to people's movements in the country. JP has already laid stress on this. The question here is not merely of its attitude to the People's Committees but of its attitude to people's movements in general. What, e.g., will its attitude be to young men and women who are working in Bihar, Bengal, Andhra and other places to awaken the oppressed so that they may smash feudal institutions, so that they may ensure that the existing laws about crop-sharing, minimum wages, tenurial security etc., are adhered to?

Finally, we should watch the Janata Party itself and see the extent to which it starts working with the people. Will it mobilize the people for conducting a census on land holdings, for tapping ground water, for educating agricultural workers about the minimum wages they are entitled to, for telling the tenants the legally permissible crop share that the landlord can extract?

All will agree that these tasks are important. All will agree that unless it works with the people on issues such as these, the Janata Party will become just another Congress and thus confirm the view of those who maintain that it in any case *is* just another Congress. It is clear that engaging in work of this kind is the only way for it to build a cadre known to and trusted by the people. It is also clear that unless such a cadre is built, many of the party's pledges just cannot be fulfilled. Thus, to cite just one instance, the bureaucracy just cannot mobilize and organize labour on the scale that is needed for guaranteeing employment to all. A party that reaches out to every nook and corner alone can do so. Hence, it will be useful to watch whether the Janata Party is on the way to becoming such a party or whether it is becoming just another electoral machine.

## And What if They Don't?

The people have been anxiously testing the electoral process for at least 10 years. In 1967 they mauled the Congress. To little effect. In 1971 they gave it massive majorities. To even worse results. In 1974 in UP they defeated two-thirds of the sitting members who sought re-election. No change. In 1977 they have again slapped the Congress soundly.

What if things still do not change? At least a few will begin losing faith in elections themselves. They will then infer that the electoral process is just a device to mislead them, to give them the illusion of choice, that the rulers have no intention of stepping out of their skin.

> Kisse to vahi purane hain
> unvān badalte jāte hain
> Kaidi ko behlāne ko
> durbān badalte jāte hain

## A WELL-DESERVED DEFEAT*

A well-deserved defeat but an ill-deserved victory.

The principal reason for the slap that the Janata has received in the South is that it has not worked either as a party or as a government. Talk of caste-alliances, of Mrs Gandhi's charisma, of the strength of regional leaders etc., should not obscure this central fact.

Lost in a fog of self-satisfaction, leaders of the Janata government have refused to listen to repeated warnings that time was running out, that they were forfeiting all the goodwill they had started with. The warnings have got nowhere. The fog has been impenetrable. Even visible impatience of the people has not awakened them. Instead of working, they have spent their time in grabbing the perquisites of office, in nursing their health, in mutual recrimination.

So, a full-blooded slap is what they deserved. And a slap is what they have got.

The Southern election results also remind us that their is no national political party left now. The Janata has been unable to make headway in the South. The Congress has evaporated. Each party of the left can scarcely get on with itself, to say nothing of its getting on with other left parties. Mrs Gandhi's party is a

*March, 1978.

coalition of regional groups.

Such a state of affairs bodes ill for the future. Coalitions of regional satrapies cannot impart either strength or a sense of purpose to our vast country.

Instead of realizing the terrible implications of this for our future, our academics and our political pundits have been peddling "decentralization" as the latest panacea. Is it the lack of formal powers that has kept the States from stemming the rot in the education system? Is it the lack of formal powers that has kept them from stemming the cancer of corruption? Has Article 370 meant that the *people* of Jammu and Kashmir have power or has it meant that a regional satrap has unquestioned power?

The trouble in our system—as the non-performance of the Janata government and the party demonstrates—is much deeper. It cannot be remedied by shuffling boxes on organization charts or redrawing lists of formal powers as between one level of government and another.

And the people will soon realize that nor can the trouble be overcome by reposing trust in one party after another. In 1967 they thought they could improve matters by trouncing the Congress. In 1971 they thought they could do so by giving it an overwhelming majority. In 1977 they thought they could do so by trusting the Janata. Now, tossed from pillar to post, they have thought that things will change by trouncing the Janata. A few more tosses and they may begin to get the message.

It is not just that we no longer have a national political party. The fact is that apart from a few regional or local groups—the Akalis in Punjab, the two DMKs in Tamil land—we no longer have parties with any cadres at all.

The latest poll again demonstrates that even elections are not now being won or lost by electoral machines. They are being won and lost on *havaas*. The Janata victory in March 1977 occurred without any organization. Mrs Gandhi's victories now owe little to any organization at the grassroots The parties, that is, have ceased to be even electoral machines.

*Havaas* can certainly decide elections. But they cannot bring about social, economic and political transformations.

This is the second fact we should bear in mind: our polity now is bereft of instruments. The bureaucracy is so demoralized that now it will not even push routine files without the cover and the lack of accountability of an emergency. And political parties are without organizations. Can we transform our society with these palsied hands?

There is a second implication, too, of the fact that our political parties are without cadres, without organizations. The polity is atomized. This means that at the local level the old oppressive groupings will now have unquestioned sway—the caste groups, the organizations of landlords, the local bands of toughs. And at levels above the locality, there will now be nothing between "the leader"—the *swadeshi* Mussolini—and the people. This atomization of the polity, this clearing away of all buffers, is the first requisite for a personal dictatorship.

The Southern results are important from this point of view. It is for this reason that while the defeat of the Janata was well deserved, Mrs Gandhi's victory, as far as the fate of a democratic polity is concerned, is ill-deserved. Just as the immediate result of the election results is to rehabilitate Mrs Gandhi, their lasting significance will be to help legitimize a personal dictatorship in the country.

For Mrs Gandhi is not hiding her intentions now. She is not doing anything surreptitiously any longer. While her opponents sit blaming each other, she, both for rehabilitating herself and for re-establishing the emergency polity she thinks our country needs, is going to the people.

She has founded a party in her name. Her partymen have openly said that "a personality cult is a good thing as long as the personality is Shrimati Indira Gandhi." While some have been telling her to shun the caucus, she has insisted on flaunting it so as to leave no one in any doubt that the caucus stands by her and she stands by it. And, most important of all, she has been campaigning on the slogan that the Eemergency was a good thing.

So great is their disillusionment with the Janata that the people have set aside the disclosures of corruption, whether these relate to Urs or to Maruti, they have set aside the disclosures of arbitrariness and brutality. Whatever their intentions, by doing so they have taken a giant step towards legitimizing a repetition of the arbitrariness, brutality and the corruption.

Our people are in the habit of having others do their work for them. That is why they have sat back after each election in the last thirty years, hoping that those they have returned in the elections would do their work for them. But this time in the Southern states they have entrusted their work to a party that has fascist genes, a party that is, as JP said recently, a focus of distilled, undiluted fascism. They will live to rue the day. They will live to see the truth of the Mahatma's maxim: when we rely on rascals to do our work, we will soon have rascals at our head.

## INDIRA GANDHI'S RESPONSIBILITY*

The fraudulent and illegal acts which Justice Shah has uncovered entail Indira Gandhi is three kinds of responsibility.

The first and gravest kind, of course, is moral responsibility. To have lied to the President, to have imprisoned thousands, to have mutilated the laws and the constitution just to hang on to office, what graver crime can there be against our country and our people? It is a sad comment on our laws that these terrible crimes do not entail criminal liability. What sort of a legal system is it which hurls a poor man into prison for seven years as an undertrial prisoner and baulks at punishing someone who has prostituted the entire State apparatus for his or her personal ends?

Given this lacuna in our laws, and given the fact that questions of moral responsibility are liable to slip off Indira Gandhi's mind as water off a duck's back, it is for the people to translate her moral culpability into political punishment. If they flock to her in spite of Justice Shah's grave indictment then they will be legitimizing the perversion of the Constitution in the future. They will then have no one to blame but themselves when she or another usurper hurls us into the June 1975 nightmare once again.

If the people remain unmoved by Justice Shah's indictment then by their very indifference they will be proving that the cancer in our polity has now gone so far as to be beyond our abilities to control it. Their indifference will prove that over the years we have become so accustomed to malfeasance that nothing will shock us now. For what greater crimes can a politician be indicted than the ones Justice Shah has uncovered against Mrs Gandhi?

*May, 1978.

There was a time when strictures by a Commission of Inquiry on even small matters used to shock people, when they used to prove fatal for the politician concerned. Remember the Das Commission? Remember the matters on which it found Pratap Singh Kairon to have misused his office? Of the numerous charges that the memorialists had put forward, Justice Das found merit in only four. He held that Kairon had abetted, if not helped, his relatives to improperly acquire two cinema houses and one cold storage, that he helped the mother-in-law of his son sell two plots of land to the Government which she should actually have surrendered as surplus land and finally, that he improperly used the services of a civil surgeon, while on an election tour. That is all. All other charges were dismissed.

Compare these matters to what Justice Shah has uncovered. Wholesale and wilful perversion of the Constitution, illegal arrests of thousands, *mala fide* legislation, manipulation of the media, institution of false cases, demoniacal demolitions of the houses of the poor. . . .The standards of malfeasance have certainly gone up in India. Raising them has been the singular contribution of Indira Gandhi and her ever-changing coterie—the L.N. Mishras, the Bansi Lals, the V.C. Shuklas, the Om Mehtas, the Gokhales.

If all this is not enough to shock our people then graver crimes will certainly be visited upon them. They will then be proving by their apathy that they can no longer safeguard democracy; for democracy cannot be safeguarded by those whose conscience is the alertness and conscience of corpses.

The second kind of responsibility that Justice Shah's reports entail for Indira Gandhi is direct criminal liability. Having people arrested on non-existent grounds, having false cases instituted against them is criminal misuse of one's office. Moreover, in the case of the textile inspectors Mrs. Gandhi is liable for prosecution even under the Prevention of Corruption Act. The Supreme Court has ruled on an earlier occasion that defrauding the public exchequer is tantamount to corruption. In the textile inspectors case, the attempt of Indira International to defraud the public exchequer by a false declaration has been established as has been the financial interest of Mrs Gandhi's relatives and her hand in having the inspectors arrested.

In relation to the grave crimes that Justice Shah has uncovered, these are minor matters. But the public should not dismiss then on this account. Rather than regarding them as minor, the public should look upon them as symbolic and should insist that Mrs Gandhi as well as all her cohorts must be prosecuted on each of these matters to the full extent of the law.

The third kind of responsibility is suggested by Justice Shah's remark that the single gravest excess of the Emergency was the way Sanjay Gandhi was allowed to function. There should be no doubt at all in the minds of the public as to who is responsible for the reprehensible and callous deeds of Sanjay Gandhi. It is Indira Gandhi alone who is responsible for setting the stage up for him, for shielding and promoting him.

Justice Das's observations on the constructive responsibility of Pratap Singh Kairon for the doings of his sons are relevant to the letter.

Readers will recall that Kairon in his counter affidavit had submitted—I am quoting from Justice Das's account of it in his report—

> 'He disclaims all responsibility, direct or indirect, if any government servant had done anything to oblige or to help his sons or relatives, for it was not done under his orders, knowledge or connivance. He concludes by saying that he has no power either morally or legally to prevent his sons from doing business and reiterates that if he had been informed that they had done anything illegally which brought them within the purview of law, he would certainly have ordered that the law should have its normal course in their case in the same manner as in the case of any other individual. He denies having passed any illegal or wrong or corrupt orders to favour his sons or any other persons.'

Do the words not have a familiar ring? Do Indira Gandhi's apologists not say exactly this today?

And this was Justice Das's verdict, even the words and phrases in it seem to have been chosen to have a bearing on what our *sevika* was later to do and say. He says:

> 'The various charges in the press and in the courts, the numerous allegations of men in public life...should certainly have

informed the mind of S. Pratap Singh Kairon about what was being thought and said about his own conduct and that of his over-zealous colleagues or subordinates. He should have realized that the allegations and insinuations thus made openly and persistently not only reflected on his own character and probity but were also bringing the government of which he was the head into hatred, ridicule and contempt.

'...The commission is free to concede that a father cannot legally or morally prevent his sons from carrying on business. But the exploitation of the influence of the father who happens to be the Chief Minister of the State cannot be permitted to be made a business of. Such exploitation cannot possibly be a legitimate business and the father's influence and powers cannot be permitted to be traded in.

'...There is no getting away from the fact that Pratap Singh Kairon knew or had more than ample reason to think or suspect that his sons and relatives were allegedly exploiting his influence and powers. But, as his own affidavit shows, he made no inquiry, gave no warning to anybody and took no step whatever to prevent its recurrence but let things drift in the way they had been going, assuming he had no hand in it.

...In view of his inaction in the face of the circumstances hereinbefore alluded to he must be held to have connived at the doing of his sons and relatives, his colleagues and the government officers.'

Remember these words when you read Justice Shah's observations on Sanjay Gandhi and also when you read Justice Gupta's forthcoming report on the Maruti plunderings.

Three operational conclusions follow directly from what has been said above.

First, all who have any residual commitment to democracy and the Rule of Law must do everything they can to educate our people about Justice Shah's findings, about their terrible import for our survival as a democracy. We should not leave this task to the Janata governments and the Janata Party. These governments and the party have proven that they have no time to go to the people and talk to them. They have time only to knife each other.

Second, the public must force the Janata government at the Centre to set up a Special Tribunal to try the principal cases of Emergency excesses that are instituted against the principal culprits of the Emergency. The Special Tribunal should be at least at the level of High Court Judges. Let the most highly respected High Court Judges in the country be selected for this purpose. But let them work full-time on the cases. Leaving matters to the lower magistracy—which showed us during the Emergency how independent and fair minded it is!—is to ensure that the cases will not get anywhere for years and years. Time is of the essence in this matter. For justice delayed to Indira Gandhi and her coterie is justice denied to the country.

Third, the people's Representation Act must be amended to ensure that anyone who has been indicted by a Commission of Inquiry after having been given an opportunity to present his version of the facts must be disqualified from holding elective office. This amendment was adopted by Jammu and Kashmir in 1967. It should now be adopted by the country as a whole.

And the amendment must be made retrospective. There is no reason to be mealy-mouthed about this. To shirk from making it retrospective will be to commit the fatal mistake that was committed by the liberals in Germany after Hittler's 1924 trial for treason—they catapulted him into prominence and power, as a historian of the era put it by "their naive adherence to principle, by their belief that democratic tolerance ought to be extended to the enemies of democracy." To shirk from making the amendment retrospective will be to give the once-and-would-be dictators another chance. And if they get another chance, will they give you a second opportunity to apply your amendment to them?

The rationale for the amendment is clear. As Justice Shah's splendid work has shown, Commissions of Inquiry can be an important device for restoring some probity to our public life. But over the years these commissions have lost their teeth. Politicians indicted by them have—like scum—floated right back to the top. The only way to restore effectiveness to the commissions is to adopt the amendment suggested above.

We should also remember that if the Janata Government at the Centre baulks at an amendment of this sort, it will not be out of any adherence to scruples. The way the Janata leaders have been knifing each other shows that they are not very particular about scruples or about principles. If they baulk at the amendment it will only be because some of their colleagues—Biju Patnaik, for one—and some of their allies—Prakash Singh Badal, for one—have themselves been indicted by commissions in the past. By baulking at the amendment the government will be showing that it is placing the interests of these individuals above the interest of the country.

All these steps must be taken. But they do not constitute a fundamental solution to the problem, nor will they be enough by themselves to deal with the threat that Indira Gandhi poses today. Today she stands as an avowed candidate of fascism, of rule by a coterie, of a personality cult. Today her rehabilitation and survival depend upon the destruction of the Rule of Law.

If the performance of the Janata governments continues to be as anaemic as it has been, the steps that have been proposed, while necessary for restoring some health to our polity, will end up helping her. For instance, what if a special tribunal is actually set up, what if it speeds up the processing of the cases against her and against her henchmen and what if all of them are indicted and imprisoned sooner than they would otherwise be? If the Janata governments go on as they have been going on during the last one year this speedier indictment would only help her become a focus of strength even sooner than she might otherwise become. Similarily, what if the People's Representation Act is amended? If the Janata governments continue at their paralytic pace, within four years Mrs Gandhi will be able to win hand somely enough to reverse the amendment and ensure, if she is so inclined, that only those who *have* been indicted by commissions can qualify for elective office.

The solution, therefore, is to compel the present governments to discharge their responsibilities and to fulfil their pledges to the people. Only to the extent to which people can compel these governments to deliver the goods will they have helped save democracy in the country.

## THREAT TO THE RULE OF LAW*

*Help from History Books*

On 9 November 1923, a provincial agitator and some seedy associates staged a *coup* in one city. It turned out to be a comic *coup* and was soon the butt of endless jokes all over Germany. The agitator himself had lost his nerve, he had fled at a crucial point. His melodramatics had appeared farcical. He and everyone else was convinced that he was finished. He was guilty of treason. He knew the punishment for it. He also knew how vulnerable he was: the fact of his complicity in the gravest crime against the State could not be denied; and he was not even a citizen of Germany. He knew that he could be deported without ceremony. Within hours of the *coup* he was contemplating suicide.

But even though it had him by the throat, the flaccid polity could not do away with him. Once again Hitler was resurrected by his enemies. Within months of the ignominous *putsch*, they had transformed a provincial agitator into the most talked-of politician in Germany.

Hitler was brought to trial for treason on 26 February 1924. The trial lasted 24 days. With more help from his enemies than he needed, Hitler turned the tables on the prosecutors. While his associates tried to wriggle out of the charge by feigning ignorance of what they had done, Hitler reversed the roles of the accused and the accuser and he argued that his treason alone was real patriotism, that those who put up with a State led by the capitulators of 1918 were the real traitors. He was given the mildest sentence for treason—five years imprisonment—and was told even while being sentenced that in all probability he would soon be released on parole. The State—nervous lest someone call it vindictive—made his "imprisonment" a vacation at public expense. He was housed comfortably with 40 of his followers, and was allowed full access to the outside world; in fact, he was enabled to use the "prison" as his party's headquarters.

Here are some passages from four well-known studies of the period. The passages tell us how an anaemic, bourgeois state—palsied by its inhibitions, compromises, corruption, by its own

*April, 1978.

## The Janata Year

culpability, by principles which it proclaims but in which it no longer believes and for seeming to abide by which it accordingly bends backwards—how such a state is unable to deal even with a sworn enemy of it. The four studies are (*a*) Bracher's *The German Dictatorship*, (*b*) Fest's *Hitler*, (*c*) Guerin's *Fascism & Big Business* and (*d*) Alan Bullock's *Hitler, A Study in Tyranny*.

### The Trial

'Never was Hitler's political ability more clearly shown than in the way he recovered from this setback (of the comic *coup*). For the man who, on 9 November 1923, appeared to be broken and finished as a political leader—and had himself believed this—succeeded by April 1924 in making himself one of the most-talked-of figures in Germany and turned his trial for treason into a political triumph, the opportunity for this lay in the equivocal political situation in Bavaria, which had saved him once before after the fiasco of 1 May.... The full story (of the *putsch*) was one which most of the political leaders of Bavaria... (because of their own complicity in it) were only too anxious to avoid being made public. Hitler exploited this situation to the full.... One of the features of the trial was the leniency with which the judges treated the accused in court, and the mildness of their rebukes to Hitler for his interruptions....'[1]

'... None of those under attack (by Hitler for their failure to be treasonous) knew how to answer these arguments. Hitler managed not only to turn the trial into a "political carnival"...but also to reverse the roles of accuser and accused... The presiding judge did not seem exactly displeased at these developments. He did not object to any of the denunciations and challenges (that Hitler) hurled at the "November criminals" and only when the applause from the audience became too stormy did he issue a mild rebuke....Hitler occassionally shouted Seisser down. For this he received no "penalty for contempt of court" which, the presiding judge declared, would have only "slight practical value." Instead he

---
[1] Allan Bullock, *Hitler, A Study in Tyranny*, Penguin, London, 1962, pp. 114-115.

was simply asked to control himself....'[2]

'... (In implicating the other Bavarian leaders) Hitler was partially successful. To begin with the court itself was by no means unresponsive to his argument. And no wonder. In it sat men who only a little while back had sympathised with him ....As for the rest, Hitler knew how to transform his defence into a public demonstration in support of his act, to stray from the theme of the trial and with national passion and prophecies of victory, to arouse the partisan audience to applause. The court, obviously impressed by the amount of public notice Hitler was attracting, tolerated this ....'[3]

## The Sentence

'... Consequently Hitler was not given a severe sentence nor was he, though still an Austrian subject, expelled from Germany ....The sentencing by the court, in April 1924, turned into a social event. Again, as often before in the course of the trial, the accused men were bedecked with flowers and nationalist symbols, while officers in full dress uniform demonstrated their sympathy ...'[4]

'... The presiding judge had a hard time cajoling the three lay judges into passing any guilty verdict at all; he had to assure them that Hitler would certainly be pardoned before serving his full sentence. The reading of the verdict was a real event for Munich society. The courtroom was crowded with spectators ready to applaud this trouble-maker with so many friends in high places. The verdict once more laid stress on the "pure" patriotic motives and honourable intentions of the defendant, but sentenced him to a minimum of five years in prison. However, he would become eligible for parole in six months.... The law called for the deportation of any troublesome foreigner, but the court decided to waive this in the case of a man "who thinks and feels in such

---

[2]Joachim C. Fest, *Hitler*, Harcourt Brace Jovanovich, New York, 1973, pp. 191-192.

[3]Karl Dietrich Bracher, *The German Dictatorship*, Praeger, 1970, p. 120.

[4]*ibid.*, pp. 120-121.

German terms as Hitler." This decision called forth a storm of approving bravos from the audience ... Hitler appeared at the window of the court building to show himself to the cheering crowd. Bouquets of flowers were piling up in the room behind him. The State had once again lost the match. ...'[5]

## Imprisonment

'Fifty miles west of Munich in the wooded valley of the Lech lies the small town of Landsberg. It was here that Hitler served his imprisonment .... In the early summer of 1924 some forty other National Socialists were in prison with him, and they had an easy and comfortable life. They ate well— Hitler became quite fat in prison—had as many visitors as they wished and spent much of their time out of doors in the garden .... Hitler's large and sunny room, No. 7, was on the first floor, a mark of privilege .... On his thirty-fifth birthday, which fell shortly after the trial, the parcels and flowers he received filled several rooms. He had a large correspondence in addition to his visitors, and as many newspapers and books as he wished. Hitler presided at the midday meal, claiming and receiving the respect due to him as leader of the party....'[6]

'Hitler was given what was almost a vacation in Landsberg castle .... The room in which Hitler daily presided over lunch was decorated with a Swastika banner .... The prison took on the air of a party headquarters ... with Hitler... receiving the tributes of his minions, and the letters, floral gifts and expressions of sympathy of the outside world ....'[7]

## The Resurrection

'... Despite the objection of the State Prosecutor and the attempts of the police to get him deported, Hitler was in fact released from prison after serving less than nine months of his sentence—and promptly resumed his agitation against the Republic. Such were the penalties for high treason in a State

---

[5]Fest, *op. cit.*, pp. 193-194.
[6]Bullock, *op. cit.*, p. 121.
[7]Bracher, *op. cit.*, p. 127.

where disloyalty to the regime was the surest recommendation to mercy. . . .'[8]

'The republican camp, for its part, also failed to put any major obstacles in the path of Hitler's resurgence. Those who did not generally sympathise with the "national" image of the Hitler movement and did not ascribe its radicalism to the youthful fervour of this super-patriot nonetheless, in naive adherence to principle, believed that democratic tolerance ought to be extended to the enemies of democracy. Moreover, the danger of revolution seemed to have abated with Hitler's turn toward legal means. Why then make much ado about a party which was nothing more than a splinter group? For years regional bans and (the country's) economic well-being were to rob Hitler of his prime weapon—the mass meeting, through which, with theatrical flair and oratory, he disseminated the most banal ideas and promises. His technique was based on two presuppositions—the exclusion of "intellectuals," whom he hated with the passion of the failed student, and the general lack of political understanding and sophistication of a population come of age in the authoritarian Wilhelmian State and which, after the shock of defeat and the crisis of the Republic, had not been able to arrive at a constructive relationship of mutual cooperation. And this factor had not changed in the years of waning radicalism. In the wings stood a new (fascist party), waiting for its main chance: a second national crisis.'[9]

'If in the beginning, when the Hitler bands were still weak, the workers' parties had answered them blow for blow there is no doubt their development would have been hampered. On this point we have the testimony of the National Socialist leaders themselves. Hitler confessed in retrospect: "Only one thing could have broken our movement—if the adversary had understood its principle and from the first day had smashed, with the most extreme brutality, the nucleus of our new movement." And Goebbels: "If the enemy had known how weak we were, it would probably have reduced us to jelly. . . .It would have crushed in blood the very beginning of our work." But

---

[8]Bullock, *op. cit.*, p. 120.
[9]Bracher, *op. cit.*, pp. 130-131.

National Socialism was not crushed in the egg; it became a force. And to resist that force, the German Socialists could conceive only one tactic: to trust the bourgeois state and ask for its aid and protection. Their *leitmotiv* was: *State, intervene*! They relied not on themselves and on the militancy of the masses but on the Prussian police.... They expected the public authorities to dissolve the Storm Troops....'[10]

And what is our *leitmotiv* today? "Ministers, Secretaries, for heaven's sake, do something."

## The Palsied Response

History teaches us three lessons for dealing with a fascist threat. First, it must be crushed; yes, crushed is the right word. Second, it must be crushed in the embryo; crushed, that is, before and not after it has done its evil. Third, to leave the task to palsied governments is to commit suicide.

The lessons of history are clear. But no one ever learns from them. Our own situation illustrates this to the letter. First, we have Mrs Gandhi and her coterie—a clear and present danger to democracy as well as to the rule of law. Second, we have a people—even the articulate and organized among them—who leave things to their leaders. And, third, we have leaders who in their turn are too busy knifing each other to do anything either about solving the country's problems or about dealing with the danger that threatens all of them even as individuals.

Consider first Mrs Gandhi's situation. She knows that the sort of matters Justice Shah has reported on will entail her criminal prosecution. She also knows that when all the affairs of Maruti have been uncovered, she will not be able to avoid constructive and in some causes direct responsibility for the doings of her son, the political Balyogeshwar.

Therefore, her rehabilitation, her very survival, depends on destroying the rule of law itself. That is why she today puts the streets as a counter to the courts and screams that she has a

---

[10]Daniel Guerin, *Fascism and Big Business*, Pathfinder Books, New York, 1973, pp. 111-112.

higher sanction as she can bring crowds out on to the streets. She foments disorder and then presents herself as the law and order candidate. She lies openly and audaciously. She hurls canards at the courts. She shrieks at the judges and the magistrates and has her followers smear the courts and the Commissions of Enquiry.

While she does all this, what do the people do? They stand by helplessly, grumbling that their government can't even take care of fifty hired *goondas*.

And what does the government do? While she goes about assaulting the rule of law itself, the government—nervous lest anyone call it vindictive—cannot even bring itself to refusing her a passport. *Badi karta hai dushman aur hum sharmae jaate hain.* . . . Indeed, it does much more than merely shy away into a corner. By its desultory performance it does all it can to destroy people's faith, not just in itself, but in the democratic framework. It brings the people to despair, till they throw up their hands—"at least she used to rule. . . . "

Its flaccid leaders sit back and let her seize the initiative on every matter. Even on the matter of Muslims and Harijans they allow, as a Cabinet Minister has himself stated in a written note, even on that they allow the very woman, who along with her son had found the final solution to their problem, the solution of castrating and killing them, they allow that very woman to put them on the defensive. How much closer to being dead can you get?

Justice Shah uncovers gross abuses. He hands them a rapier of a report. Hardly any one of them reads it. They turn the report over to a Committee of Secretaries. The Secretaries are horrified. The report leaves them no option but to recommend her criminal prosecution. But they will be damned if they recommend that. What if they recommend it and it backfires politically? What if it does not backfire but she comes back? So they tell the Cabinet to wait. Wait for the second report, they say, then place both before the public, watch public reaction and act accordingly, they mumble. Thus is freedom guarded—by an inert Cabinet on the one side and by a committee of plasticine wonders on the other. Thus is democracy given a magnificent choice between death on the one side and suicide on the other.

"It is all a failure of leadership," say the ringside pandits. Leadership, my foot. After all, this is not the first time that a bunch has squandered such an enormous amount of goodwill. Remember Mrs Gandhi in January 1972? The empress of our hearts, wasn't she? And within a year she too had squandered all that goodwill. Was that too "failure of leadership?" What about the leaders of the left parties, the trade unions, the student movement? Have they been any less successful in forfeiting all the goodwill they had? Why then is it that only those who are bound to fail as leaders reach the top of our political system? The trouble, as you will realize in attempting to answer that question, lies much deeper than in "failure of leadership."

"But do you mean that the criminals of the Emergency should be denied the normal protection of the rule of law?" Recall but one sentence from the passages cited earlier—recall the help rendered to Hitler by those who "in naive adherence to principle, believed that democratic tolerance ought to be extended to the enemies of democracy." That apart, this solicitude has nothing to do with dedication to the rule of law. It is pusillanimity and nothing else. The very people who proclaim at their cocktail parties that the Emergency criminals should be allowed to use clauses and sub-clauses to ward off justice forever, those very people have never raised an eyebrow when the same clauses and sub-clauses have been used to hurl the poor into prisons, when they have been used to keep them there for upto seven years as under-trial prisoners.

What we are witnessing today in relation to the Emergency criminals is not the rule of law but the destruction of it. We are witnessing how the bourgeois rule of law is destroyed—members of the class itself destroy it for their personal aggrandisement and the bourgeoise is unable to muster up the firmness needed to bring these blackguards to book.

Today, two features of our legal system are being bared for all to see. First, it cannot catch criminals provided they are influential and well connected. Second, it cannot catch them for their principal crimes against the people and the State. You will notice that if any of the stars of the Emergency are ever indicted, he will not be indicted for his inhumanity, for his callousness, for his crimes against the people, for their wilful and wholesale perversion of the Constitution, but for violating some rule of business, for not issuing notices in time, for not following some procedure.

Thus, we have our "leaders" and our "laws." We have our judges too. Judges represented at the top by a judge who one day upholds the fascist decision of a clique to deny six hundred and fifty million the right to *habeas corpus*, who the next day wishes he had had the courage to resign rather than pronounce that judgement, who the day after addresses one of the principal culprits of the Emergency again and again as "a very responslble member of society." And readers send in "letters to the editor" complimenting him for having the courage to say that he had not the courage when it was needed.

Then we have our seedy leftists busy abusing each other. And finally we have the liberals—busy rearranging furniture on the deck of the Titanic; nay, busy holding seminars about rearranging furniture on the deck of the Titanic.

At the top of the heap sits a political leadership that is as culpable as the Bavarian leadership at the time of the 1923 *putsch*, and therefore as keen to prevent the full story from coming out. Who among them—in the ruling party or out—will save us from the impending avalanche of fascism?

Will Jagjivan Ram? During the Emergency his speeches in its favour were as skilfully worded as his speeches against it have been since then. For samplers, read just two of his speeches—the two he made while piloting the Proclamation of the Emergency through Parliament in July 1975.

Will the ailing strong man from Meerut save us? Find out about the numerous negotiations—before as well as during the Emergency—that he has conducted with Indira Gandhi before you pin your hopes on him.

Is Brahmananda Reddy going to save the country from fascism? Revelations before Justice Shah establish him as Reddy-the-ever-ready resigner. He is always quick to surrender his authority and position rather than risk taking a stand. When Indira Gandhi tells him of her plan to declare an emergency and arrest all the opposition leaders, he demurs for a brief moment: "there already is an emergency in force, madam, you can arrest everyone under that itself." She persists. And he caves in: "you know what is best for the country, Madam, so you can decide." V.C. Shukla is pursuing the censorship policy with great zeal. He does not bother about preparing the grounds on account of which some action is to be taken. By happenstance the Home Ministry is the one that has to examine the adequacy of the grounds before sanctioning the step. Does Reddy use this opportunity? Not at all. He just transfers the power to act under that clause to the Ministry of Information & Broadcasting!

Or consider Raghuramaiah, already a jewel in the Janata crown. Will he stand up to the fascist threat? He is the one who beat the drums on Sanjay's visit to Andhra and declared at a public meeting: "My grandfather served your great-grandfather, my father served your grandfather, I have served your mother, I and my children will serve you forever." He has now affirmed before Justice Shah that he had pushed through the Boeing deal within a single day after Dhawan, the Additional PA to the PM, spoke to him—he pushed it through in all nervous haste even though the Public Investment Board as well as the Planning Commission had disapproved of the deal. In the same testimony he recalled how, when he was Minister for Parliamentary Affairs, he had secured the resignations of ministers after ministers on the mere asking of the same Dhawan.

Who do you think went overboard congratulating Indira Gandhi on the tenth anniversary of her election as PM for "her amazingly firm and far seeing leadership?" Who recalled "the somewhat reluctance" (*sic*) with which she had decided to contest the election and yet how her decision to do so "has proved to be the most significant decision in the life of our country?" Who do you think waxed eloquent thus? None other than the heir to the glorious heritage of Chatrapathi Shivaji— Yashwantrao Balwantrao Chavan himself. Will *he* save us from fascism?

To rely on these fellows to save us from the impending fascist avalanche is to rely on superannuated buffaloes to see us across a mine field.

## THE VIGOROUS DEBATE*

In the penultimate paragraph of his second report Justice Shah

---

*June, 1978.

observes that he "would reckon (his Commission's) achievements not by the number or seriousness of the punitive actions taken against persons who had transgressed the laws, but by the nature and extent of the remedial and ameliorative actions that follow the labours of the Commission."

In the last paragraph Justice Shah observes that he would regard the Commission's labours "amply rewarded" "if the Commission's observations should generate a public debate on some of the vital issues focussed on by the Commission with the object of devising corrective machinery and remedial action."

Two weeks have gone by since the reports were made public. Have you noticed the vigour of the debate that has ensued? The vigour has seen about the same with which corpses must debate matters at the dead of night in graveyards.

As an exercise, glance through the four national English papers of the last two weeks. A couple of editorials each and some extracts from the reports used as fillers on the sixth or seventh page. That is all.

Now, the reason cannot be that Justice Shah and his team have taken unduly long over their task. Quite the contrary. There just has not been a single commission in India or elsewhere which has covered as much ground with as much dispatch as the Shah Commission has. Many talk idly about the Nuremburg trials asserting that those are the sorts of trials we should have had for the Emergency culprits. Have they cared to find out how long those trials took?

So, the reason cannot be lack of dispatch. Nor can it be that the questions Justice Shah has discussed are unimportant. Indeed, they are matters of the life and death for a free society. Each case on which Justice Shah has given his findings raises fundamental issues about our system—about the administration, the police, the magistracy, about a supposedly sovereign but in fact diarrhoeal Parliament, about the nature of Law. And in each instance Justice Shah is at pains to go beyond the individuals who did wrong, in each instance he draws our attention to the larger issues that lie behind the particular act of malfeasance. Do our Nuremburg-enthusiasts recall the earnestness with which an entire continent debated the central question raised at those trials—the question of an individual's responsibility for a collective guilty? And do they recall how ravaged that continent then

## The Janata Year

was by a war of unprecedented ferocity. The difference is not between the Nuremberg trials and the Shah Commission but in the societies to which these exercises were addressed.

So, the reason cannot be that the issues that Justice Shah has commented on are not important. Nor can the excuse be that his findings are ambiguous or that his prose is muffled. Indeed, there has not been a single commission in India during the last 30 years that has expressed itself in such unequivocal terms as the Shah Commission. Justice Shah's pen is a surgeon's knife.

Nor, finally, can the papers troop out the standard excuse "pressure from Government." The Janata government unable to do anything itself, would, if anything, be only too happy if the newspapers did its work for it.

To discover the reason for the anaemic comment by our press on these vital matters, we have to look at Justice Shah's reports in a larger context. It isn't that for some special reason our papers have been less than vigorous in discussing Justice Shah's findings. They are equally flaccid in disscussing every issue you can think of. Their stupor on the Shah reports is just their habitual stupor.

Lest this sound a harsh judgement, I shall cite a few examples.

Atrocities on Harijans have been much talked of in the past few months. To assess the vigour of our press you should calculate, first, the square inches of column space devoted to airing this issue, then the proportion of this which was devoted to merely reporting the statements of assorted leaders on the matter ("Mrs. Gandhi says atrocities have increased," "Charan Singh says they have decreased") and, finally, the proportion devoted to actually investigating the incidents where they occurred.

Alternatively, consider trade union matters. Next time you read about a strike ask yourself whether the papers have told you any more than the fact that the strike has occured. Have they helped you gather the background to the strike—for instance, have they told you anything about the type of negotiations that preceded the strike? Have they helped you discover the cause of the strike—for instance, have they given data about how the wages and working conditions of the striking labours compares with those of other workers in that industry or in the neighbourhood, about how the trend of wages in the industry or the unit compares with the trend of salaries, rentier income and profits of that industry or unit? Have they helped you learn anything about the nature of the strike—for instance, have they told you anything about the relative roles of the local unions and the national unions? Finally, find out whether the resolution of the issues at stake makes as much news as the strike itself. When agreement is finally reached, does your paper inform you about the terms on which it has been reached? Does it tell you anything about how these terms compare with terms negotiated elsewhere in the neighbourhood or the industry?

If the answer in each instance is "no" then in what sense is the press performing its elementary function—that of informing the people?

"But you have picked up issues involving labour, Harijans, etc. The answer is simple: these are issues involving the poor. The press is of and for the middle and upper classes. That is why it does not investigate them in depth."

This is a part of the answer. But, I fear, the lesser part. After all, the press does not display any zest even in investigating issues that concern the middle and upper classes. Education is a good example. A few months ago one-third of our universities were closed because of troubles of various kinds. How many of our newspapers informed us about the causes and nature of the troubles that led to the closures? How many of them told us anything whatsoever about the conditions on which teaching in some of the universities was resumed?

Or take freedom itself for that matter. Editor after editor trooped up to Justice Shah and told him about the threats he was subjected to, about how the restrictions during the Emergency prevented him from taking up issues that were vital for freedom. But what about the record since April last year of the press on issues involving freedom and civil liberties? How many papers have taught us anything about conditions in our jails? How many have investigated cases of individual under-trial prisoners and educated us about the way in which they are kept in jail for years and years? How many have taught us anything about conditions in police lock-ups and the methods of police interrogation?

Every society—even as it ruthlessly examines its shortcomings—must learn to build on its successes. How many of our papers have informed us about the innovative experiments that are being carried out and that have proved successful in various spheres in our country?

The reason for the criminal neglect of these issues as of Justice Shah's reports is not "pressures of the Government" or "restrictions by the owners." The reason is laziness.

Shuffling boxes on organization charts, passing laws guaranteeing press freedom, providing constitutional safeguards won't help. A recommendation of the Verghese group on AIR and TV autonomy will illustrate the point.

To safeguard autonomy the group suggested among other things that Akash Bharati should be overseen by a Board of Trustees. To fortify the independence of the members of this Board it suggested that they should have the status of Supreme Court Judges. Now, the one thing that you can be certain about a man, who, in order to stand up, needs the prop of the status of a Supreme Court judgeship is that he is not going to stand up when the crisis comes. Did those judges of the Supreme Court whok neeled down before Indira Gandhi on the *habeas corpus* case, did they lack the status of Supreme Court Judges?

You cannot have autonomous institutions without autonomous individuals. You cannot have a vigilant press with watchdogs who have grown fat and lazy. That is why they cannot safeguard our freedom. That is why others cannot safeguard their freedom.

## CAN THE EXHAUSTED DEFEND FREEDOM?*

Many of our politicians suffered during the Emergency. They suffered physically; they were incarcerated. Many others—academics, journalists and even some civil servants—lived in fear. But none of this has had any lasting influence on their conduct. Like addicts, like hardened criminals, they have relapsed into their old ways. Everyone exhorts them to change. Everyone warns them that unless they do so they will help bring those 19 months back. To no avail!

The exhortations, the warnings do not reckon with a crucial

*February, 1978.

fact: the middle class in India today is exhausted, it has just about given up. It doesn't even have the energy to stand up. Where will it get the much greater energy needed to change course?

This exhaustion, this premature, almost tubercular, fatigue is the principal trait of the middle class today. We are often told, for instance, that our civil servants, our academics are interested in nothing but their careers. But this is only a part of the picture. Even careers are not pursued with verve. A bit of licking here, a little malicious gossip—and that too in anaemic officialese—about our colleagues there. That is about all there is to our careerism.

Our press is truly representative in this respect. The Emergency and its censorship were a handy excuse: few worked, most sat back saying that it was no use investigating any lead as the results would not be published in any case. But what is the excuse today?

One does not have to go by the stories about how senior editors of some of our national dailies tumble out of their offices at three or three-thirty and after that none of them knows, none of them cares to find out, what is appearing in his paper the next day. One does not have to go by these stories. One can go by the results. You should take the papers of any month and find out what proportion of the space is taken up by advertisements; what proportion is filled with genuine investigative reporting; and what proportion of this last is the result of leg work outside the metropolitan areas. Indeed, you will often notice the same story, indeed the identical text, in different papers, each of which tells its readers that the story, the text is "by our special correspondent." Can such a press fight for its freedom?

This exhaustion of our professions, of our middle class, is important because free institutions, free debate, "freedom" such as it has been, has in the last 30 years mainly been a middle-class affair. Scholars who have reflected upon these matters tell us that when we got independence we already had a substantial, articulate and in some respects well-organized middle class. In particular, the state apparatus—manned overwhelmingly by the middle class—was "overdeveloped" in relation to the base. The interests of the colonial power had seen to that. The industrial bourgeosie was weak. The landed interests were not organized;

in many areas they had yet to fight off the feudal holdovers, the zamindars and other intermediaries.

The middle class, accordingly, had considerable room for manoeuvre. It used this to strengthen its own position vis-a-vis the owners of industry and land. All that talk about socialism, for instance, was a handy device to put the owners of land and industry on the defensive. The one way to make a tycoon wait upon you is to shout "socialism" and set up procedures that require your *dhobi*-mark at every step.

Of course, economic and social realities forced the middle class, even as it was trying to aggrandize its position, to act out its real function—as an agent of the propertied. Thus, it shouted "socialism," but also ensured that in practice it was diluted so as not to hurt the propertied.

These are "the good old days" that are fading away before our eyes. For now the owners of industry and of land are strong, they are well-organized. And the middle class is demoralized and exhausted.

The stage is thus set for out-and-out capitalist growth, in industry as well as in agriculture. And this has little to do with whether this party is in power or that. The individuals who occupy office merely determine whether one rationalization will be used for the course of events or another.

Today the talk is of the importance of agriculture. This will merely result in a larger proportion of public investment being earmarked for the landed interests. That will mean that there isn't enough of public investment left for the industrial sector ("and in any case public sector units are under-utilized as well as ill-managed")—a perfect setting for lifting all restraints from the private industrialist. And the quickest way for the private industrialist to grow is to produce goods which the rich want and to do so by using readily available, imported, capital-intensive technology. Hence are doors opened to foreign capital even as we talk of self-reliance.

"But aren't the interests of the landed classes and of the owners of industry irreconcilable? Will there not be a conflict among them and will the middle class not be able to play one off against the other?"

This is no more than academic wishful thinking. The interests of the two are reconcilable and today they happen to coincide in matters big as well as small. Both, for instance, are interested in preserving and enlarging an economic system based on private property. Or consider a detail: the owners of industry want a large and growing marketed surplus from agriculture, and who can supply this surplus but the big farmers? The former would, therefore, support larger allocations out of public funds to agriculture and both together would ensure that these funds go to the bigger farmers. Similarly, both will cooperate to crush the fulcrum which inconveniences them both—organized labour.

Planning and similar rituals cannot but be killed in the process. In the early fifties these were required for building up the infrastructure and providing the basic goods that would ultimately be needed for capitalist growth. Now the infrastructure is in place, units producing basic goods are limping along below capacity. What was an aid then—the planning paraphernalia—is a shackle now. This—and not the lack of dynamism of some Deputy Chairman or the incompetence of some members of the Planning Commission—is what accounts for the progressive euthanasia of planning since the mid-sixties.

Just as we can be certain that the stage is set for out-and-out capitalist growth, so can we be certain about its consequences for freedom. Capitalist growth—with its goods for the rich, including the rich of other countries, with its capital-intensive techniques—cannot but intensify dualism in our society. This intensification cannot be brought about without sitting upon labour, agricultural as well as industrial. And that, in turn, cannot be done without crushing the freedom of association, of speech.

This then is the prospect before us. And the middle class is too exhausted to defend these freedoms. Indeed, so exhausted is it, so demoralized by the drift over which it has presided, that it wants to abdicate; it actually wants someone else to take over. It is thus ripe for the demagogue—someone who will ride to the sound of conches, someone who exudes self-confidence and aplomb, someone who promises to do our work for us, someone who promises to take upon himself the burden of solving our problems, of getting things done, of just carrying. It is ripe for a political Sai Baba.

"Even capitalist growth requires agents. Will the middle class not at least be required for this purpose?"

The new rulers will certainly need agents, but they will not find them in the middle class. They will find them among the lumpen, the toughs, who are completely bereft of values, of standards, who are completely alienated from the present set-up. To keep the people in line the new rulers will need whips. These wet noodles of the middle class won't do.

# 14   Lessons of an Inquiry

In May last year JP asked nine of us to investigate the deaths of hundreds of young men and women in alleged encounters in Andhra Pradesh. Our group was headed by the eminent jurist, V.M. Tarkunde.

We reported our findings in two interim reports, "Encounters are Murders" and "The Killings in Guntur."

Our hopes and objectives were quite modest. As all of us believed that an alert and concerned citizenry is the only bulwark of a free society. The people—as many of them as we could reach—were our primary audience. We hoped that as the entire country had just experienced a dictator's heel, a large enough number would pay attention to how their brothers were being treated by their own society. After all, what was involved here was not just the murder of human rights, but of human beings. We also hoped that by the end of the exercise we would be able to ensure the indictment of at least a few officials for murder and complicity in murder. This would, we reasoned, deter at least a few policemen from killing people when they were ordered to do so the next time around.

Apart from releasing the reports to the public we brought our findings to the attention of the Prime Minister and the Home Minister. We requested them to institute a judicial inquiry into

## Lessons of an Inquiry

the killings in encounters. We pointed out that the inquiry must be ordered by the Central Government as the State Government was itself to be the subject of investigation.

The Prime Minister agreed that this should be done. Officials of the Andhra Pradesh Government, in particular of its Home Department and those of the Centre's Home Ministry, now set to work to thwart the Prime Minister's wishes. They manoeuvred things in such a way that two days before the Prime Minister was to return from his visit to the UK, the Home Minister announced in Parliament that with his concurrence the State Government (and not the Centre) was appointing a commission to investigate the matter.

At his press conference immediately after his return, the Prime Minister was asked what the Government proposed to do about the findings of the Tarkunde Committee. Innocent of the Home Minister's announcement, he spoke the truth—that he had already ordered that an inquiry be instituted by the Central Government. This announcement was flashed by AIR as well as by Samachar.

We met the Prime Minister within a day of his announcement. We told him that we were as heartened by his announcement as we had been dismayed by the announcement of the Home Minister. That was the first he had heard of the decision that officers had pushed through behind his back. But it was too late; the deed had been done the way the bureaucrats wanted it done. All he could do was reprimand an official.

I mention this as just one of many instances that can be cited. Similar manoeuvrings were to thwart our requests on the terms of reference, the protection of witnesses, the fact that policemen who had been directly involved in the killings should be at least posted out of the areas in which the killings had occurred, and so on.

In each instance the manoeuvrings were by the civil servants ("civil," yes sometimes, but whose "servants"?) and policemen. In each instance their machinations prevailed against the wishes and inclinations of the political leaders.

Once Justice Bhargava started his work, Andhra Pradesh officials and policemen did all they could to keep him from getting at the facts. As the inquiry progressed, they had ample reason to be alarmed. It was clear that the judge was having little difficulty in seeing through their concocted accounts. At one stage Justice Bhargava ordered the CBI to investigate our reports of police efforts to intimidate and harass the witnesses. The police had reason to believe that the CBI inquiry had gone against them.

Cornered, they have now persuaded the State Government to issue an edict that henceforth Justice Bhargava must hold his hearings in camera. This is a slap on the people's face. Predictably all voluntary organizations—including the group that had been nominated by JP—have withdrawn from the proceedings. In all probability Justice Bhargava will himself refuse to conduct the inquiry under these circumstances.

The policemen and the bureaucrats have won again. But at whose expense? At the expense of the Tarkunde Committee or at the expense of rule of law? What are the general lessons that emerge from an effort such as that of the Tarkunde Committee?

I think our experience yields five lessons. The first three concern the conduct of the inquiries by voluntary bodies and the last two concern the system under which we all live.

First, inquiries of the kind undertaken by the Tarkunde Committee should be undertaken only if the members of the committee are willing and able to devote almost all of their time to the work. Such was not the case in our committee. After the first few months almost all the burden was carried by two or three members based in Hyderabad. This seriously impaired the effectiveness of our functioning.

Secondly, the inquiries should be undertaken only if the group has close links with workers' and peasants' organizations. We could collect the evidence we did because three of our members had the confidence of such organizations. We could not collect as much evidence as we should have collected (given the enormous amount that is there in the terrorized countryside of Andhra Pradesh) because our contacts with the workers and peasants are not as wide, as deep, and as strong as they should be. It is precisely for the same reason, and because of the extreme weakness of a genuine people's movement in Andhra Pradesh, that we could not even protect the witnesses who had testified before us from the blandishments and threats of the police.

Thirdly, contacts—"personal equations," as the phrase goes —with high-ups in the system are of no use when you are trying to question—much more change—the system itself. Because our group was headed by V.M. Tarkunde, we had direct access to the Prime Minister and I believe, we had support of his sincere conviction that justice must be done in this case. The access and the support was not able to thwart the bureaucrats and the policemen as the latter were working in the interests of the present state of affairs and we were not. Similarly, at least three of our members had close contacts with the national Press. In spite of this we were not able to persuade the Press to take a sustained interest in an issue that questioned the basic premises of the system of which the Press is a part.

Fourthly, we have again been taught that as Gandhi used to say, law is but the convenience of the powerful. When members of the ruling class break the law—even when they smother law under their heels as did the Emergency culprits—the clauses and sub-clauses protect them. When the dispossessed and poor are killed, the same clause and sub-clauses prevent even an inquiry into the facts.

This strength of the rulers is, in fact, weakness. For this is precisely how the bourgeois rule of law destroys itself. On the one side, seeing its operation the poor perceive no stake in it: therefore, they never rise to its defence. On the other, individual adventurers in the ruling class violate the law for their own aggrandisement (the Emergency provides a recent example). But the ruling class is unable to punish its own kind and thus signals the once and would-be usurpers and their once and would-be henchmen that there are no penalties to riding rough-shod over the institutions of the bourgeoisie itself.

Finally, it is quite clear that our residual liberalism cannot be stirred into action on any issue, however grave. Malfeasance, corruption, subversion of the constitution, perversion of the State apparatus, even murder, as in the present case—every issue will find us looking the other way. Our work on the encounters provided us much documentation of this fact.

In spite of much effort, for instance, we were unable to enthuse the generality of lawyers in Andhra Pradesh to take an interest in a matter that was so vital to the rule of law. Similarly, we placed an appeal for contributions in publications that reached perhaps three-quarters of a million readers. We received less than Rs 3,000 in return. Finally, the Press, in spite of the obvi ous importance of our conclusion (that citizens had in fact been murdered in cold blood), in spite of the fact that we had given the relevant names of the victims and before Justice Bhargava, of the policemen who had killed, in spite of the fact that we had indicated the precise locations where the crimes had taken place, in spite of all this the Press did not follow-up work on its own. A couple of investigative reports, and that is all. Contrast this with the space and effort it devoted to the Nanavati murder case some years ago and to the Vidya Jain murder case more recently.

Yes, the cancer is too far gone now. It will be cured only by the patient's death.